Palgrave Studies in European Union Politics

Series Editors
Michelle Egan
American University
Washington, USA

Neill Nugent
Manchester Metropolitan University
Manchester, UK

William E. Paterson
Aston University
Birmingham, UK

Following on the sustained success of the acclaimed European Union Series, which essentially publishes research-based textbooks, Palgrave Studies in European Union Politics publishes cutting edge research-driven monographs. The remit of the series is broadly defined, both in terms of subject and academic discipline. All topics of significance concerning the nature and operation of the European Union potentially fall within the scope of the series. The series is multidisciplinary to reflect the growing importance of the EU as a political, economic and social phenomenon.

Editorial Board
Laurie Buonanno (SUNY Buffalo State, USA)
Kenneth Dyson (Cardiff University, UK)
Brigid Laffan (European University Institute, Italy)
Claudio Radaelli (University College London, UK)
Mark Rhinard (Stockholm University, Sweden)
Ariadna Ripoll Servent (University of Bamberg, Germany)
Frank Schimmelfennig (ETH Zurich, Switzerland)
Claudia Sternberg (University College London, UK)
Nathalie Tocci (Istituto Affari Internazionali, Italy)

More information about this series at
http://www.palgrave.com/gp/series/14629

Christian Adam · Michael W. Bauer ·
Miriam Hartlapp · Emmanuelle Mathieu

Taking the EU to Court

Annulment Proceedings
and Multilevel Judicial Conflict

Christian Adam
Geschwister Scholl Institute
of Political Sciences
Ludwig-Maximilians-Universität
München
Munich, Germany

Miriam Hartlapp
Otto Suhr Institute of Political Science
Freie Universität Berlin
Berlin, Germany

Michael W. Bauer
Jean-Monnet Chair for Comparative
Public Administration
and Policy-Analysis
German University of Administrative
Sciences Speyer
Speyer, Germany

Emmanuelle Mathieu
Institute for Political Studies
University of Lausanne
Lausanne, Switzerland

This book is open access thanks to the generous support of the Swiss National Science Foundation and Freie Universität Berlin.

ISSN 2662-5873   ISSN 2662-5881 (electronic)
Palgrave Studies in European Union Politics
ISBN 978-3-030-21628-3   ISBN 978-3-030-21629-0 (eBook)
https://doi.org/10.1007/978-3-030-21629-0

© The Editor(s) (if applicable) and The Author(s) 2020, corrected publication 2020. This book is an open access publication.
Open Access This book is licensed under the terms of the Creative Commons Attribution 4.0 International License (http://creativecommons.org/licenses/by/4.0/), which permits use, sharing, adaptation, distribution and reproduction in any medium or format, as long as you give appropriate credit to the original author(s) and the source, provide a link to the Creative Commons license and indicate if changes were made.
The images or other third party material in this book are included in the book's Creative Commons license, unless indicated otherwise in a credit line to the material. If material is not included in the book's Creative Commons license and your intended use is not permitted by statutory regulation or exceeds the permitted use, you will need to obtain permission directly from the copyright holder.
The use of general descriptive names, registered names, trademarks, service marks, etc. in this publication does not imply, even in the absence of a specific statement, that such names are exempt from the relevant protective laws and regulations and therefore free for general use.
The publisher, the authors and the editors are safe to assume that the advice and information in this book are believed to be true and accurate at the date of publication. Neither the publisher nor the authors or the editors give a warranty, expressed or implied, with respect to the material contained herein or for any errors or omissions that may have been made. The publisher remains neutral with regard to jurisdictional claims in published maps and institutional affiliations.

Cover credit: Magic Lens/Shutterstock; all rights reserved, used with permission

This Palgrave Macmillan imprint is published by the registered company Springer Nature Switzerland AG
The registered company address is: Gewerbestrasse 11, 6330 Cham, Switzerland

The original version of the book frontmatter was revised: Author corrections to Funding details and List of figure have been incorporated. The correction to the book frontmatter is available at https://doi.org/10.1007/978-3-030-21629-0_9

ACKNOWLEDGEMENTS

The beginning of this project dates back to 2005. Back then, Miriam and Michael participated in a workshop on EU policy-making at the Max Planck Institute for the Study of Societies in Cologne, Germany. When discussing our papers, we discovered that EU annulment cases constituted decisive turning points in our respective policy case studies. We became curious whether this was a mere coincidence or whether there was more to annulment cases from a policy analytical perspective. As we found virtually no political science literature on annulment litigation, we decided to work more systematically on this topic. This was the beginning of an intellectual journey that led to the present monograph.

After some initial data mining and the development of a first paper on the issue, the Young Scholar Fund of the University of Konstanz kindly supported the project—and Christian Adam joined in. Together with Christian, we brought the annulment project to a new level of theoretical analysis and empirical data basis. In 2013, Christian submitted his doctoral thesis on the politics of judicial review in a closely related area. Around that time, Emmanuelle Mathieu completed our team on a grant from the German Research Institute for Public Administration Speyer funded by the German Leibniz Association. Since then, we have addressed selective aspects of annulments in the EU multilevel system in controversial discussions among the four of us and in several conference papers and journal articles published inter alia in the *European Journal of Political Research*, the *Journal of Common Market Studies*, and the *Journal of European Integration*. This book constitutes as complete a picture of the role that annulment conflicts play in the EU multilevel system as we were able to deliver. It has been a truly collaborative endeavour of hard but exciting work, especially over the last four years.

The production of this book received much help. We are indebted to numerous people and institutions. Over forty experts in a wide range of regional national administrations and EU institutions patiently answered our questions in what often turned out to be very long interviews. We are thus grateful to all our discussion partners in the German, Saxon, Bavarian, Spanish, Galician, and Basque administrations; in the European institutions—especially the Legal Service of the European Commission; in various law firms; and in private and public companies.

We are particularly grateful to Michael Blauberger, Mark Dawson, Markus Jachtenfuchs, Daniel Kelemen, Ellen Mastenbroek, Susanne K. Schmidt, and Michael Zürn for valuable input at earlier stages of the project. A special thanks goes to the participants of the workshop 'Implementation and Judicial Politics: Conflict and Compliance in the EU Multilevel System', supported by the Fritz Thyssen Foundation. We organized this workshop hosted by the Berlin Social Science Center, WZB, on behalf of the German Research Institute for Public Administration Speyer in March 2016. The debates we led at our workshop turned out to be a defining moment for our theorizing of annulment litigation. Furthermore, we are indebted to many dear colleagues who challenged and commented upon our research papers on various occasions and thus shaped our thinking of annulment litigation.

We would also like to thank our student assistants for their support in coming to grips with an immense amount of empirical data: Paula Protsch, Julia Feldkötter, Sabine Mehlin, Frieder Bürkle, and Charly Uster. A special appreciation goes to Nora Wagner, Tamara Ulrich, and Kim Greenwell, who helped us finalize the manuscript—a challenging task by itself that was made more complicated by the geographical dispersion of our team.

Speyer	Michael W. Bauer
Berlin	Miriam Hartlapp
Munich	Christian Adam
Lausanne	Emmanuelle Mathieu
2019	

PRAISE FOR *TAKING THE EU TO COURT*

"This is an excellent book on the link between politics and law. In the growing political science literature on the Court of Justice of the European Union, the authors have managed a real *tour de force* in showing to what extent initiating action for annulment is, in fact, a political decision of stakeholders. Empirically rich and theoretically subtle, the book is a must-read for anyone interested in understanding legal conflict management in a multi-level system such as the EU."
—Sabine Saurugger, *Sciences Po Grenoble, Laboratoire Pacte, France*

Contents

1 The Neglected Politics Behind EU Annulment Litigation   1

2 Towards an Analytical Framework to Study Annulments in the EU   21

3 The Legal Background   51

4 Studying Annulment Actions   73

5 Motivations: When Conflict Leads to Litigation   83

6 Litigant Configurations: Turbulence and the Emergence of Complex Configurations   127

7 Litigant Success: How Litigant Configurations Relate to Legal Outcomes   155

8 The Political Side of EU Annulment Litigation   189

Correction to: Taking the EU to Court   C1

Annexes	207
References	211
Index	233

About the Authors

Christian Adam is Assistant Professor at the Geschwister Scholl Institute for Political Science at the Ludwig Maximilians Universität München (LMU Munich). He received his B.A. at the University of Konstanz, where he also obtained his doctorate in 2013. Christian Adam completed his M.A. program at the University of St. Gallen (HSG) and his CEMS Master in International Management in collaboration with the London School of Economics and Political Science. In his work, he tries to find ways to explain institutional (mis-)behavior and institutional change. In this context, he is particularly interested in the perceived legitimacy of democratic and legal institutions and in the perceived legitimacy of institutional change. The origins and consequences of political conflict that take the form of litigation have taken an important role in this regard. He coauthored the book *On the Road to Permissiveness? Change and Convergence of Moral Regulation in Europe* (2015), and his articles have appeared in such peer-reviewed journals as *Policy Sciences*, the *Journal of Common Market Studies*, the *Policy Studies Journal*, and *Administrative Review*.

Michael W. Bauer holds the Jean Monnet Chair for Comparative Public Administration and Policy Analysis at the German University of Administrative Sciences Speyer and is a part-time Professor at the School of Transnational Governance, European University Institute, Florence. He was Professor at the Humboldt University Berlin (2009–2012) and at the University of Konstanz (2004–2009). He studied in Mannheim,

Vienna, Frankfurt am Main, and Berlin and received a Master's degree in Politics and Administration from the College of Europe Bruges (1997). From 2000 to 2002, Michael worked as a post-doctoral fellow at the Max Planck Institute for Research on Collective Goods in Bonn, prior to which he conducted his Ph.D. at the European University Institute in Florence (1997–2000) under the supervision of Adrienne Héritier. His research focuses on international bureaucracies, multilevel governance, European integration, and policy implementation. Michael has published widely in public policy, public administration, and European integration journals. His collaborations include *The European Commission of the Twenty-First Century* and *Dismantling Public Policies: Strategies, Constrains and Outcomes*, as well as 'The State, the Economy, and the Regions: Theories of Preference Formation in Times of Crisis', published in 2016 in the *Journal of Public Administration Research and Theory*. He recently coedited a special issue of the *Journal of European Public Policy* about international bureaucracies' role in policy making, a handbook of the European administrative system, and a monograph about the changing politics of the European Union budget.

Miriam Hartlapp is Professor of Comparative Politics: Germany and France at the Freie University Berlin (FU). Before joining the FU in April 2017, she held chairs at Leipzig (2014–2017) and at Bremen University (2013–2014), worked at the Max Planck Institute for the Study of Societies in Cologne, at the International Labour Organization in Geneva, and led a Young Independent Research Group at the WZB Berlin Social Science Center. She is coauthor of *Complying with Europe: The Impact of EU Minimum Harmonisation and Soft Law in the Member States* (2005, winner of the 2007 EUSA Best Book in EU Studies Prize) and *Which Policy for Europe? Power and Conflict Inside the European Commission* (2014). Her research focuses on governance in the EU multilevel system, particularly the European Commission and the role of France and Germany in the EU, comparative implementation, (non-)compliance and enforcement, and regulation of economic, employment, and social policies. Currently, she is academic coordinator of an EU-funded interdisciplinary project on European Union soft-law research and is leading an ANR-DFG project on the effects of EU soft law across the multilevel system.

Emmanuelle Mathieu is a Lecturer at the University of Lausanne. Before this appointment, she was a Marie Curie research fellow at the Barcelona Institute for International Studies. She has worked at the German Research Institute for Public Administration Speyer; at the European University Institute, where in 2014 she defended her thesis, written under the supervision of Adrienne Héritier; and at the Catholic University of Louvain. Her research is located at the crossroads between multilevel governance, European governance, and regulatory governance. She has worked on coordination in multi-actor regulatory environments, on the EU regulatory space, on litigation and conflict in the EU, and on regulatory governance in developing countries. Her book *Regulatory Delegation in the European Union: Networks, Committees and Agencies* was published in 2016. Her work also appeared in *Regulation & Governance*, *Public Administration* and *West European Politics* among other journals in the field. She recently coedited, with Christian Adam and Miriam Hartlapp, a special issue of the *Journal of European Integration* about the impact of the public policy context on the power of the CJEU.

Abbreviations

ANOVA	Analysis of Variance
CAP	Common Agriculture Policy
CARUE	Conference for Issues Related to the European Union
CFI	Court of First Instance
CFSP	Common Foreign and Security Policy
CJEU	Court of Justice of the European Union
COM	European Commission
DecaBDE	Decabromodiphenyl ether
DG	Directorate General
ECB	European Central Bank
ECJ	European Court of Justice
EFTA	European Free Trade Association
EP	European Parliament
EPSO	European Personnel Selection Office
EU	European Union
EURES	European Employment Services
GC	General Court
MS	Member States
NAFOR	European Union Naval Force
NGO	Non-Governmental Organization
OHIM	Community Trademark Office
PNR	Passenger Name Records
SAAP	State Aid Action Plan
TEU	Treaty on European Union
TFEU	Treaty on the Functioning of the European Union
UK	United Kingdom
US	United States of America

LIST OF FIGURES

Fig. 1.1	Total number of actions for annulment by year of initiation	11
Fig. 1.2	Share of actions for annulment by policy sector	12
Fig. 1.3	Share of actions for annulment by defendant	13
Fig. 1.4	Total actions for annulment by type of applicant	14
Fig. 2.1	Horizontal conflicts	35
Fig. 2.2	Vertical conflicts	36
Fig. 2.3	Complex horizontal conflicts	37
Fig. 2.4	Complex vertical conflicts	39
Fig. 5.1	Annulment actions and treaty changes	100
Fig. 6.1	Complex litigant configurations over time	130
Fig. 7.1	Success rate over time	168
Fig. 7.2	Litigant success by litigant configuration	169
Fig. 7.3	Success rates for simple and complex configurations	172

LIST OF TABLES

Table 1.1	Cases cited in this chapter	16
Table 2.1	Cases cited in this chapter	40
Table 3.1	Cases cited in this chapter	67
Table 5.1	Overview of the four motivational logics for litigation	93
Table 5.2	Cases cited in this chapter	118
Table 6.1	Simple and complex cases in vertical conflicts (1957–2012)	131
Table 6.2	Most frequent complex actors' configurations in vertical conflicts (1957–2012)	131
Table 6.3	Simple and complex cases in horizontal conflicts (1957–2012)	132
Table 6.4	The Council and the Commission in complex configurations (1957–2012)	132
Table 6.5	T-test on the relative frequency of complex litigant configurations in years with and without treaty changes	139
Table 6.6	Cases cited in this chapter	150
Table 7.1	Pairwise comparison of configuration-specific differences in success rates	170
Table 7.2	Cases cited in this chapter	184
Table A.1	List of interviews	208

xxi

CHAPTER 1

The Neglected Politics Behind EU Annulment Litigation

In September 2016, Ireland and Apple announced that they were taking the European Commission to the Court of Justice of the European Union (CJEU).[1] They questioned the legality of a Commission decision that demanded that Ireland reclaim billions of euros from Apple, the multinational technology company.[2] The Commission regarded the Irish tax arrangement with Apple as violating European Union (EU) state aid law. According to the Commission, Apple enjoyed an undue tax advantage that it had to pay back. The subsequent Commission decision was thus bound to have ample consequences for both Ireland and Apple. Yet although the decision would flush thirteen billion euros into the Irish public budget, the Irish government was dominated by the fear of losing jobs if business-friendly tax deals with Apple and other companies were no longer an option. In addition, Apple's profits would take a considerable cut, putting pressure on its management and sending shivers through its shareholders. On the other side of this conflict, the Commission strongly emphasized its obligation to prevent collusive tax pacts that might spiral into self-defeating fiscal competition among member states.

Despite the political drama surrounding the case, little attention was paid to the supranational legal instrument—the annulment procedure—used as a last resort by Apple to prevail in this conflict with the Commission. According to EU law, the annulment procedure constitutes the only legal route to contest a supranational act or particular Commission decision about the national implementation of European policies (Article 263 TFEU).[3] By launching an annulment action against the EU executive, Apple was thus asking to review the lawfulness of the supranational decision, hoping that the Court would find it to be in violation of EU law and therefore annul it. Ireland actively and officially supported Apple's case in court by intervening with legal arguments in its favour, while the Commission found a legal supporter in the European Free Trade Association Surveillance Authority. Even the United States government tried to take on an active role by supporting Apple and Ireland in court. The Court rejected the United States' application, however, and denied it formal access to these court proceedings.[4]

The extraordinary attention the Apple case received most likely stemmed from the involvement of a world-famous company and the enormous amount of money that was disclaimed by politicians. However, the case also carries substantial political implications for the emerging EU multilevel order. 'If the Commission prevails in court, the decision will reset the balance of power on tax policy in Europe. While governments will still be able to set their own tax rates, the Commission will have established itself as a watchful referee of how national rules are implemented. Success on appeal for Apple and Ireland might relieve some of that pressure and give national governments more leeway', analysed the Financial Times (Houlder et al. 2016). Whether the Court will rule in favour of the Commission or in favour of Ireland and Apple is still an open question at the time of writing. At any rate, this instance highlights that annulment actions have become an important legal battleground for EU policy making and system development.

If one single annulment decision can crucially affect the future balance of power in tax policy in the EU, then what about the other several dozens of annulment cases that are decided each year? Are they equally important? The frank answer to this question is that we do not know. Considering the potential impact of EU annulment actions, it is striking that they evaded the focus of students of the European multilevel system for so long. In view of this gap, the aim of this book is to explore EU annulment actions and their political relevance for EU multilevel governance.

As we will argue in this book, annulment actions are part of the struggle over policy decisions and system development in the emerging multilevel political order of the EU. They often represent what seems like a measure of last resort with which national governments, regional governments, interest groups, companies, and even other EU institutions try to fight off interferences of (other) EU institutions. Moreover, we will argue that the initiation of an action for annulment is by no means an automatic and legalistic reaction to EU institutions breaching their mandates and overstepping their competences. Even blatant breaches of EU law will only attract annulment litigation when this is in the political and/or financial interest of stakeholders. At the same time, even where the pleas for actions for annulment seem highly dubious, with very slim chances for success, initiating an action for annulment can be in the political and/or financial interest of some actors. Simply put, annulment actions are a legal instrument that is typically used for political reasons and often has the power to yield significant political consequences as a result of its impact on policy content, political procedures, and the EU's constitutional order. This calls for political science research to complement legal scholarship on annulment actions. The common multilevel nature of annulment conflicts underlines yet again the importance of understanding the EU as a multilevel system. If we fail to understand the role of these conflicts in which public actors from multiple levels of government, as well as interest groups, companies, and EU institutions, directly accuse (other) EU institutions of violating EU law, we arguably fail to understand a substantial part of this multilevel system. This book intends to improve our understanding of these conflicts by focussing first on the motivation of actors to litigate, second on the configurations of actors involved, and third on the outcome of the rulings and their effect on policy substance and competence distribution in the EU multilevel system.

Unsurprisingly, annulments as devices of EU law have so far been the concern primarily of legal scholarship. As we argue in the following chapters, to understand the role of annulment actions within the EU multilevel system, it is essential to consider their political dimension as well (Bauer and Hartlapp 2010; Adam et al. 2015; Adam 2016; Hartlapp 2018; Mathieu et al. 2018). Without investigating their political nature, without looking at the underlying motivations of actors, and without gauging the potential impact of such litigation, our understanding of annulments will remain partial and inadequate. As the Apple case suggests, annulments may be politically and economically highly relevant— in our view, reflecting an increasingly important feature of emerging multilevel conflict over supranational decision making and implementation. This makes annulment litigation a fascinating subject for political scientists, especially for those interested in multilevel politics and EU policy making.

Against this background, this book provides a political perspective of EU annulments, combining qualitative and quantitative empirical insights and theoretical analysis. Essentially, our argument centres around two concepts: actors' motivations and actor configurations.

First, we argue a legalistic understanding of actions for annulment that expects annulment actions to emerge only when the suspicion that an EU institution has breached its mandate and overstepped its competences falls short of the empirical reality. Instead, annulments are regularly initiated in the attempt to influence policies and competence allocation in the EU by a variety of actors with different motivations. The literature on private litigants typically presumes that companies are motivated by financial gains, while non-governmental organizations go to court to push forward ideological and policy preferences. This presumption seems overly simplistic for the context of litigating public actors that are motivated by keeping or expanding institutional competences in addition to seeking policies and material gains. Here, motivations cannot simply be presumed, but instead must be uncovered by research. To do so, it is essential to identify and analyse the conflict that underlies and precedes the decision to litigate. We distinguish four ideal types of motivations for litigation: material gains, institutional competences, ideology and policy preferences, and political trust. We derive these motivations by analysing actors' problems, demands, and preferences within the multilevel policy process that gives rise to annulment litigation. This allows us to describe actors' motivations for going to court (why they consider litigating), as well as the conditions that influence *when* actors go to court, such as the legal opportunity structures and the merits of a case. On this basis, we try to move beyond simple risk-benefit analysis to explain litigation behaviour. After all, for some motivations, it is very difficult to quantify the expected benefits of litigation. Moreover, different actors feel very differently about legal uncertainty and even the slim chances of legal success. In fact, we have to take into account that for public litigants, even losing cases can be beneficial for them (Adam et al. 2015).

Second, next to motivations, our argument puts actor configurations centre stage. Sometimes, annulment conflicts are fought between just one applicant and one defendant EU institution—a member state litigating against the Council of the European Union, or a private company litigating against the Commission, for example. Quite frequently, however, the litigant configuration in court is much more complex than that, including actors from multiple levels of government, and private and public actors on both sides of the conflict. While we are far from able to predict the emergence of such complex constellations in individual cases, we present evidence that suggests that the emergence of complex multilevel configurations is more likely during times of institutional turbulence at the EU level, for example, in times of treaty change or—at a smaller scale—in response to disruptive policy changes. In such situations of institutional turbulence, established legal paths and orders become unsettled. Moreover, the incentives to go to court increase in times of turbulence. This is because disrupted legal regimes create more legal grey areas for the Court to colour in with its rulings. After all, the Court has not had the chance to interpret and specify new or altered treaty articles or directives. Provoking influential precedent rulings is more likely to occur soon after turbulence and can be very valuable to litigants for a number of reasons. Particularly when there is a chance to have the Court colour in rather large legal grey areas due to turbulence, litigation can be chosen for various motivations, be it for material gain, to gain institutional competences, of to attain ideological goals. For the same reason that institutional turbulence increases the stakes for potential litigants on either side of conflicts, it also makes court rulings less predictable. Since there is no long history of court rulings interpreting new or modified treaty articles or directives, the Court's take on these new and revised legal acts remains unknown until such a history of rulings is established. Existing case law cannot easily be used to predict court behaviour without considerable uncertainty. Therefore, institutional turbulence creates legal uncertainty and incentives to try to provoke precedent rulings. This not only incentivizes more actors to take an active role in annulment litigation resulting in a greater number of complex actor configurations. This also creates a situation in which the success rate for these complex actor configurations is much closer to 50% than for simple actor configurations. Simply put, when court rulings are easy to foresee—as would be the case with a long history of relevant court rulings on an issue—fewer actors will be drawn to take an active part in annulment proceedings than when court rulings are rather difficult to foresee; that is, where chances of success are close to 50:50. Consequently, we argue that we should not be too quick to attribute the significantly different success rates for simple versus complex actor configurations to a causal impact of the actor configuration on the judges at Luxembourg. Instead, it rather indicates that the legal cases that give rise to simple actor configurations are significantly different from the cases that trigger complex actor configurations in court.

Annulment actions thus serve one rather clearly defined legal purpose: to keep supranational institutions in (legal) check. And yet we hope to convincingly show that at the same time, they also serve various political purposes. These political purposes reach all the way from gaining political trust from domestic constituents, to reaching ideological goals, to expanding institutional competences, all the way to hoping for material gains. While (Article 258 TFEU) infringement proceedings have helped the Commission to push the Europeanization of national policies ahead (e.g. Tallberg 2002), and preliminary reference proceedings (Article 267 TFEU) have helped to boost the European integration process (e.g. Burley and Mattli 1993), it is more difficult to pinpoint the role of annulment actions. Annulment proceedings have helped to restrict the power and influence of EU institutions in some areas but also helped to expand their competences in other areas. Most importantly, however, annulment actions have given various types of actors and the Court the chance to continuously adjust and fill in the (legal) gaps within the developing EU polity. Thereby, they have influenced not only policy content but also the competences of EU institutions and their relationship to member states, regional governments, interest groups, companies, and citizens.

POLICY AND INSTITUTIONAL RELEVANCE
OF ANNULMENTS

Annulment actions are thus one important channel for judicial review in the EU. Judicial review is a process under which the actions of public actors are subject to the review of the judiciary. The competent court may invalidate an executive or legislative decision for being unlawful or unconstitutional. Judicial review is a key element of the checks and balances in the separation of powers. It allows the judiciary to put a halt on executive or legislative decisions that go beyond their competences.

Research in the area of law and politics provides abundant examples of how judicial review can lead to far-reaching policy and institutional changes. Many social movements have used judicial review to push forward their agenda, achieving impressive results in some cases thanks to the United States Supreme Court's relative judicial openness in certain policy issues, such as the defence of minorities (Meyer and Boutcher 2007). We also know from the literature on federalism that judicial review can lead constitutional courts to play a prominent role in the redefinition of central-regional competence distribution (Laufer and Münch 1998; Swenden 2006, 79–89).

In the EU, judicial review through annulment actions can have far-reaching policy and institutional impacts. The policy impact of annulments is particularly visible in the context of state aid policy. EU state aid policy prohibits governmental subsidies to economic actors when they distort competition on the internal market (there are nevertheless exceptions to this rule under specific circumstances). The crucial and decisive task of assessing whether a subsidy is compatible with the internal market belongs to the Commission. How the Commission interprets the compatibility with the internal market is often subject to examination that also includes the Court and the case law it has produced in the past. Annulment actions, raised against the Commission's state aid decisions, have therefore often contributed to clarifying the conditions under which the Commission may and may not prohibit national aids. Thereby, these annulment rulings have not only affected the substance of state aid policy but also influenced the balance of power between the Commission and the member states.

One example for the effect of annulment litigation on the balance of power between the Commission and the member states is case T-21/06, initiated by Germany in 2006. In the course of its annulment ruling, the Court legitimized the Commission's newly established practice of tying acceptable state aid provision to the occurrence of market failure. In the specific case, Germany had subsidized two private broadcasting companies (ProSiebenSat.1 and RTL Group) in order to successfully rollout digital TV receivable through antenna in the Berlin-Brandenburg area. The Commission declared these aids illegal and justified this decision with reference to the newly established concept of market failure: the subsidy is authorized only if it was an effective and proportionate instrument to address a market failure. This connection between market failure and the legality of national state aid policy was not included in the treaties. It was only established in the Commission's State Aid Action Plan (SAAP) adopted in 2005 (European Commission 2005, 4). Due to the indeterminate legal nature of this concept, its introduction would ensure a maximal level of discretion for the Commission. This is why in its advisory statement during the consultation period of the SAAP in 2005, the German government explicitly complained that the concept of market failure as introduced by the Commission was not an appropriate foundation for assessing national state aid (Federal Republic of Germany 2005, 3). The Commission's use of the market failure concept in this particular case provided Germany with the opportunity to involve the CJEU to either revoke or specify the role of market failure in the context of state aid control. Germany, however, lost this case and helped to clarify that the Court would accept market failure as a criterion for evaluating the legality of state aid measures. Due to the substantial room for interpretation this concept gives to the Commission, this annulment conflict has arguably tilted the balance of power over state aid policy further towards the Commission.

Annulments can also have significant effects on national politics, as the following case dealing with suckler-cow premiums (C-344/01) indicates. This case, related to EU agricultural funds, had a profound impact on the relationship between central and regional levels of government in Germany. In Germany, as is often the case in federal or regionalized countries, the practical management of EU agricultural funds is delegated to lower levels of government—in the German case, to the *Länder* (German states). In case a state fails to comply with EU requirements in terms of supervision and control of how the funds are spent, the Commission refuses to refinance the corresponding amount of money to the member state. In Germany, this sanction primarily hurt the federal budget from which the money had been advanced, because no compensation rule that would transfer the financial burden of the sanction to the non-compliant state's budget existed. The German federal government had been eager to change this situation. But because of the states' collective opposition to such a change, the status quo remained. Yet this situation changed in response to the so-called suckler-cow premiums case, which took place during lengthy negotiations between the federal government and the states about important reforms of German federalism. This was yet another instance in which the Commission found that several German states had failed to follow EU rules when paying out premiums to farmers for suckler cows and imposed financial sanctions. Again, the federal government would be stuck with these sanctions without a mechanism to divert them to the noncomplying states. In this situation, annulment litigation must have seemed like an obvious course of action. After all, in the event of success in court, the financial sanction would just disappear. Even more importantly, in the opposite outcome of legal defeat, the court ruling would put further pressure on the states to compromise about the redistribution of financial responsibilities in case of financial sanctions related to the spending of EU money. When the Court ruled against Germany, the federal government was able to instrumentalize the ruling and managed to successfully negotiate an amendment to the German constitution (Article 104a), specifying that where the *Länder* are the regional entities implementing Germany's supranational responsibilities, 15% of resulting financial corrections would be covered by the federal budget, while 85% would from then on be covered by the *Länder* budgets (Adam et al. 2015). In other words, the German federal government lost this annulment case, rather successfully leaving a mark in the German constitution.

Moreover, annulment actions can also have a profound impact on the distribution of competences between EU institutions. The *ERTA* case (C-22/70) is proof of this. Here, the Commission sued the Council for having prevented the Commission from negotiating an international agreement in the field of transport. Traditionally, member states would negotiate international trade agreements only in those areas of external policy where the EU is not competent. In that case, the Council had authorized member states to negotiate and conclude an international transport agreement that included social rules for the protection of drivers. While the Council claimed that transport was a national competence (currently, Article 95 TFEU), the Commission felt that the Council had overstepped its competences and launched an annulment to shift the legal base so negotiation powers would fall on the Commission (today Article 207 TFEU). The Court additionally granted that the existence of an *acquis communautaire* harmonizing social provisions in transport (Regulation 543/69) necessarily vested any international agreement in community powers—consequently excluding concurring powers of member states in trade negotiations. This legal interpretation implied that the Commission could expand its external policy competences to areas where the EU holds internal competences. This became known as the principle of implied powers and was further developed and eventually codified in the Nice Treaty (Cremona 2011), leaving a lasting effect in primary law.

Such far-reaching institutional adjustments triggered by annulment actions may also take place below the level of formal treaty changes, for example, through the modification of administrative practices. After having lost numerous annulment rulings on the application of the post-Lisbon comitology structure, the Commission secretariat general issued an internal guideline to its policy directorate generals to be particularly vigilant during law making. Annulment cases had the effect of limiting the Commission's influence on the delegation and implementation of acts. To compensate its loss of influence at the level of comitology, the Commission changed its approach, favouring the inclusion of detailed policy preferences in the drafting of legislative acts. Because of annulment actions, the Commission thus developed a new procedural strategy consisting of fixing things at an earlier stage rather than leaving room for policy making to the Council and the European Parliament (EP) via implementing and delegating acts (COM_1).[5]

In all these examples, annulment actions emerged from conflicts among a few actors and appear, at first sight, to be of minor importance because they seemed to deal merely with sector-specific issues and individual implementation decisions. Nevertheless, they brought about long-lasting and far-reaching formal and informal policy and institutional adaptations to the EU multilevel system, at times shifting the balance of policy-making powers. In the digital TV case, for example, a conflict between the Commission on one hand and Germany and two broadcasting companies on the other resulted in a wide extension of the Commission's room for interpreting EU state aid law, thanks to the Court's acknowledgement of the concept of market failure. In the suckler-cow premiums case, a conflict between Germany and the Commission on an apparently highly technical issue allowed the federal state to significantly reshape its financial relationship with German states in agriculture policy with respect to paying for supranational fines. An annulment case also coined the far-reaching and now famous doctrine of implied powers, allowing the Commission to significantly expand its competences in external affairs to the detriment of the Council and of the member states. Finally, annulment actions also led the Commission to revise its procedural strategy with a view to maximizing its influence on EU policies, leading to the expansion of detailed legislation to the detriment of delegation and implementing comitology acts. There should thus be no doubt that annulment actions play a crucial role in the EU's multilevel system. Ignoring the political role of annulment conflicts carries the risk of missing important aspects of how conflicts shape policy contents and policy process in the EU's multilevel system.

ANNULMENT OVER TIME AND ACROSS POLICY AREAS: EMPIRICAL EVIDENCE

Annulments are relevant not only in qualitative terms; they also emerge in quite significant numbers. Due to expanding competences of the European Commission and other EU institutions, such as the EP, the need to keep these supranational institutions in check via judicial review has increased over time, and so has the number of annulment cases directed against legal acts adopted by these institutions. Since the 1960s, there has been a clear increase in the number of annulment actions filed against EU institutions (see Fig. 1.1). At the same time, this increase is characterized by fluctuations. Chapter 5 offers a much closer look at the peaks and lows in the number of annulment actions over time.

But annulment actions have not only increased in number. They have also captured more and more policy sectors, slowly spreading across the whole spectrum of policy sectors in which EU institutions have become

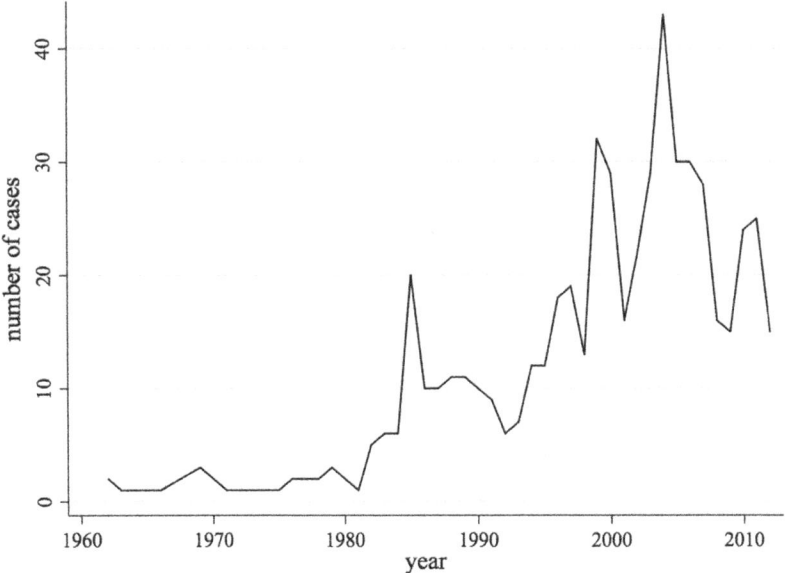

Fig. 1.1 Total number of actions for annulment by year of initiation (*Source* Own collection based on Stone Sweet and Brunell [2007] and updated from CURIA [cut off 31 December 2012])

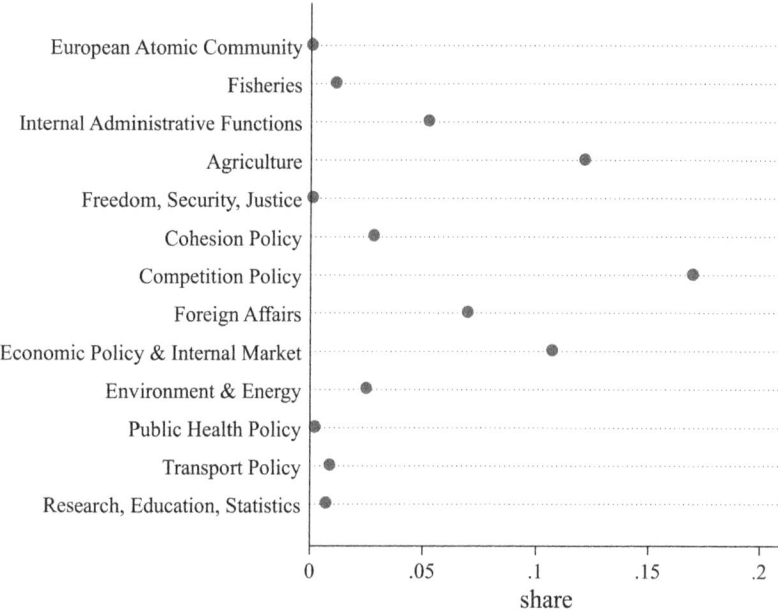

Fig. 1.2 Share of actions for annulment by policy sector (*Source* Own collection based on Stone Sweet and Brunell [2007] and updated from CURIA [cut off 31 December 2012])

active (see Fig. 1.2). While annulment actions occurred early in traditional areas of EU activity—such as agriculture or state aid and competition policy—expansion of supranational competences in foreign affairs (broadly defined with external affairs, trade policy, and foreign and security policy) have been accompanied by rising numbers for annulment actions in those areas, too.

Quite importantly, all major EU institutions have been confronted with annulment actions. While filing actions for annulment was initially meant to be a way for national governments to keep the High Authority—as predecessor of today's Commission—in check, actions for annulment are no longer raised only against the supranational executive. Around 20% of the annulment actions are directed against the Council, the EP, or the European Central Bank (ECB). The bulk of annulment cases—around 80%—however, still object to executive measures adopted by the Commission (see Fig. 1.3).

1 THE NEGLECTED POLITICS BEHIND EU ANNULMENT LITIGATION 13

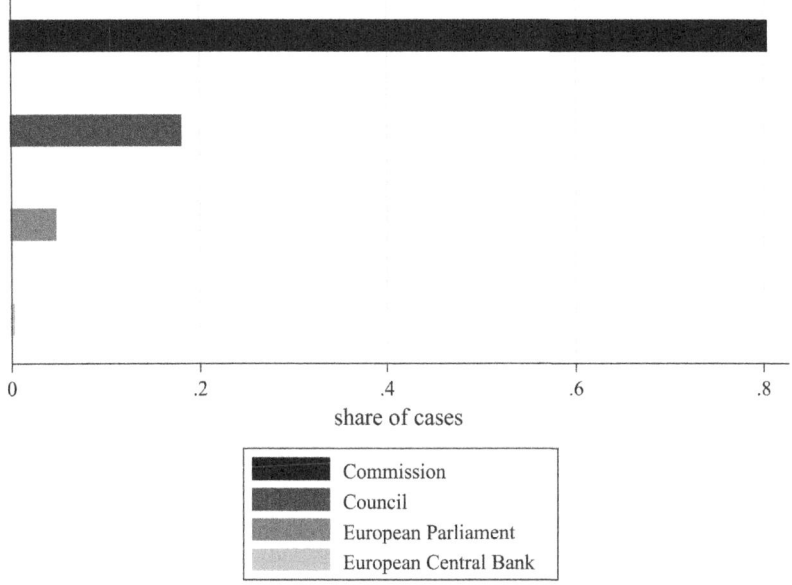

Fig. 1.3 Share of actions for annulment by defendant (*Source* Own collection based on Stone Sweet and Brunell [2007] and updated from CURIA [cut off 31 December 2012])

A look at the types of actors that initiate actions for annulment completes the rather complex picture we have drawn so far. While initially, annulment litigation was thought to be an instrument of judicial control for national governments against supranational institutions, today, a rather broad range of litigants launch annulment actions. Figure 1.4 indicates that private actors (individuals, companies, and interest groups), regional entities (regional or local authorities), national governments (i.e. member states), as well as EU institutions themselves actively use and initiate annulment actions in their struggles with (other) EU institutions. By 2012, private actors initiated the majority of annulments. Among public claimants, member states and EU institutions file a similar number of annulments. Subnational public actors are clearly less active.[6]

Concerning applicants, we observe interesting dynamics over time. The number of actions initiated by private applicants has boomed.

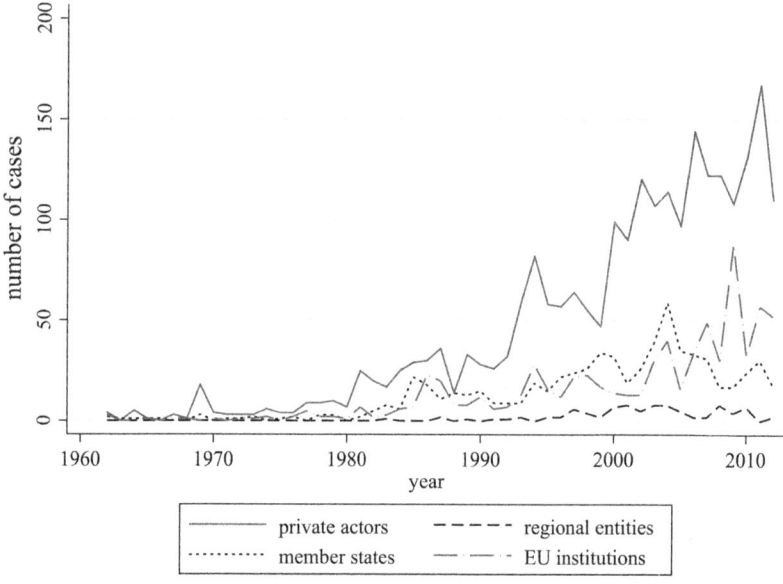

Fig. 1.4 Total actions for annulment by type of applicant (*Source* Own collection based on Stone Sweet and Brunell [2007] and updated from CURIA [cut off 31 December 2012])

Remarkably, EU institutions themselves increasingly sue each other, a tendency that has consolidated over time and even exceeded the number of actions initiated by the member states in the mid-2000s (Hartlapp 2018). At the same time, national governments have become somewhat more reluctant to litigate against EU institutions. As for regional actors, they have consistently been among the least active applicants.[7] We thus see an interesting changing structure of conflict cleavages over time in annulment litigation (Adam 2018).

These changes over time and the increased diversity in the type of litigants are partly the result of the evolution of actors' standing rights. The conditions under which each type of actor (other than member states governments, the Commission, and the Council) can initiate annulment actions are detailed in the treaties. Their interpretation by the Court and the corresponding treaty-based provisions have, however, evolved over time, leading to an extended access to the CJEU in the form of judicial review for an ever greater variety of litigants (Arnull 1995, 2001; see also Chapter 3). To some extent, these developments regarding standing rights for different actors factor into the empirical patterns of annulment litigation that we observe. And yet, the development of these standing rights was driven by politically motivated annulment litigation in the first place. Actors that had not enjoyed the right to initiate annulments or had only limited rights to do so, such the EP, for example, bring litigation despite little to no chance of being admitted to the Court in the hope of provoking influential precedent rulings extending their standing rights; something the EP managed to accomplish with their annulment action in the so-called *Chernobyl* case (70/88 *Parliament v. Council*).

In sum, empirical patterns of annulment litigation suggests that actions for annulment have become an increasingly relevant judicial tool in the struggle over policy content and decision competences in the EU. Corresponding with the expansion of EU competences over time and across policy fields, the rising powers of EU institutions such as the EP and the ECB, the need for (and use of) judicial review has also grown in proportion. Initially restricted to actions against the Commission in a limited number of policy sectors such as agriculture and state aid, the use of annulment actions rose in frequency, covered an ever greater range of policy fields, and came to be directed against virtually all EU institutions. The list of applicants has grown more heterogeneous as well. Private actors, regional authorities, the EP, and EU institutions themselves file annulment actions ever more frequently.

STRUCTURE OF THE BOOK

The next chapter has two parts (Chapter 2). First, we review the literature on multilevel governance, public policy, and judicial politics in the EU and highlight what the analysis of annulment actions brings to each of these literatures. Secondly, this allows us to identify three questions (on motivations, actor constellations, and outcomes of the rulings and effects) that organize the litigation chain we present in our book. Next, we present the legal background of annulment actions (Chapter 3) to the extent that it structures opportunities and constraints for our policy actors when considering raising annulment actions. We proceed with a presentation of our data collection strategy and of the logic behind the empirical analysis that we employ (Chapter 4). We do so before presenting three chapters that present empirical evidence and develop theoretical arguments related to our four research questions. The first of these empirical chapters explores the different types of motivations underlying public actors' decisions to turn policy conflicts into annulment actions (Chapter 5). The second empirical chapter explores the factors behind the emergence of complex and multilevel actors' constellations in annulment proceedings (Chapter 6). The third empirical chapter covers our last two questions: the impact of actors' constellations on success in court and the impact of annulment actions on the multilevel policy conflicts they originate from (Chapter 7). The conclusion summarizes our findings and wraps up our main argument, while also suggesting avenues for further research in the area (Chapter 8).

We hope that this book makes a strong case for the need to understand annulment actions as a class of legal proceedings with political intent and impact in EU multilevel policy making. Yet even if we only manage to set out a new area waiting for empirical analyses in the field of law and politics—or just add to the intellectual controversy over the political importance of EU annulments, for that matter—we will be satisfied. Annulment litigation has become too important to continue being ignored by political analysis.

CASES CITED

See Table 1.1.

Table 1.1 Cases cited in this chapter

C-22/70	Judgment of 31 March 1971, *Commission v. Council*, C-22/70, EU:C:1971:32
C-344/01	Judgment of 4 March 2001, *Germany v. Commission*, C-344/01, EU:C:2004:121
T-21/06	Judgment of 6 October 2009, *Germany v. Commission*, T-21/06, EU:T:2009:387
T-892/16	Order of 15 December 2017, *Apple v. Commission*, T-892/16, EU:T:2017:925f

Notes

1. Throughout this book, we refer to the Court of Justice of the European Union as 'the Court'. Thereby, we typically refer to both the Court of Justice and the General Court, depending on the competent court in the respective case, without specifying this court more specifically.
2. Order of 15 December 2017, *Apple v Commission*, T-892/16, EU:T:2017:925f.
3. TFEU stands for Treaty on the Functioning of the European Union. A list of abbreviations is provided at the beginning of the book.
4. The legal dispute did not end there. Despite the pending annulment decision, Ireland is obliged to recover the state aid deemed illegal. As Ireland's progress was too slow in the eyes of the Commission—several deadlines for calculating and collecting the illegal state aid were missed by the Irish government—the Commission decided to take Ireland to the Court of Justice for failure to implement the Commission decision, in accordance with Article 108(2) of the TFEU (see http://europa.eu/rapid/press-release_IP-17-3702_en.htm, accessed 4 October 2017). In response to this, Ireland collected the money from Apple in September 2018; funds are currently being held in escrow while the annulment case is still pending in court.
5. The acronym COM indicates that the interviewee works for the European Commission. The logic behind codifying the interview sources is explained in more detail in Chapter 4. All interviews conducted in the preparation of this research are listed in the Annex.
6. In some countries, subnational authorities have formal agreements with their national governments stating that in case a subnational government wants to file an annulment against EU institutions, the case is formally brought forward by the member state's central administration.
7. Regional governments and private actors face stricter legal requirements than governments or EU institutions for CJEU consideration of the cases that they raise (cf. Chapter 3).

References

Adam, C. (2016). *The politics of judicial review: Supranational administrative acts and judicialized compliance conflict in the EU*. Basingstoke, UK: Palgrave Macmillan.

Adam, C. (2018). Multilevel conflict over policy application—Detecting changing cleavage patterns. *Journal of European Integration*, *40*(6), 683–700.

Adam, C., Bauer, M. W., & Hartlapp, M. (2015). It's not always about winning: Domestic politics and legal success in EU annulment litigation. *Journal of Common Market Studies*, *53*(2), 185–200.

Arnull, A. (1995). Private applicants and the action for annulment under Article 173 of the EC treaty. *Common Market Law Review, 32,* 7–49.
Arnull, A. (2001). Private applicants and the action for annulment since CODORNIU. *Common Market Law Review, 38,* 7–52.
Bauer, M. W., & Hartlapp, M. (2010). Much ado about money and how to spend it! Analysing 40 years of annulment cases against the European Union Commission. *European Journal of Political Research, 49,* 202–222.
Burley, A.-M., & Mattli, W. (1993). Europe before the court: A political theory of legal integration. *International Organization, 47*(1), 41–76.
Cremona, M. (2011). External relations and external competences of the European Union: The emergence of an integrated policy. In P. Craig & G. de Burca (Eds.), *The Evolution of EU Law* (pp. 217–268). Oxford, UK: Oxford University Press.
European Commission. (2005, June 7). *State aid action plan—Less and better targeted state aid: A roadmap for state aid reform 2005–2009.* COM (2005) 107 final. http://eur-lex.europa.eu/LexUriServ/LexUriServ.do?uri=CEL-EX:52005DC0107:EN:NOT. Accessed 9 April 2013.
Federal Republic of Germany. (2005). *Stellungnahme der Bundesregierung der Bundesrepublik Deutschland zum 'Aktionsplan staatliche Beihilfen' vom 5.10.2005.* http://ec.europa.eu/competition/state_aid/reform/comments_saap/37982.pdf. Accessed 7 December 2017.
Hartlapp, M. (2018). Power shifts via the judicial arena: How annulments cases between EU institutions shape competence allocation. *Journal of Common Market Studies, 56*(6), 1429–1445.
Houlder, V., Barker, A., & Beesley, A. (2016, August 30). Apple's EU tax dispute explained: The consequences of the commissions complaint and the wider implications of its ruling. *Financial Times.* https://www.ft.com/content/3e0172a0-6e1b-11e6-9ac1-1055824ca907.
Laufer, H., & Münch, U. (1998). *Das föderative System der Bundesrepublik Deutschland.* Stuttgart, Germany: UTB.
Mathieu, E., Adam, C., & Hartlapp, M. (2018). From high judges to policy stakeholders: A public policy approach to the CJEUs power. *Journal of European Integration, 40*(6), 653–666.
Meyer, D., & Boutcher, S. (2007). Signals and spillover: Brown vs. Board of Education and other social movements. *Perspectives on Politics, 1,* 81–93.
Stone Sweet, A., & Brunell, T. L. (2007). *Data set on actions under Article 230: 1954–2006. NEWGOV Project.* San Domenico di Fiesole, Italy: Robert Schuman Centre, European University Institute.
Swenden, W. (2006). *Federalism and regionalism in Western Europe: A comparative and thematic analysis.* Basingstoke, UK: Palgrave.
Tallberg, J. (2002). Paths to compliance: Enforcement, management, and the European Union. *International Organization, 56,* 609–643.

Open Access This chapter is licensed under the terms of the Creative Commons Attribution 4.0 International License (http://creativecommons.org/licenses/by/4.0/), which permits use, sharing, adaptation, distribution and reproduction in any medium or format, as long as you give appropriate credit to the original author(s) and the source, provide a link to the Creative Commons license and indicate if changes were made.

The images or other third party material in this chapter are included in the chapter's Creative Commons license, unless indicated otherwise in a credit line to the material. If material is not included in the chapter's Creative Commons license and your intended use is not permitted by statutory regulation or exceeds the permitted use, you will need to obtain permission directly from the copyright holder.

CHAPTER 2

Towards an Analytical Framework to Study Annulments in the EU

Annulment actions are a legal weapon in the political fight between actors. The aim of engaging in annulment litigation is to shape the making of public policies and to influence the distribution of competences or the flow of funds. To explore the politics of annulments, our starting point is the proposition that courts can only speak in reaction to litigation initiated by actors enmeshed in complex policy conflicts. In that perspective, the Court of Justice of the European Union (CJEU) and its rulings are just a result of conflicts deliberatively escalated to the judicial arena in the struggle between opposing actors to trigger favourable decisions that serve their regulative and redistributive interests. Annulment actions can thus be conceived as tools employed by stakeholders fighting to defend their interests in a multilevel policy context. With this analytical vantage point come several questions. Most importantly, we must answer the question of how to conceptualize annulment conflicts and their underlying struggles. What are the relevant analytical questions to raise? In this chapter, we seek orientation from existing scholarly works in order to develop an analytical framework allowing us to engage in the empirical analysis of annulment actions and the respective motivations of actors.

In the following, we engage with three specific strands of literature that potentially enrich and orient our understanding of annulment litigation. They do so from different angles and thus contribute to different aspects of our research. First, scholars interested in multilevel governance and evolution of the European Union's (EU's) political system inform our understanding of how conflict emerges in the EU. Second, public policy analysis forms our view on implementation and the role of judicial proceedings in EU policy making. Moreover, third, judicial politics underline that actors strategically shape legal conflicts. Based on communalities and differences with the arguments presented in these strands of literature, we develop three specific research questions, which will further guide our empirical analysis of EU annulment conflicts in the remainder of this book. In a nutshell, we argue that analyses of annulment litigation need to focus on three aspects. First, we need to analyse the motivations—particularly those of public actors—to understand why they raise such cases. Second, we need to assess the actor configurations that characterize and influence judicial proceedings. Third, we must identify judicial outcomes (who loses and who wins?) along with their impact on policy substance and distribution of competence in the EU multilevel setting.

Research Questions

Essentially, we address three research questions. They are related to (1) the use of annulment actions, (2) their structure, and (3) their outcome and impact.

Our first question deals with the emergence of annulment actions: why do actors decide to litigate? The EU's multilevel policy process involves many distinct actors located at different governmental levels and active in different arenas. As a result, a wide array of interests, political preferences, values, cultures, and understandings interact and sometimes clash in the policy process. Conflicts between these actors have been widely studied in the context of policy making in the legislative arena. Sometimes, however, these policy conflicts are resolved within the judicial arena. Annulment actions constitute one legal channel for resolving some of these policy conflicts within the judicial arena. The question, however, is what motivates actors to turn to annulment actions to pursue their goals in the EU's multilevel policy context?

The second question deals with the structure of annulment actions. On a descriptive level, we ask about which actor configurations characterize annulment actions. The multilevel governance approach conceives EU governance as composed of a variety of interactions between a wide range of actors in the EU public policy process. What kind of actor configurations can we observe in annulment actions? Who litigates most and why? Are the conflict lines observable in the policy process reflected in litigation constellations? Which alliances and lines of cooperation are we likely to observe, and why? On a more analytical level, we therefore ask about determinants of different actor configurations and explore the impact of structure in this regard.

Third, we explore the outcome of annulment actions (i.e. rulings). How often are annulment actions successful, and why? Are some actors more likely to win than others? And are some actor configurations more successful than others? Most importantly, we explore the question of how certain we can be that any observed link between litigant configuration and judicial outcome results from a causal impact of that litigant configuration on the Court and not from unobserved factors that give rise to different litigant configurations and legal outcomes at the same time. In this regard, we also assess the impact of annulment actions on the multilevel policy context and on policy stakeholders and explore whether legal success in court is always aligned with political success or not. The discussion below will elaborate these different lines of inquiry.

MULTILEVEL GOVERNANCE AND CONFLICT IN THE EU

Much of the literature on multilevel governance looks at the EU as a specific political system. It provides important insights on actors and shapes our thinking on how conflict emerges from their interactions in the European political arena. Since the early 1990s, the EU system has been increasingly characterized as multileveled. In contrast to classical political systems, the multilevel concept stresses vertical collaboration, the multiplicity of actors taking part in EU governance, and the loose coupling of levels and arenas (Marks 1993; Marks et al. 1996; Hooghe 1996; Benz and Eberlein 1999; Hooghe and Marks 2001; Tatham and Bauer 2014b). The multilevel governance perspective focuses—at least conceptually—on the opportunities emerging from interaction, coordination, and cooperation of governments and non-state actors on multiple levels, forming institutional linkages and politics beyond a clear hierarchy (Tatham and Bauer 2014a). Implicitly, in these interactions, conflicts about policy and the distribution of competences play a key role. They do so, for example, in the form of rivalry between subnational actors and national governments in their relationship with the EU (Hooghe and Marks 2001, 115). However, the conceptualization of the conflict surrounding multilevel governance arrangements has been afforded less room than the analysis of new forms of collaboration and engagement. On the rare occasions that policy conflict gets more attention, as in the cases with the joint decision trap (Scharpf 1985, 2006; Falkner 2011), multilevel conflict is conceived as a constraint for collective action. Conflict is typically associated with a form of blockage rather than as a dynamic process able to escalate diverging views to an eventual (court) decision. Thus, although conflict is implicit in this literature, it has not been a central concern for multilevel governance scholars. Consequently, it seems fair to stress the limitations of existing works on EU multilevel governance when it comes to the emergence of conflicts among actors of various political levels, the mediation of such conflict over policy decisions by the judiciary, and the potentially resulting new dynamics, feedback effects, and structuring elements for public policy. To be fair, Stone Sweet (1999) and Kelemen (2011) have laid some groundwork for analysing the role of legal conflict from a perspective of multilevel governance. In particular, Kelemen's argument about an emerging Eurolegalism stresses how features of the EU system link to litigation. Yet these works focus on the emergence of court rulings rather than their specific characteristics and outcomes.

It is not that multilevel conflict has been completely absent from pertinent scholarly conceptualizations. Empirical accounts found that the propensity for multilevel conflict has increased in the EU in recent decades (Bauer and Trondal 2015a, b). This rise has occurred for a number of reasons. With the intensification of EU integration in level and scope (Biesenbender 2011; Börzel 2005), there was just more to argue about. Since each treaty change increased the scope of issues the EU is able to legislate, the potential for disagreement about how to legislate, implement, and enforce legislative decisions automatically expands.

Besides, with the delegation of new powers to the supranational level, the boundaries of the competences and the precise procedures applying to the related decision-making processes often become—before accepted routines emerge—a matter of contest (see, for example, Farrell and Héritier 2007; Hartlapp 2018). Thus, the legal transfer and the practical wielding of new supranational powers do increase the potential for national resistance (Saurugger and Terpan 2013; Crespy and Saurugger 2014; Mathieu and Bauer 2018), as well as for conflicts between supranational and national authorities. Even in spite of an increasingly differentiated integration process (Holzinger and Schimmelfennig 2012), the trend towards vesting ever more competence at the supranational level remains unbroken; every revision of the founding treaties has conferred more powers to Brussels. Therefore, it does not come as a surprise that the potential for contesting the usage of these powers and the proper application of emerging rules become ever more likely (Bauer 2001).

If the range of issues to argue about has increased, so has the number and diversity of actors taking part in the policy process. At the institutional level, the days when the Commission and the Council were the sole relevant actors of EU policy making are long gone. With the increasing influence of the European Parliament (EP) (Corbett et al. 2011), the formal integration of the Council of the European Union (Naurin and Wallace 2008), political moves of the European Central Bank (Glöckler et al. 2016), and the boom of EU agencies, EU regulatory networks, and various types of committees (Dehousse 1997; Christiansen and Kirchner 2000; Egeberg 2006), the EU institutional landscape has become considerably more complex. First, each new actor comes with its own institutional interests, which may clash with those of the preexisting actors. Second, as these emerging actors are gradually empowered, their incentive and capacity to engage in conflictive relationship with the remaining actors increase as well (Bauer and Becker 2014). Enlargement has had a similar effect, as it increased the diversity of interests and political preferences (Meardi 2000; Kvist 2004) and generated distributional tensions between the member states (Pluemper and Schneider 2007). In short, with the growth of the EU and changes in its institutional setting, the propensity for tensions and conflicts among its components has increased (Ege et al. 2018). Indeed, the heterogeneity of identities, interests, and situations among actors pertaining to the same political system increases the likelihood of conflict (Blau 1977; Horowitz 1985). Yet the constitutional and therefore locked-in status of much of EU governance and the high number of veto players make it very difficult for each institution individually to influence the course of EU policies via the legislative channel. These rising constraints have been shown to foster informal politics (Christiansen and Neuhold 2013) and may well encourage the use of litigation as an alternative strategy to achieve political objectives (Swenden 2006, 79).

At the same time, the EU's policy process shifted from technocracy to a more contentious style of decision making. From the mid-1980s, with the turn from government to governance and with the broadening scope of issues covered by EU policies, a multitude of interest groups (financial institutions, industry, non-profit organizations, and regional and local governments) began to mobilize and intervene in the policy process, intensifying the political pressures on decision-taking elites (Mazey and Richardson 1993; McLaughlin and Greenwood 1995; Tömmel and Verdun 2008). Subnational governments have also entered the picture, with the establishment of representative offices in Brussels (Bauer 1996) and via their participation in regional policy making through the partnership principle (Bauer 2002). Far from fostering consensual decision making across governmental levels, this has fuelled political conflict and rivalry between central and subnational governments (Hooghe and Marks 2001, 115; Trondal and Bauer 2017).

In parallel, not only has the EU policy process been permeated by interest groups and subnational actors, it has also become increasingly vulnerable to pressures from public opinion (Hooghe and Marks 2009; Hix 2011). The popular opposition to the EU project expressed by citizens via referenda (Danish rejection of the Maastricht Treaty in 1992, French rejection of the Constitutional Treaty in 2005, and the recent British refusal to remain in the EU) has further made clear that public opinion matters. As they take part in the confrontation of interests that mark the EU political process, public opinion, interest groups, and subnational governments have significantly increased the potential for conflict in the EU.

Finally, in the last few years, the rise of tensions and crises on the global scene has intensified the potential for conflict within the EU. With the financial crisis and Great Recession, the explosion of armed conflicts in its southern and eastern neighbourhood, and the ascent of a new nationalism, the EU has been jumping from one crisis to another. Caught between gravity and urgency, the EU and the member states search for ways to manage and solve these crises. The results are often situations with high distributional stakes, which increases the propensity for conflict, as illustrated by the Greek crisis, the refugee crises, and the Brexit process. Solidarity crumbles with the growing divergence of interests between net donors and net recipients of EU spending policies (Scharpf 2017), between the Visegrad Group and the remaining member states about refugees, and between pro-European and Euro-sceptics—to name just a few of the cleavages along which the EU currently risks being broken apart.

In sum, we see a changing nature of the EU political system and of policy making towards ever greater complexity and ever greater fragmentation. Competence and influence are shared and contested between many more actors at different levels than was traditionally the case. Kelemen (2011) argues that this has led to the substitution of consensus-oriented styles of policy making and embedding of policy struggles within networks with a more adversarial style of policy making and conflict. Such policy making—much like in the United States—increasingly relies on the threat and use of litigation. The strength of his argument is to link system features to litigation, therewith providing much support for an increasing relevance of litigation, including annulment actions. At the same time, the argument raises many new questions that engage more deeply with the link between system and litigation.

When do multilevel policy conflicts among the different actors populating the EU lead to litigation? What motivates policy actors to take the judicial step and turn to courts? Litigation may make sense for private actors that do not formally take part in the policy decision-making process. To them, activating judicial policy making through judicial review may appear as a promising mechanism. Litigation is more puzzling, however, when initiated by public actors who do take part in the EU decision-making process and most likely have done so in the very process from which the contested act or decision emerged. Yet annulment actions are regularly raised by member states, the Commission, the Council, and the EP. Why do these public actors litigate? What do they expect from a CJEU ruling? Which benefits do they draw from engaging in judicial proceedings? These are a first set of key questions that will structure our research.

Even more so, the multilevel structure of EU governance creates conflict that exhibits a multilevel structure as well. In fact, raising awareness of the fact that the EU's governance arrangement is characterized by multilevel actor configurations and thus requires interaction, cooperation, and coordination among different kinds of policy stakeholders and policymakers at different levels of government has been one of the main achievements of research on multilevel governance. When analysing annulment actions as one mechanism to resolve such multilevel conflicts, we should thus assess to what extent multilevel conflict configurations translate into multilevel litigant configurations during judicial proceedings.

After all, annulment proceedings do not always comprise only one applicant attacking only one defendant. While those simple configurations make up for the majority of cases, there are a significant number of judicial conflicts that exhibit a more complex structure, where several actors can simultaneously challenge one EU measure or where additional policy stakeholders decide to intervene in the conflict in support of the applicant or the defendant. Annulment conflicts are thus often complex, multi-actor, and multilevel. So far, however, we know rather little about the conditions under which multilevel governance systems give rise to simple and/or complex judicial conflicts.

EU POLICY MAKING AND LITIGANT CONFIGURATIONS

Research on EU policy making, the second literature strand relevant to our interest in annulment actions, provides insights into actors' motivations to engage with litigation. Students of EU public policy making have explored the interaction between judicial proceedings and policy making. Some are interested in the effect of litigation on policy making, others on litigation during implementation as a later stage in the policy cycle.

There is an important body of research on judicial policy making and, more generally, on the increasingly prominent role of courts in policy making and governance (Stone Sweet 1999; Hirschl 2008). In the EU, we know that the Court has played a crucial role in the construction of the EU legal order (Burley and Mattli 1993; Stone Sweet and Brunell 1998) and in favour of market integration and harmonization (Alter and Meunier-Aitsahalia 1994; Scharpf 2010). More recent work has emphasized the influence of rulings in other areas such as social policy (Conant 2006; Martinsen and Falkner 2011), gender equality, environmental issues (Cichowski 2007), health care policy (Martinsen 2015), and gambling policy (Adam 2015). Thus, litigation matters politically because it shapes public policy.

Frequently, these studies explore interactions between the Court, the legislative process, and other relevant stakeholders in detail, even if the overall impact of rulings on policy making is constrained (Martinsen 2015; Mathieu et al. 2018). Yet while a great share of this literature is interested in understanding court agency and the power of the CJEU to influence the course of integration, the full scope of the Court's agency and power relative to other actors and forces in EU policy making is yet to be determined. Among other things, this is due to the prevalence of different theoretical perspectives on the Court and the methodological difficulty inherent in researching court agency when decisions are taken behind closed doors (Vauchez 2015).

In contrast to these studies, this book focuses mainly on motivations and structural conditions that lead to litigation. In this context, we distinguish political and legal opportunity structures that influence actors' decisions to turn conflict into litigation. In his seminal study on anti-nuclear protest movements, Herbert Kitschelt showed that differences in the openness of national political systems for input and differences in their capacity to implement policies shape the level of protest (Kitschelt 1986; see also Epp 1998; Boyle 1998). Where more access points exist in a political system, for example through separation of powers between the executive and the legislature or centralization of the state, there are fewer structural opportunities for protest and litigation.

While political opportunities certainly play a role in the use of litigation, the literature on social movements' legal mobilization shows that legal opportunities are decisive. Some even argue that legal opportunity structures explain more of the across-country variation in litigation than the respective political opportunity structures (Hilson 2017). Legal opportunity structures comprise two elements: access to courts and legal stock (Hilson 2002; Vanhala 2011). From a procedural perspective, access is enabled or constrained by laws on *locus standi* or standing rights of the claimant to file suits, court control of their docket, or length of procedures (Vanhala 2012), as well as by rules about who carries the costs of legal procedures. In addition, what matters from a substantive perspective is available precedent case law and the relevant statutory basis to which the conflict can be linked. This legal stock helps lawyers formulate and carry through with legal disputes (Andersen 2005). Social movements obviously have alternative instruments at their disposal to push forward their policy goals. They can rely on lobbying, public protest, or litigation (Bouwen and McCown 2007). The literature found that the extent to which they rely on litigation is highly dependent on the relative openness of the legal system in which they are operating. Where access to courts and judicial review is restrained, social movements tend to turn away from litigation and favour other strategies. By contrast, in countries with a largely unrestricted access to courts, social movements are much more active within the judicial arena (De Fazio 2012).

Turning to EU studies, Alter and Vargas explain variation in the use of litigation strategies to push for equal pay with a combination of political and legal opportunity structures (Alter and Vargas 2000). Conant et al. (2017) state that the increasing relevance of formal law and lawyers who interact with cultural and legal institutions go hand in hand with rises in litigation activity. Besides legal and political opportunity structures they deem micro-level characteristics, such as information or available resources in the form of in-house lawyers or pro bono legal advice as well as identity politics, to be important. Hartlapp (2018) has shown that differences in the level of litigation between the Council, the EP, and the Commission can be explained by their different organizational characteristics. According to her, organizational structures inside and across EU institutions must be taken into account when trying to understand legal mobilization in horizontal annulment actions. In the legislative process, the Council can assure its positions most easily. The Commission as agenda setter, in contrast, faces the strongest incentives to mobilize. The EP does so as well to an increasing extent, particularly since the Treaty of Maastricht entered into force. According to Hartlapp (2018), the internal decision-making process provides the Commission with the greatest freedom to launch annulment actions, the Parliament is somewhat constrained by a possible negative vote in the plenary, while the Council needs proactive agreement from all member states to launch an annulment. However, her analysis also indicates that agency inside these institutions matters a great deal.

More generally, mobilization studies have addressed the link between the rise and the impact of litigation. While litigation has initially raised much enthusiasm among social movements, researchers found that judicial success was generally unable to bring about the social changes pursued (Scheingold 1974; Handler 1978, 24; Rosenberg 1991). Nevertheless, social movements were able to draw indirect benefits from litigation, such as raising their own legal capacity and the public awareness of their cause. Litigation was able to consolidate movements' struggling culture and collective identity and thereby triggered mobilization and support to improve their bargaining position in the political arena and change predominant legal understandings and paradigms (Scheingold 1974; Lobel 1994; McCann 1994, 1998, 2008). All of this echoes the argument by Adam et al. (2015) that member states use annulment actions without always aiming at judicial success, as judicial success can be unrelated or even negatively related to the litigant's goal of raising an annulment action in the first place (see also the examples presented in Chapter 1).

Besides its relevance for policy making, litigation also matters at later stages in the policy cycle. We discern three ways in which judicial proceedings matter for implementation and compliance research. Research

2 TOWARDS AN ANALYTICAL FRAMEWORK TO STUDY ANNULMENTS IN THE EU   31

has repeatedly shown that subnational actors play a decisive role during policy implementation. The national failure to comply with EU law and the subsequent initiation of the infringement procedure by the Commission are often related to conflicts taking place within the member states. For example, the dispersion of powers within the member states (visible as veto players interfering in the implementation of EU policies), can favour implementation failures (Haas 1998; Haverland 2000; Mbaye 2001; Guiliani 2003). Likewise, compliance conflicts with the Commission relate to national party politics (Treib 2003, 2010) and interest-representation systems (Lampinen and Uusikylä 1998; Mbaye 2001). Where such conflicts lead to late or incorrect implementation, subnational actors, in particular private actors, may litigate before national courts to bring their state into compliance with EU law (Börzel 2000; Van der Vleuten 2005; Hartlapp 2008; Hofmann 2016).

Following the top-down perspective of the first generation of American policy implementation scholars (e.g. Pressman and Wildavsky 1973; Dunsire 1978; Sabatier and Mazmanian 1979), EU implementation studies often have an inherent pro-compliance bias. Litigation is either an indicator of an instance in which the Commission has been able to uncover implementation failure (i.e. litigation emerges when member states fail to comply with EU law) or even as an indicator showing how implementation outcomes improved over time. When analysing the role of judicial proceedings in the policy process, implementation scholars want to uncover the conditions of implementation failure. They analyse the conditions under which legal proceedings are used in the EU's system of multilevel governance to bring domestic policies in line with existing European requirements (Mbaye 2001; Hartlapp 2005; Börzel et al. 2010; Steunenberg and Rhinard 2010; Börzel et al. 2012).

From this classical top-down implementation perspective, litigation can be interesting whenever it helps us to capture implementation outcomes and to understand compliance failure. This perspective overlooks, however, that litigation can be chosen as a strategic option by the Commission to advance their goals in the EU policy process (Schmidt 2000; Blauberger and Weiss 2013). By threatening to trigger CJEU-driven policy making in areas where the Council resisted legislation proposed by the Commission, the Commission has managed to change the Council's default position, coaxing member states into action. Related scholarship analyses how policy actors can strategically use the shadow of litigation in order to influence the policy process (Falkner 2011).

Here, litigation or the threat of litigation matters because it affects the Council's calculations of the cost benefits of adopting new legislation and, as a consequence, affects the balance of power between the Commission and the Council.

Finally, litigation can be looked at as a component of the struggles taking place between implementing actors, along the lines of the bottom-up approach of the American policy implementation literature (Lipsky 1971, 1980; Elmore 1979; Barret and Fudge 1981). Here, turning the implementation perspective on its head, implementation is conceptualized to depend primarily on the multiple actors at the application level. From this perspective, conflict and struggle is not an anomaly but rather a natural component of the policy process. Consequently, litigation is best understood as part of these struggles about the outcome of EU public policy making.[1]

In sum, the literature on implementation, compliance, and Europeanization has so far underlined three ways in which judicial proceedings interact with the EU public policy process. First, scholars interested in compliance have shown that proceedings can help improve national compliance with EU legislation. Second, we also know that the shadow of litigation can be used by the Commission to increase its power vis-à-vis the Council in the EU policy-making process. Third, it has shown that domestic politics often determines the way in which member states react to the CJEU's rulings. With these analytical focal points, this literature has predominantly focused on the impact of the judicial proceedings (or the threat thereof) on multilevel policy dynamics. However, what about the inverse relationship? How do multilevel politics affect the emergence of litigation?

If we combine the insights concerning litigation from the multilevel governance literature and from the implementation and Europeanization literature, it should be clear that litigation and jurisprudence do not emerge in a political vacuum. Neither does annulment litigation. On the one hand, we need to study the impact of annulment rulings by analysing how they feed back into conflictive multilevel policy processes. Who are the winners and losers of annulment actions? Are actors losing the legal battle also always losing the underlying political battle? On the other hand, we need to assess how annulment litigation emerges from (supranational) compliance failures as well as from more general dysfunctionalities and conflicts in the multilevel governance process. What can different kinds of litigant configurations tell us about the underlying political conflicts in this regard?

JUDICIAL POLITICS AND JUDICIAL SUCCESS

Finally, the literature on judicial politics and judicial behaviour provides obvious insights that need to be taken into account in any kind of analysis of annulment litigation. In the EU context, the question of judicial behaviour relates to how judges of the CJEU make their decisions. Legalists emphasize judicial objectivity, claiming that judges' decisions are predetermined by EU law (Barav 1979). They reject the idea that judges' decisions are influenced by political or ideological preferences. Judges' work is conceived as purely technical, apolitical, and based on methodologies of legal interpretation. Yet several alternative models of judicial behavioural models, strongly informed and influenced by judicial politics in the United States, have been developed. Proponents of an attitudinal model of judicial decision making claim that judgements and legal interpretations are never fully determined by the objective merits of a case or by a specific legal method (Segal and Spaeth 2002, 53). Rather, there is a margin of interpretation of the law and of the case. This gives judges a lot of freedom within these margins and grey areas, which they can use to rule in accordance with their ideological preferences. In the case of the CJEU, judges are said to be ideologically biased in favour of European integration (Mattli and Slaughter 1998). Moreover, there are proponents of a strategic approach to judicial behaviour. This approach acknowledges judges' discretion and the need for interpretation, too. Yet proponents of the strategic approach contend that judges cannot freely use their freedom for interpretation to impose their ideologically preferred outcomes. Since they rely on the acceptance of their judgements and wish to uphold their authority as a well-accepted institution, they have to take the expectations of key litigants and societal stakeholders into account as well. In this sense, they will adjust their judgements to the specifics of the respective (political or social) situation and rule in a way that will avoid widespread disagreement and political retaliation (Segal and Spaeth 2002, 100). In the context of the CJEU, for example, judges' capacity to follow their preference for EU integration is argued to be limited by the anticipated reactions to their rulings by key member states (Garrett et al. 1998; Carrubba et al. 2008; Larsson and Naurin 2016; Dederke and Naurin 2018). The presumed need to rule strategically in order to avoid non-compliance or political retaliation constrains the Court's formal independence. Carrubba et al. (2008) show, for example, that when a large number of powerful member states oppose the Commission in court, the Commission's chances for success are substantially lower than when it does not face such an opposition. According to Carrubba and his colleagues, this effect is due to the Court's anticipation of the member states' reactions to its rulings. When several strong member states take part in a judicial conflict, the Court may anticipate that a ruling that would be negative for them could be neutralized through legislative override. Besides, member states enjoying the status of strong political power in Brussels are less vulnerable to reputation pressures and, therefore, are more likely (than weak member states) not to comply with a ruling that is problematic for them.

Interestingly, the scholarly debate about whether or not the CJEU is in fact contained by member state influence (Conant 2002) is—by and large—a debate about whether the Court is independent or not. Consequently, this debate risks losing track of the possibility that the Court might be very independent in some context but rather constrained in other contexts. According to Mathieu et al. (2018), it is, however, essential to keep this possibility in mind and to explore to what extent the policy context from which litigation emerges systematically mediates the Court's behaviour. This policy context might lead the Court to be more concerned with strategic concerns, giving it more room for ideologically biased interpretations, or it might confront the Court with very different kinds of legal questions. Since extant research has mainly looked at CJEU behaviour in the context of preliminary reference procedures, it has mainly looked at the involvement of member state governments submitting legal briefs to the Court. Whenever we deal with actions for annulment, however, we are likely to encounter a more diverse and complex actor constellation, which can include member state governments, regional governments, interest groups, companies, and EU institutions all at the same time. In light of extant research on judicial behaviour, this empirical fact highlights the need to analyse the conditions that give rise to such complex actor configurations. Moreover, it feeds the interest in whether these litigant configurations influence the Court in any kind of way. In any case, an exploration of the role and impact of annulment litigation cannot ignore judicial behaviour and the potential relationship between potentially quite complex actor configurations and judicial behaviour.

CONCEPTUALIZING MULTILEVEL ANNULMENT CONFLICT

Actor configurations in multilevel policy conflicts and in annulment actions are key analytical interests to us. Essentially, we distinguish between horizontal and vertical annulment conflicts depending on the location of the main opponents in the multilevel system. Moreover, we distinguish between simple and complex actor configurations.

Horizontal v. Vertical Conflict

In cases in which supranational institutions litigate against another supranational institution, the cleavage is horizontal. The conflict runs between actors situated at the same level of the EU system. Take the EP as an example. Traditionally, the EP held powers to decide about non-compulsory budget spending and has used these competences to strategically expand its powers, for example by increasing non-compulsory expenditures. When the Council challenges the legality of the general budget (e.g. C-34/86), it carries conflict between the two EU institutions to the judicial arena. Such conflict may emerge between other institutions situated at the supranational level of the EU system, too. We refer to these cases as horizontal cases, since both opponents are located at the supranational level (see Fig. 2.1).

In contrast, in actions initiated by actors from the national level—whether these are national governments, regional entities, or private actors—the dominant conflict cleavage is vertical. Therefore, we refer to these cases as vertical conflicts throughout the book (see Fig. 2.2). Good examples for this are conflicts over the appropriation of EU funds when these supranational funds are spent and administered by national entities. Where EU institutions try to interfere in a legally binding way with how to spend and administer that money or decide that national entities

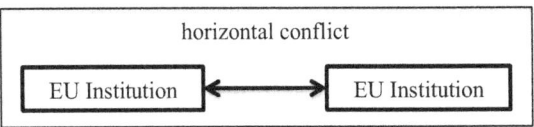

Fig. 2.1 Horizontal conflicts (*Source* Own compilation)

Fig. 2.2 Vertical conflicts (*Source* Own compilation)

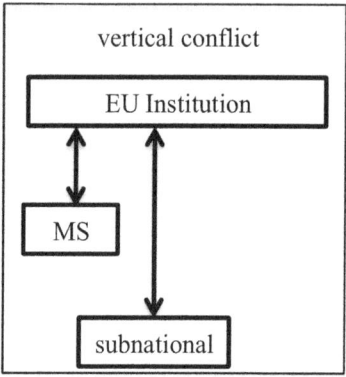

have misspent that money, we often witness vertical conflict that regularly leads to annulment litigation with vertical actor configurations (as depicted in Fig. 2.2).

Based on the location of the applicant for legal action within the multilevel system, we thus distinguish between different kinds of annulment conflicts. Since the legal defendant in these situations is always situated at the EU level, this distinction is mainly driven by the location of the applicant at either the national level (vertical conflicts), or the supranational level (horizontal conflicts).

Simple v. Complex Conflicts

Moreover, we consider conflicts to have complex actor configurations where they involve more than one actor on either side of the judicial conflict. Whereas the primary conflict cleavage determines whether conflicts are considered as vertical or horizontal conflicts, the annulment conflicts are often characterized by additional secondary conflict cleavages. Member state governments or other EU institutions can join horizontal conflicts by acting either as additional litigant or as intervener in support of the supranational litigant. Thereby, these horizontal conflicts acquire an additional vertical conflict cleavage. In these cases, the member state and the supranational institution form a multi-actor, and in fact multilevel, alliance against the defending EU institution. Importantly, however, this vertical cleavage can exist on either side of the conflict.

Member state governments can act in ways other than in support of applicant institutions. They can also oppose them by joining the case in support of the defendant. In these cases, the litigant institution faces a multi-actor defence coalition. We can even find configurations characterized by a situation in which multi-actor applicant coalitions confront multi-actor defence coalitions (see Fig. 2.3). All of these multilevel horizontal conflicts are complex conflicts. Such a conflict configuration emerged, for example, over the regulation of the hazardous substance decabromodiphenyl ether (DecaBDE) in which the EP and Denmark, with the support of Finland and Sweden, initiated, actions for annulment against the Commission, which was itself supported by the United Kingdom (C-14/06).

Yet complexity is not always induced by the involvement of member state governments joining horizontal conflicts. Additional EU institutions that join cases on the side of the applicant institution or on the side of the defendant institution can also induce complexity. A good example of this is the negotiation of an agreement between the EU and the United States of America on the processing and transfer of passenger

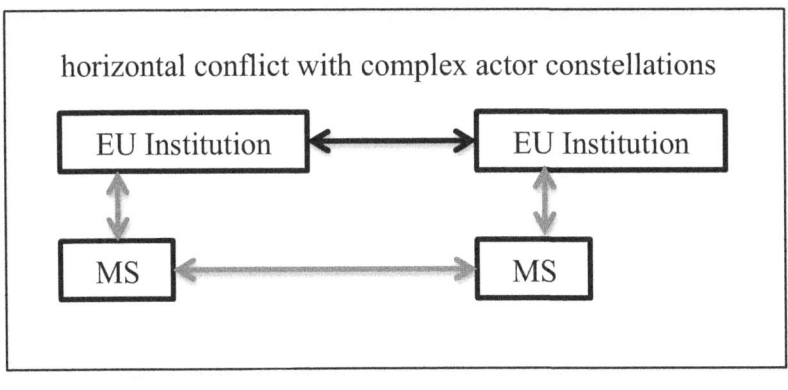

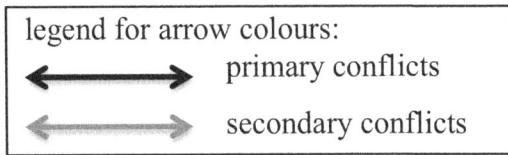

Fig. 2.3 Complex horizontal conflicts (*Source* Own compilation)

name record data. The Council had proposed that air carriers should be allowed to transfer the data to the United States Department of Homeland Security, while the EP—being concerned with citizens' data privacy—questioned this practice. Sharing these concerns, the European Data Protection Supervisor sided with Parliament once an action for annulment was initiated (joined cases C-317/04 and C-318/04). On the defendant side, the Council found support from the European Commission and the United Kingdom, all of whom defended the agreement in court (Hillion and Wessel 2009, 576). Whenever such secondary cleavages are relevant, we consider conflicts to be complex actor configurations as opposed to simple actor configurations.[2]

Similarly, vertical cases can also be characterized by more than one conflict, with additional and important secondary conflict lines. Other member state governments might object to the application for annulment and join to support the defending EU institution. The same is true for other subnational actors. This way, the conflict between two member state governments can find expression in them supporting different sides in the conflict as illustrated schematically (see Fig. 2.4).

A Multilevel and Multi-step Analytical Approach

This conceptual approach guides and structures the remainder of this book. While we address each research question individually, our analytical goal is to formulate a more general argument about how elements of the public policy process and elements of the judicial process feed into each other to determine the political role of actions for annulment. While the policy context of the cases may explain actors' decision to take use annulments, these decisions influence—but do not determine—eventual litigant configurations. In turn, the litigant configuration representing the structure of the legal conflict is able to affect the legal discourse during proceedings. After all, litigants take part in proceedings because they hope to influence these in their favour. The information and arguments made by the different kinds of litigants can influence—but hardly determines—the Court's interpretations and judgement. These interpretations and judgements not only determine legal winners and losers, but also affect the policy substance and the distribution of competences in the EU's system of multilevel governance by influencing current and future policy context from which new conflicts arise.

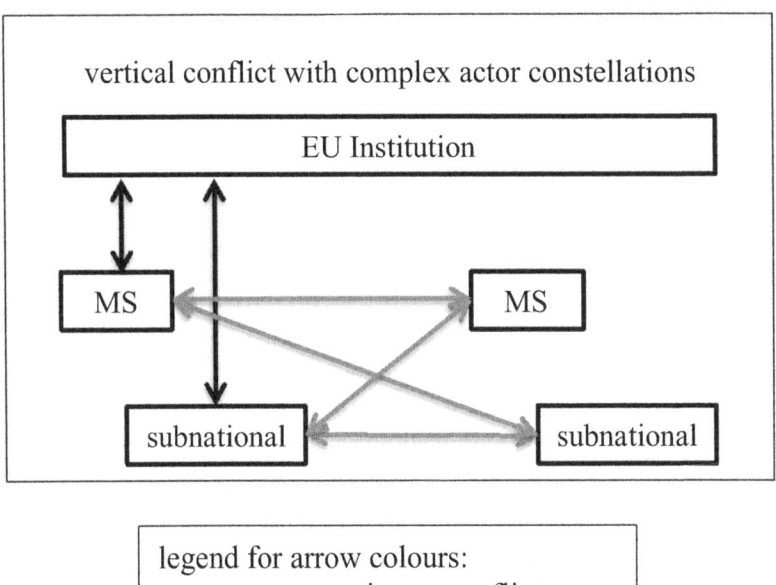

Fig. 2.4 Complex vertical conflicts (*Source* Own compilation)

The process that in the end determines the impact of court rulings thus resembles an analytical chain that has been studied already. Referring to a filtering process, delta, or funnel, these works look at the chain of events as a narrowing passageway and seek to understand what shapes the eventual litigation (Klages 1983; Glenn 1999; Van Waarden and Hildebrand 2009). In contrast, the principal contribution of this book consists of promoting a comprehensive approach to studying the role of judicial proceedings by analysing them within multiple interrelated steps as one element within a continuous multilevel policy process. Thereby, we try to go beyond looking merely at the use of litigation, at litigant configurations, or at judges' decisions in isolation. Instead, we consider them to be linked in a chain-like fashion. A comprehensive understanding of annulment litigation in the multilevel system must take this chain-like linkage into account. This view has affinities with the policy-cycle perspective (Easton 1965), composed of distinct phases that feed into each other (agenda setting, policy making, policy implementation, evaluation, agenda setting). Likewise, the way judicial proceedings intervene in the multilevel policy process can be looked at as a sequential chain, where multilevel policy conflicts lead to litigation and structures litigant configuration. This, in turn, affects judicial outcomes, which, through their policy and institutional impacts, feed back into the multilevel policy process. The chain-like approach that centres on litigants as the starting point to policy change is thus very similar to the bottom-up approach within the implementation literature.

Based on this analytical and conceptual foundation, the next chapter will provide the relevant information about the legal background of annulment actions (Chapter 3). We will then briefly explain our methodological approach (Chapter 4) before presenting three empirical chapters addressing the questions mentioned above. First, we will explore the motivations underlying policy actors' use of annulment actions (Chapter 5). Second, we will address the rise of complex actor constellations in annulments proceedings (Chapter 6). We will finalize our empirical investigation with judicial success and the impact of annulment actions (Chapter 7) before we draw general conclusions in a final chapter (Chapter 8).

CASES CITED

See Table 2.1.

Table 2.1 Cases cited in this chapter

C-34/86	Judgment of 3 July 1986, *Council v. Parliament*, C-34/86, EU:C:1986:291
C-317/04; C-318/04	Judgment of 30 May 2006, *Parliament v. Council*, Joined Cases C-317/04 and C-318/04, EU:C:2006:346
C-14/06	Judgment of 1 April 2008, *Parliament v. Commission*, C-14/06, EU:C:2008:176

NOTES

1. Following this line of reasoning, some authors integrated court rulings and the CJEU into Europeanization research emphasizing the way national struggles co-shape the policy implementation process. These works discuss conflict structures in the national arena as an explanation for national

response to the CJEU's case law (Blauberger 2012, 2014; Schmidt 2012, 2014).
2. In a recent article on Norwegian Supreme Court judgements, Skiple et al. (2016) use a similar but wider definition of complex cases identified 'through the number of third parties supporting a litigant (i.e. legal intervenient), the number of justices who voice their opinion and the number of words in the majority opinion' (Skiple et al. 2016, 9).

REFERENCES

Adam, C. (2015). Gambling: Erosion and persistence of domestic sports betting monopolies. In C. Knill, C. Adam, & S. Hurka (Eds.), *On the road to permissiveness? Change and convergence of moral regulation in Europe* (pp. 206–233). Oxford, UK: Oxford University Press.

Adam, C., Bauer, M. W., & Hartlapp, M. (2015). It's not always about winning: Domestic politics and legal success in EU annulment litigation. *Journal of Common Market Studies, 53*(2), 185–200.

Alter, K. J., & Meunier-Aitsahalia, S. (1994). Judicial politics in the European Community: European integration and the pathbreaking Cassis de Dijon decision. *Comparative Political Studies, 26*(4), 535–561.

Alter, K. J., & Vargas, J. (2000). Explaining variation in the use of European litigation strategies: European Community law and British gender equality policy. *Comparative Political Studies, 33*(4), 452–482.

Andersen, E. A. (2005). *Out of the closets and into the courts legal opportunity structure and gay rights litigation*. Ann Arbor: The University of Michigan Press.

Barav, A. (1979). The judicial power of the European Economic Community Symposium: Conference on comparative constitutional law. *Southern California Law Review 53*, 461–526.

Barrett, S., & Fudge, C. (Eds.). (1981). *Policy and action*. London: Methuen.

Bauer, M. W. (1996). Die Verbindungsbüros der Deutschen Länder bei der Europäischen Union in Brüssel. *Verwaltungsrundschau, 42*(12), 417–420.

Bauer, M. W. (2001). *A creeping transformation? The European Commission and the management of EU structural funds in Germany*. Dordrecht, The Netherlands: Kluwer Academic (Library of Public Policy and Public Administration).

Bauer, M. W. (2002). The EU 'partnership principle': Still a sustainable governance device across multiple administrative arenas? *Public Administration, 80*(4), 769–789.

Bauer, M. W., & Becker, S. (2014). The unexpected winner of the crisis: The European Commissions strengthened role in economic governance. *Journal of European Integration, 36*(3), 213–229.

Bauer, M. W., & Trondal, J. (Eds.). (2015a). *The Palgrave handbook of the European administrative system*. Basingstoke: Palgrave Macmillan.

Bauer, M. W., & Trondal, J. (2015b). The administrative system of the European Union. In M. W. Bauer & J. Trondal (Eds.), *The Palgrave handbook of the European administrative system* (pp. 1–28). Basingstoke: Palgrave Macmillan.

Benz, A., & Eberlein, B. (1999). The Europeanization of regional policies: Patterns of multi-level governance. *Journal of European Public Policy, 6*(2), 329–348.

Biesenbender, J. (2011). The dynamics of treaty change: Measuring the distribution of power in the European Union. *European Integration Online Papers (EIoP), 15*(5), 1–24.

Blau, P. M. (1977). *Inequality and heterogeneity: A primitive theory of social structure*. London: Macmillan.

Blauberger, M. (2012). With Luxembourg in mind ... the remaking of national policies in the face of ECJ jurisprudence. *Journal of European Public Policy, 19*(1), 109–126.

Blauberger, M. (2014). National responses to European court jurisprudence: West European politics. *West European Politics, 37*(3), 457–474. https://doi.org/10.1080/01402382.2013.830464.

Blauberger, M., & Weiss, M. (2013). If you can't beat me, join me! How the Commission pushed and pulled member states into legislating defence procurement. *Journal of European Public Policy, 20*(8), 1120–1138.

Börzel, T. A. (2000). Why there is no southern problem: On environmental leaders and laggards in the European Union. *Journal of European Public Policy, 7,* 141–162.

Börzel, T. A. (2005). Mind the gap! European integration between level and scope. *Journal of European Public Policy, 12*(2), 217–236.

Börzel, T. A., Hofman, T., & Panke, D. (2012). Caving in or sitting it out? Longitudinal patterns of non-compliance in the European Union. *Journal of European Public Policy, 19*(4), 454–471.

Börzel, T. A., Hofmann, T., Panke, D., & Sprungk, C. (2010). Obstinate and inefficient: Why member states do not comply with European law. *Comparative Political Studies, 43*(11), 1363–1390. https://doi.org/10.1177/0010414010376910.

Bouwen, P., & Mccown, M. (2007). Lobbying versus litigation: Political and legal strategies of interest representation in the European Union. *Journal of European Public Policy, 14*(3), 422–443.

Boyle, E. H. (1998). Political frames and legal activity: The case of nuclear power in four countries. *Law and Society Review, 32*(1), 141–174.

Burley, A.-M., & Mattli, W. (1993). Europe before the court: A political theory of legal integration. *International Organization, 47*(1), 41–76.

Carrubba, C. J., Gabel, M., & Hankla, C. (2008). Judicial behavior under political constraints: Evidence from the European Court of Justice. *American Political Science Review, 102*(4), 435–452.

Christiansen, T., & Kirchner, E. J. (2000). *Committee governance in the European Union.* Manchester, UK: Manchester University Press.

Christiansen, T., & Neuhold, C. (2013). Informal politics in the EU. *Journal of Common Market Studies, 51*(6), 1196–1206.

Cichowski, R. A. (2007). *The European court and civil society.* Cambridge, UK: Cambridge University Press.

Conant, L. J. (2002). *Justice contained: Law and politics in the European Union.* Ithaca, NY: Cornell University Press.

Conant, L. J. (2006). Individuals, courts, and the development of European social rights. *Comparative Political Studies, 39*(1), 76–100.

Conant, L., Hofmann, A., Soennecken, D., & Vanhala, L. (2017). Mobilizing European law. *Journal of European Public Policy, 25*(9), 1–14. https://doi.org/10.1080/13501763.2017.1329846.

Corbett, R., Jacobs, F., & Shackleton, M. (2011). *The European Parliament.* London: John Harper.

Crespy, A., & Saurugger, S. (2014). Resistance to policy change in the European Union: An actor-centered perspective. *Cahiers Du Cevipol, 2014*(1), 1–20.

Dederke, J., & Naurin, D. (2018). Friends of the Court? Why EU governments file observations before the Court of Justice. *European Journal of Political Research, 57*(4), 867–882. https://doi.org/10.1111/1475-6765.12255.

De Fazio, G. (2012). Legal opportunity structure and social movement strategy in Northern Ireland and Southern United States. *International Journal of Comparative Sociology, 53*(1), 3–22. https://doi.org/10.1177/0020715212439311.

Dehousse, R. (1997). Regulation by networks in the European Community: The role of European agencies. *Journal of European Public Policy, 4*(2), 246–261.

Dunsire, A. (1978). *The execution process: Implementation in a bureaucracy.* Los Gatos, CA: Martin Robertson.

Easton, D. (1965). *A framework for political analysis.* Englewood Cliffs, NJ: Prentice Hall/Harvester Wheatsheaf.

Ege, J., Bauer, M. W., & Becker, S. (2018). *The European Commission in turbulent times: Assessing organizational change and policy impact.* Baden-Baden, Germany: Nomos.

Egeberg, M. (2006). *Multilevel Union administration: The transformation of executive politics in Europe.* New York: Palgrave Macmillan.

Elmore, R. F. (1979). Backward mapping: Implementation research and policy decisions. *Political Science Quarterly, 94*(4), 601–616.

Epp, C. R. (1998). *The rights revolution: Lawyers, activists, and supreme courts in comparative perspective*. Chicago: University of Chicago Press.

Falkner, G. (Ed.). (2011). *The EU's decision traps: Comparing policies*. Oxford, UK: Oxford University Press.

Farrell, H., & Héritier, A. (2007). Contested competences in the European Union. *West European Politics, 30*(2), 227–243.

Garrett, G., Kelemen, R. D., & Schulz, H. (1998). The European Court of Justice, national governments, and legal integration in the European Union. *International Organization, 52*(1), 149–176.

Glenn, H. (1999). *Paths to justice: What people do and think about going to law.* Oxford, UK: Hart Publishing.

Glöckler, G., Lindner, J., & Salines, M. (2016). Explaining the sudden creation of a banking supervisor for the euro area. *Journal of European Public Policy, 24*(8), 1135–1153. https://doi.org/10.1080/13501763.2016.1184296.

Guiliani, M. (2003). Europeanization in comparative perspective: Institutional fit and national adaptation. In K. Featherstone & C. M. Radaelli (Eds.), *The politics of Europeanization* (pp. 134–155). Oxford, UK: Oxford University Press.

Haas, P. M. (1998). Compliance with EU directives: Insights from international relations and comparative politics. *Journal of European Public Policy, 5*(1), 17–37.

Handler, J. F. (1978). *Social movements and the legal system: A theory of law reform and social change*. Cambridge, MA: Academic Press.

Hartlapp, M. (2005). *Die Kontrolle der nationalen Rechtsdurchsetzung durch die Europäische Kommission*. Frankfurt: Campus Verlag.

Hartlapp, M. (2008). Extended governance: Implementation of EU social policy in the member states. In I. Tömmel & A. Verdun (Eds.), *Innovative governance in the European Union: The politics of multilevel policymaking* (pp. 221–236). Boulder, CO: Lynne Rienner.

Hartlapp, M. (2018). Power shifts via the judicial arena: How annulments cases between EU institutions shape competence allocation. *Journal of Common Market Studies, 56*(6), 1429–1445.

Haverland, M. (2000). National adaptation to European integration: The importance of institutional veto points. *Journal of Public Policy, 20*(1), 83–103.

Hillion, C., & Wessel, R. A. (2009). Competence distribution in EU external relations after ECOWAS: Clarification or continued fuzziness? *Common Market Law Review, 46*(2), 551–586.

Hilson, C. (2002). New social movements: The role of legal opportunity. *Journal of European Public Policy, 9*(2), 238–255.

Hilson, C. (2017). *Protest and litigation against nuclear power in the 1970s: Exploring political and legal opportunity structure*. Paper presented at CES Glasgow 2017.

Hirschl, R. (2008). The judicialization of politics. In K. E. Whittington, D. R. Kelemen, & G. A. Caldeira (Eds.), *The Oxford handbook of law and politics* (pp. 1–23). Oxford, UK: Oxford University Press. https://dx.doi.org/10.1093/oxfordhb/9780199604456.013.0013.

Hix, S. (2011). *The political system of the European Union* (3rd ed.). Basingstoke, UK: Palgrave Macmillan.

Hofmann, A. (2016). *Legal rights and practical effect: Why the European Commission supports access to justice for interest groups*. Conference Paper: Workshop implementation and judicial politics: Conflict and compliance in the EU multi-level system.

Holzinger, K., & Schimmelfennig, F. (2012). Differentiated integration in the European Union: Many concepts, sparse theory, few data. *Journal of European Public Policy, 19*(2), 292–305.

Hooghe, L. (1996). *Cohesion policy and European integration: Building multi-level governance*. Oxford, UK: Oxford University Press.

Hooghe, L., & Marks, G. (2001). *Multi-level governance and European integration*. Lanham, MD: Rowman & Littlefield.

Hooghe, L., & Marks, G. (2009). A postfunctionalist theory of European integration: From permissive consensus to constraining. *British Journal of Political Science, 39*(1), 1–23.

Horowitz, D. L. (1985). *Ethnic groups in conflict*. Berkeley: University of California Press.

Kelemen, R. D. (2011). *Eurolegalism*. Cambridge, MA: Harvard University Press.

Klages, H. (1983). Ursachenfaktoren der Inanspruchnahme der Ziviljustiz. *Deutsche Richterzeitung, 10*, 395–436.

Kitschelt, H. P. (1986). Political opportunity structures and political protest: Anti-nuclear movements in four democracies. *British Journal of Political Science, 16*(1), 57–85.

Kvist, J. (2004). Does EU enlargement start a race to the bottom? Strategic interaction among EU member states in social policy. *Journal of European Social Policy, 14*(3), 301–318.

Lampinen, R., & Uusikylä, P. (1998). Implementation deficit—Why member states do not comply with EU directives? *Scandinavian Political Studies, 21*(3), 231–251.

Larsson, O., & Naurin, D. (2016). Judicial independence and political uncertainty: Assessing the effect of legislative override on the European Court of Justice. *International Organization, 70*(2), 377–408.

Lipsky, M. (1971). Street-level bureaucracy and the analysis of urban reform. *Urban Affairs Quarterly, 6*, 391–409.

Lipsky, M. (1980). *Street-level bureaucracy*. New York: Sage.

Lobel, J. (1994). Losers fools and prophets: Justice as struggle. *Cornell Law Review, 80*, 1331–1421.

Marks, G. (1993). Structural policy and multilevel governance in the EC. In A. Cafruny & G. Rosenthal (Eds.), *The state of the European Community: The Maastricht debates and beyond* (Vol. 2, pp. 391–410). Harlow, UK: Longman.

Marks, G., Scharpf, F. W., Schmitter, P. C., & Streek, W. (Eds.). (1996). *Governance in the European Union*. Thousand Oaks, CA: Sage.

Martinsen, D. S. (2015). *An ever more powerful court? The political constraints of legal integration in the European Union*. Oxford, UK: Oxford University Press.

Martinsen, D. S., & Falkner, G. (2011). Social policy: Problem solving gaps, partial exits and court-decision traps. In G. Falkner (Ed.), *The EUs decision traps: Comparing policies* (pp. 128–145). Oxford, UK: Oxford University Press.

Mathieu, E., Adam, C., & Hartlapp, M. (2018). From high judges to policy stakeholders: A public policy approach to the CJEUs power. *Journal of European Integration, 40*(6), 653–666.

Mathieu, E., & Bauer, W. M. (2018). Domestic resistance against EU policy implementation: Member states motives to take the Commission to court. *Journal of European Integration, 40*(6), 667–682.

Mattli, W., & Slaughter, A.-M. (1998). Revisiting the European Court of Justice. *International Organization, 52*(1), 177–209. https://doi.org/10.1162/002081898550590.

Mazey, S., & Richardson, J. J. (1993). *Lobbying in the European Community*. Oxford, UK: Oxford University Press.

Mbaye, H. A. D. (2001). Why national states comply with supranational law: Explaining implementation infringements in the European Union 1972–1993. *European Union Politics, 2*(3), 259–281.

McCann, M. W. (1994). *Rights at work: Pay equity reform and the politics of legal mobilization*. Chicago: University of Chicago Press.

McCann, M. W. (1998). How does law matter for social movements? In B. G. Garth & A. Sarat (Eds.), *How does law matter?* Evanston, IL: Northwestern University Press.

McCann, M. W. (2008). Litigation and legal mobilization. In K. E. Whittington, D. R. Kelemen, & G. A. Caldeira (Eds.), *The Oxford handbook of law and politics* (pp. 1–25). Oxford, UK: Oxford University Press. https://dx.doi.org/10.1093/oxfordhb/9780199208425.003.0030.

McLaughlin, A., & Greenwood, J. (1995). The management of interest representation in the European Union. *Journal of Common Market Studies, 33*, 143–156.

Meardi, G. (2000). Trojan horse for the Americanization of Europe? Polish industrial relations towards the EU. *European Journal of Industrial Relations, 8*(1), 77–99.

Naurin, D., & Wallace, H. (Eds.). (2008). *Unveiling the Council of the European Union: Games governments play in Brussels*. Basingstoke: Palgrave Macmillan.

Pluemper, T., & Schneider, C. J. (2007). Discriminatory European Union membership and the redistribution of enlargement gains. *Journal of Conflict Resolution, 51*(4), 568–587.

Pressman, J. L., & Wildavsky, A. B. (1973). *Implementation: How great expectations in Washington are dashed in Oakland—Or, why it's amazing that federal programs work at all, this being a saga of the Economic Development Administration as told by two sympathetic observers who seek to build morals on a foundation of ruined hopes*. Berkeley: University of California Press.

Rosenberg, G. N. (1991). *The hollow hope: Can courts bring about social change?* (1st ed.). Chicago: University of Chicago Press.

Sabatier, P., & Mazmanian, D. (1979). The conditions of effective implementation: A guide to accomplishing policy objectives. *Policy Analysis, 5*(4), 481–504.

Saurugger, S., & Terpan, F. (2013). Analyser les résistances nationales à la mise en œuvre des normes européennes: une étude des instruments daction publique. *Quaderni, 80,* 5–24.

Scharpf, F. W. (1985). Die Politikverflechtungs-Falle. Europäische Integration und deutscher Föderalismus im Vergleich. *Politische Vierteljahresschrift, 26*(4), 323–356.

Scharpf, F. W. (2006). The joint-decision trap revisited. *Journal of Common Market Studies, 44*(4), 845–864.

Scharpf, F. W. (2010). The asymmetry of European integration, or why the EU cannot be a social market economy. *Socio-Economic Review, 8*(2), 211–250.

Scharpf, F. W. (2017). *Vom asymmetrischen Euro-Regime in die Transferunion – und was die deutsche Politik dagegen tun könnte* (MPIfG Discussion Paper 17/15). Cologne, Germany: Max Planck Institute for the Study of Societies.

Scheingold, S. (1974). *The politics of rights: Lawyers, public policy, and social change*. New Haven, CT: Yale University Press.

Schmidt, S. K. (2000). Only an agenda setter? The European Commissions power over the council of ministers. *European Union Politics, 1*(1), 37–61.

Schmidt, S. K. (2012). Who cares about nationality? The path-dependent case law of the ECJ from goods to citizens. *Journal of European Public Policy, 19*(1), 8–24. https://doi.org/10.1080/13501763.2012.632122.

Schmidt, S. K. (2014). Judicial Europeanisation: The case of Zambrano in Ireland. *West European Politics, 37*(4), 769–785. https://doi.org/10.1080/01402382.2014.919775.

Segal, J. A., & Spaeth, H. J. (2002). *The Supreme Court and the attitudinal model revisited*. Cambridge, UK: Cambridge University Press.

Skiple, J. K., Grendstad, G., Shaffer, W. R., & Waltenburg, E. N. (2016). Supreme Court justices economic behaviour: A multilevel model analysis. *Scandinavian Political Studies, 39*(1), 73–94. https://doi.org/10.1111/1467-9477.12060.

Steunenberg, B., & Rhinard, M. (2010). The transposition of European law in EU member states: Between process and politics. *European Political Science Review, 2*(3), 495–520.
Stone Sweet, A. (1999). Judicialization and the construction of governance. *Comparative Political Studies, 32*(2), 147–184.
Stone Sweet, A., & Brunell, T. L. (1998). Constructing a supranational constitution: Dispute resolution and governance in the European Community. *American Political Science Review, 92*(1), 63–81.
Swenden, W. (2006). *Federalism and regionalism in Western Europe: A comparative and thematic analysis*. Basingstoke: Palgrave.
Tatham, M., & Bauer, M. W. (2014a). Competence ring-fencing from below? The drivers of regional demands for control over upwards dispersion. *Journal of European Public Policy, 21*(9), 1367–1385.
Tatham, M., & Bauer, M. W. (2014b). Support from below? Supranational institutions, regional élites, and governance preferences. *Journal of Public Policy, 34*(2), 237–267.
Tömmel, I., & Verdun, A. (Eds.). (2008). *Innovative governance in the European Union: The politics of multilevel policymaking*. Boulder, CO: Lynne Rienner.
Treib, O. (2003). Die Umsetzung von EU-Richtlinien im Zeichen der Parteipolitik: Eine akteurszentrierte Antwort auf die Misfit-These. *Politische Vierteljahresschrift, 44*(4), 506–528.
Treib, O. (2010). Party politics, national interests, and government—Opposition dynamics cleavage structures in the convention negotiations on EU social policy. *European Union Politics, 11*(1), 119–142.
Trondal, J., & Bauer, M. W. (2017). Conceptualizing the European multilevel administrative order: Capturing variation in the European administrative system. *European Political Science Review, 9*(1), 73–94.
Van Der Vleuten, A. (2005). Pincers and prestige: Explaining the implementation of EU gender equality legislation. *Comparative European Politics, 3*, 464–488.
Vanhala, L. (2011). *Making rights a reality? Disability rights activists and legal mobilization*. Cambridge, UK: Cambridge University Press.
Vanhala, L. (2012). Legal opportunity structures and the paradox of legal mobilization by the environmental movement in the UK. *Law and Society Review, 46*(3), 523–556.
Van Waarden, F., & Hildebrand, Y. (2009). From corporatism to lawyocracy? On liberalization and juridification. *Regulation and Governance, 3*(3), 259–286. https://doi.org/10.1111/j.1748-5991.2009.01059.x.
Vauchez, A. (2015). Methodological Europeanism at the cradle: Eur-lex, the Acquis and the making of Europe's cognitive equipment. *Journal of European Integration, 37*(2), 193–210.

2 TOWARDS AN ANALYTICAL FRAMEWORK TO STUDY ANNULMENTS IN THE EU 49

Open Access This chapter is licensed under the terms of the Creative Commons Attribution 4.0 International License (http://creativecommons.org/licenses/by/4.0/), which permits use, sharing, adaptation, distribution and reproduction in any medium or format, as long as you give appropriate credit to the original author(s) and the source, provide a link to the Creative Commons license and indicate if changes were made.

The images or other third party material in this chapter are included in the chapter's Creative Commons license, unless indicated otherwise in a credit line to the material. If material is not included in the chapter's Creative Commons license and your intended use is not permitted by statutory regulation or exceeds the permitted use, you will need to obtain permission directly from the copyright holder.

CHAPTER 3

The Legal Background

Litigation describes the process of taking disputes to court. With the help of Article 263 TFEU (Treaty on the Functioning of the European Union) annulment litigation, different kinds of actors can take to the Court of Justice of the European Union (CJEU) disputes with European Union (EU) institutions over the legality of these institutions' actions. The Court will review the legality of these actions and decide whether to declare them void.

Annulment actions thus constitute an important part of the EU's system of judicial protection (Arnull 2011), which also comprises the infringement procedure and the preliminary reference procedure. The infringement procedure, set out in Article 258 TFEU, allows the Commission to address and challenge member states' violations of EU law. In this context, the Commission enjoys the privilege of transferring cases to the EU's judicial arena whenever member states fail to modify their application of EU law in response to reasoned opinions in which the Commission explains why it believes the respective member state to be in violation of its treaty obligations and demands further information and appropriate adjustments from the member state (Tallberg 2002; Börzel 2003; Hartlapp 2005, chapter 6). Even though most infringement proceedings do not reach this judicial phase, infringement cases eventually brought before the Court still represent a substantial part of its overall workload (Arnull 2006, 35; Falkner 2018). In contrast, the activation of the CJEU in the context of Article 267 TFEU preliminary

© The Author(s) 2020
C. Adam et al., *Taking the EU to Court*,
Palgrave Studies in European Union Politics,
https://doi.org/10.1007/978-3-030-21629-0_3

reference procedures is the privilege of national courts. Under this procedure, national courts can refer to the CJEU questions regarding the interpretation of the treaty and the validity and interpretation of acts of the institutions, bodies, offices, or agencies of the EU. Preliminary rulings have played a significant role in the development of Community law, as it is through these exchanges between national courts and the CJEU that crucial concepts, such as, for example, the direct effect and the supremacy of EU law, have been developed (Craig and de Burca 2011, 461). As such, preliminary reference proceedings have been an important channel through which the constitutionalization of the European treaties has emerged. This channel has been turned from being an instrument to assure equal application of EU law before domestic courts into being an instrument to challenge national laws and even national constitutional law in breach of EU law in national courts (Alter 1998).

Yet while research on the role of infringement procedures on the Europeanization of national policies, as well as research on the role of preliminary rulings on the trajectory of European integration, abound in political science research, actions for annulment have attracted much less attention from this group of scholars. This is rather striking. After all, the action for annulment is the only legal instrument with which member states, EU institutions, and even citizens, companies, interest groups, and regional governments can directly activate the CJEU and ask for judicial review. Annulment actions thus constitute a direct road to Luxembourg without having to take a detour through national courts, although—as will be discussed below—this direct route is not open to all applicants under all circumstances at all times.

While we are mainly interested in the political role of annulment litigation, this is hardly possible without appreciating the legal background. To understand why disputes are taken to court, we need to understand the legal context specifying when actors will actually be able to go to court successfully. The use of any legal instruments will be influenced by rules regulating their use. This is the essence of the message conveyed by the literature on legal opportunity structures. Depending on the options a legal system provides, for example the rights attributed to certain kinds of actors to file suits in particular constellations, actors' decisions to take recourse to litigation are conditioned, with respective effects (Andersen 2006; Conant 2006; Hilson 2002; Wilson and Rodriguez Cordero 2006; Vanhala 2012). Social movements' litigation strategies provide good examples. The more open the legal system is for bringing policy-related decisions into the legal arena, the more options social movements enjoy to employ litigation in the struggle for their cause. However, legal access is nothing "static" or a priori given nor refused forever. Quite the opposite. The judges tend to develop the underlying law in their judgements; their judgements on individual cases thus bring novel interpretations that, in turn, often influence constitutional or treaty-base revisions. Therefore, rules regulating the access to courts in certain matters may change over time—thus altering the dynamic of the policy processes due to a redistribution of access rights to litigate (Wilson and Rodriguez Cordero 2006). As we want to understand policy stakeholders' decisions to litigate with the help of annulment actions, the legal framework regulating these actors' capacity to launch annulment cases are of great interest. Before this background, this chapter revisits the EU legal framework that specifies the use of annulment actions.

This endeavour is actually quite challenging. After all, political scientists are inclined to quickly skim such legal elaborations or to skip them completely when these elaborations seem detailed and technical. This is a pity, however, since knowing this legal background is important for understanding the political role of any kind of legal instrument. At the same time, no matter how detailed and technical those writers with a background in political science think their writings are, it will be tough for them to meet the high standards of legal scholarship. We try to find a compromise that is as accessible as possible to political scientists without being perceived by legal scholars of annulment actions to be overly simplistic and superficial. This means that the following cannot be a complete history of relevant case law and judicial interpretations on annulment actions. Instead, we try to eclectically describe the most important legal developments that seem relevant to understanding the political role of annulment litigation in the EU.

Actions for Annulment: Some Essentials

Annulment actions have been a part of the treaties ever since the Treaties of Rome. Since the Treaty of Lisbon, we find the legal provisions guiding the application of actions for annulment in Article 263 TFEU.[1] This article essentially defines three key aspects that determine the possibility of initiating a successful action for annulment: the range of legal acts that can be challenged, the grounds on which legal acts will be annulled, and the types of actors that may initiate annulment proceedings. More specifically, Article 263 comprises six paragraphs. In the first paragraph, the treaty lists the type of acts that can be reviewed by the Court. The second paragraph deals with privileged applicants and the grounds that may justify starting an annulment. The third paragraph is about semi-privileged applicants, and the fourth is about non-privileged applicants. A new fifth paragraph specifies conditions related to non-privileged applicants, and the last paragraph presents the time limit for initiating annulment actions.

Until 1989, the European Court of Justice was solely responsible for decisions on annulment actions. This changed with the creation of the Court of First Instance, which relieved the Court from many of these cases. This was the case at least at the first instance of these cases, whereas the European Court of Justice remained responsible for appeals against annulment judgements by the Court of First Instance. Initially, the Court of First Instance was competent on annulment actions brought by private applicants (mainly regarding competition policy). In 1993 and 1994, it became competent to examine all annulment action cases initiated by private parties (Bellamy 2010, 35–36). In 2004, the Court of First Instance's competences have been further extended. Among other things, it is charged with deciding actions initiated by the member states that are directed against the Commission and against the Council in certain cases in the fields of state aid and (external) trade protection. Moreover, it should hear actions for annulment brought against the Council that resulted from the exercise of its implementing powers, and it was charged with deciding actions directed against the European Central Bank (ECB) (Fairhurst 2010, 182). The Treaty of Lisbon further rearranged the distribution of competences between the two Courts. Not only does it rename the Court of First Instance the General Court, it also charged this General Court with hearing all actions for annulment, except those that involved only EU institutions (e.g. horizontal cases), and actions brought by the member states against the European Parliament (EP) or the Council as long as these had not already been transferred to the Court of First Instance in 2004.

When deciding annulment cases, both Courts have and will assess whether actions are founded based on four legal grounds specified in Article 263(2) that applicants may invoke: lack of competence, infringement of an essential procedural requirement, infringement of the treaties or of any rule of law relating to their application, or misuse of powers.

There are two main types of lack of competence. The first constitutes a breach of the principle of conferral entailed in Article 5(2) Treaty on European Union, which stipulates that the EU may act only in those areas in which it has been conferred powers through the treaties. However, the Court has generally relied on a generous interpretation of the powers conferred to the EU (Hartley 2007, 398). For example, it has developed the doctrine of implied powers (*ERTA* C-22/70) and has only rarely recognized a breach of the principle of conferral (Horspool and Humphreys 2012, 255). The second type of lack of competence occurs where an EU institution breaches the principle of institutional balance by overstepping the powers of another EU institution. Frequent conflicts between the Council and the EP arose in this context about the appropriate legal basis for legislative action. Since the influence of the EP in the decision-making process depends on the legal basis on which an act or a policy is adopted, the Court was often called to assess whether an act of the Council was adopted under the correct legal basis. This type of situation has also been addressed through the second ground for annulment: the infringement of essential procedural requirements.

A classic example of violation of procedural requirement is the failure to consult an EU body when the procedural rules applying to the decision required the consultation of that body. In *Roquette* (C-138/79), for example, the Court annulled a measure adopted by the Council under the consultation procedure because the Council had adopted the act without the opinion of the EP. Moreover, the obligation to provide an adequate statement of reasons, in particular a statement of the legal basis upon which the measure is adopted, constitutes another important procedural requirement for annulment actions. Finally, the breach of the rights of defence (e.g. the right to be heard, or access to documents for stakeholders during the preparation of the act) is also frequently used to justify an annulment action.

The third ground to invoke annulments is the infringement of the treaty or any rule relating to its application. This is the widest ground for actions in annulment. It covers not only all constitutive treaties and Community legal acts but also some of the EU's international agreements, as well as unwritten general principles of law that have been developed by the Courts themselves (Türk 2009, 127–128), such as the principles of legal certainty and legitimate expectations. These principles are particularly relevant when the Community adopts rules that concern events that lie in the past. Retroactive rules are allowed only when the public interest weights more than the private interest in the maintenance of the status quo. The other three important principles are the principles of equality, proportionality, and fundamental rights.

Finally, the actions of EU institutions will be annulled when these institutions have misused their powers in taking that action. More specifically, a misuse of powers seems to have occurred when disputed measures 'appear[s], on the basis of objective, relevant and consistent evidence, to have been taken with the exclusive or main purpose of achieving an end other than that stated or evading a procedure specifically prescribed by the Treaty' (T-415/03). Annulment actions based on misuse of powers are, however, rarely successful because of the difficulty for applicants to provide objective evidences of the motives of the author of the act (Türk 2009, 142–145) and thus attract fewer litigation decisions.

From a legal perspective, a thorough explanation of the grounds on which one initiates an action for annulment is obviously essential. From a political science perspective, however, it is interesting to see that in practice, the majority of annulments that we coded were not initiated with reference to any single one of those grounds. Instead, applicants typically try to make the case for several of these grounds at the same time.

It is important to highlight that successful actions for annulment must not only be founded, they also must be initiated within the appropriate time limits stipulated in Article 230(5). Specifically, proceedings 'shall be instituted within two months of the publication of the measure, or of its notification to the plaintiff, or, in the absence thereof, of the day on which it came to the knowledge of the latter, as the case may be'. This can be quite a demanding deadline for potential applicants. After all, in case no action for annulment reaches the Court before this deadline, it considers that all potential applicants have implicitly accepted the legality of the EU legal act. For example, in the event that member states fail to challenge an unwelcome decision by the Commission on domestic state aid arrangements with an action for annulment, they miss the chance to have the Court review the legality of the decision later on. Consequently, if member states simply ignore such a decision by the Commission, the Commission can involve the Court under the infringement procedures without running the risk of having the Court review the legality of that decision in the process of these proceedings. Consequently, actions for annulment are imminent manifestations of conflict that indicate conflict without substantial delay. Moreover, they are not simple substitutes for infringement proceedings but fulfil their own distinct legal role.

In case actions for annulment are founded—based on any of the legal grounds discussed above—and have been initiated in time, the Court shall, according to Article 231(1), declare the respective EU legal act void. That means the Court deprives this legal act of its legal effect. In fact, the annulment of the act applies retroactively and has effect *erga omnes* in that annulments apply generally and are not limited to the applicant.

But before the Court will even assess whether an action for annulment is founded, it will first evaluate whether the case is admissible at all. Two aspects that have raised considerable controversy in this regard are the types of legal acts that can be subjected to annulment review and the types of actors that can make use of annulment actions. In fact, the wording of Article 263 TFEU has been modified several times since its original conception with respect to these two questions. Most of these treaty changes have been motivated by the intent to accommodate the Court's interpretation of both aspects within its respective case law at the time. While legal scholars continue to criticize the restrictive rules that make it difficult—particularly for private actors to access the Court through annulment actions—this evolution has overall led to a considerable extension of the list of reviewable acts and of eligible applicants.

An Evolving Set of Reviewable Acts

Article 263(1) lists the type of acts that can be reviewed by the Court of Justice under the annulment regime. These are legislative acts, acts of the Council, acts of the Commission, and acts of the ECB, other than recommendations and opinions. Acts of the EP and of the European Council, as well as acts of bodies, offices, or agencies of the EU can also be reviewed—as long as these acts are intended to produce legal effects vis-à-vis third parties.

Primary law thus explicitly states that annulment actions can be initiated against EU legislative acts. These legislative acts are defined within Article 289 TFEU as those legal acts adopted under the ordinary legislative procedure or under the special legislative procedure. The ordinary legislative procedure corresponds to the former co-decision procedure, which grants equal weight to the EP and the Council in the decision-making process. Special legislative procedures replace the former consultative, cooperation, and assent procedures. In those procedures, the Council of the EU is the main legislator, while the EP is less influential as its role is restricted to consultation or approval. Moreover, in Article 263(1), primary law also explicitly holds that annulment actions can be directed against acts of the Council, the Commission, and the ECB, other than recommendations and opinions.

While these provisions seem rather clear on a first glance, they have been the subjects of quite a few legal controversies. Very prominently, the Commission and the Council found themselves in disagreement over whether atypical actions, other than clearly reviewable regulations, directives, and decisions other than the explicitly non-reviewable recommendations and opinion, should also be reviewable through annulment actions. In *ERTA* (C-22/70), the Court declared for the first time that instead of focusing on the form of a challenged act, it would first consider its substance when reviewing the applicability of an action for annulment. The specific conflict erupted over the renegotiation of the European Agreement concerning work of crews of vehicles in international road transport in the context of the United Nation's Economic Commission for Europe. This agreement specified regulatory aspects such as standardized rest periods for drivers. In preparation of these negotiations at the international level, EU member state governments had discussed their negotiation strategy within a Council meeting and had synthesized the results of these discussions within written proceedings. The Commission demanded that the Court declare these proceedings void since it saw itself competent and responsible for negotiating this treaty at the international level. While the Court in this case has left a substantial mark on the organization of the EU's external relations,[2] it also influenced the annulment procedure itself by stating that according to its interpretation of the treaties, annulment actions could be initiated against 'all measures adopted by the institutions, whatever their nature or form' as long as they were 'intended to have legal effects' (C-22/70). With this interpretation, the Court substantially extended the range of acts subject to annulment actions to also involve atypical acts, such as, for example, conclusions adopted by the Council, letters written by the staff of the Commission, or oral decisions (Türk 2009, 12).

While the question of what constituted such legal effects remained, however, the Court clarified in *IBM*, more than ten years after *ERTA*, that it considered acts to be exerting legal effect when they are 'binding on, and capable of affecting the interests of, the applicant by bringing about a distinct change in his legal position' (C-60/81). With this interpretation, the Court has also made clear that simply disguising legal acts as non-binding acts by label would be insufficient to make them immune to review through annulment litigation. In case C-57/95, the Court, for example, annulled a communication issued by the Commission because it saw this communication as having clear legal effects for the member states.

Moreover, in *Les Verts v. European Parliament* (C-294/83), the Court further extended the range of reviewable acts by including those acts adopted by the EP that have legal effects vis-à-vis third parties. Since the original treaty provision had not listed the EP as a potential defendant in annulment litigation (Arnull 2000, 182–183), legal acts by the EP were not considered to be the subject of annulment litigation. Yet with the extended competences of the EP, this provision came to be questioned more and more strongly. In this specific case, the French ecological nonprofit *Les Verts*, a predecessor of the French party Les Verts, Confédération Écologiste—Parti Écologiste, which subsequently became the party Europe Écologiste—Les Verts, had initiated a series of actions for annulment against various EU institutions over the allocation of EU funds to reimburse political information campaigns in the context of the European elections in 1984. Specifically, they claimed that by the manner in which (in this case) the bureau of the EP had allocated these funds, the Parliament had unduly used its power to favour those parties that had already been elected to the EP before the 1984 election. With this application for an annulment of how these funds were allocated, the Court had to consider whether it would even be competent to review the legality of actions by the EP. Interestingly, at the oral stage in the proceedings, the EP held that its legal acts could not be subjected to annulment litigation at least as long as the Parliament itself did not have the right to challenge other institutions' legal acts via annulment litigation. This was an interesting suggestion that could have helped the Parliament to either reject the legal challenge in this case or at least gain the right to bring annulment cases against other EU institutions itself. As the advocate general and the Court did not follow this reasoning, this became known only for adding the EP to the list of potential defendants in annulment litigation. With the Maastricht Treaty, the member states followed up on this by formally extending the list of reviewable acts of Article 263 to include acts of the EP, acts adopted jointly by the EP and the Council, and acts adopted by the ECB.

Particularly the last episode in this brief overview over the evolution of actions reviewable through actions for annulment highlights the fact that actions for annulment emerge where EU institutions are competent to adopt binding legal acts or where these institutions presume to have this right. Consequently, the historical pattern of annulment litigation is reflective of the (successful) strive for increasing competences by EU institutions. As long as EU institutions are unable to adopt typical legally binding acts and as long as they do not try to impose legal effects in other ways, actions for annulment are irrelevant. Yet, as the example of the EP has indicated, as soon as EU institutions start to gain competences and try to use these competences to influence politics, they start to attract actions for annulment.

The (presumed) right to adopt legally binding acts not only shapes empirical patterns of annulment litigation by influencing the list of potential defendants. It also influences the sector-specific prevalence of annulment litigation. Institutions' ability to adopt legally binding acts can vary from policy sector to policy sector as well as over time. For example, the Commission's competence to adopt legally binding measures varies across sectors (Franchino 2007). While the Commission may adopt legally binding decisions in the field of competition law, it does not enjoy this privilege to the same extent in the contexts of the EU's social policy or public health policy. Consequently, it cannot be surprising that we find a higher number of actions for annulment in the context of competition law than in the context of public health policy. Similarly, we see more actions for annulment in the context of state aid policy, as the Commission is able to enforce EU state aid law by adopting legally binding decision. In contrast, wherever the Commission fulfils its role as guardian of the treaties on the basis of adopting reasoned opinions in the context of infringement proceedings, we do not observe many actions for annulment. After all, reasoned opinions do not fall under the category of reviewable acts. Overall, this creates an exciting tension; while actions for annulment are particularly frequent in areas where EU institutions have far-reaching competences, they can be particularly influential in areas in which EU institutions are just starting to fight for these competences. After all, an aggressive push for more binding influence by an EU institution is likely to attract an action for annulment and will give the Court a chance to weigh in on whether this institutional power grab is compatible or incompatible with EU law.

An Evolving List of Applicants

The unique feature of actions for annulment is that they allow actors to directly activate the Court. Yet EU law does not grant this right to all types of actors to the same extent. Different types of actors enjoy different privileges to directly challenge EU institutions at the CJEU. In fact, EU law distinguishes between so-called privileged applicants, semi-privileged applicants, and non-privileged applicants, where privileged applicants are the major institutional actors, the group of semi-privileged applicants consists of the more peripheral EU institutional actors, and the group of non-privileged applicants basically comprises regional governments, interest groups, companies, and individual citizens.[3]

Privileged applicants, listed in Article 263(2), do not have to fulfil any specific conditions for initiating annulment actions. When evaluating the admissibility of a case, the Court does not evaluate the standing rights of these applicants. Individual member states, the Council, the Commission, and since 1992, the EP make up the group of such privileged applicants. With respect to individual member states, the right to initiate annulment proceedings is limited to its governmental authorities and 'cannot be extended to regional governments' or self-governing communities, regardless the extent of their powers' (joined cases T-32/98 and T-41/98, as well as joined cases T-132/96 and T-143/96). The Court thus treats regional authorities as non-privileged applicants (see below).

Semi-privileged applicants can be admitted to initiate an action for annulment when they are able to demonstrate that they do so 'for the purpose of protecting their prerogatives'—as stipulated in Article 263(3). In contrast, privileged applicants are admitted even when cases do not involve their individual prerogatives. Today, the Court of Auditors, the ECB, and the Committee of the Regions make up this category of semi-privileged applicants. Before 1992, the EP was a part of this group as well. The inclusion of a semi-privileged group of applicants has been the result of an evolving EU polity and an evolving jurisprudence of the Court. Before the Treaty of Maastricht, the treaties only spoke of privileged and non-privileged applicants; with the EP not being part of the privileged applicants. Yet over time, the Parliament not only passively gained more power but also tried to actively increase its influence. Since these developments went hand in hand, the Parliament was able to make more and more convincing cases that the Council and the Commission were trying to interfere with its (newly gained) prerogatives. In *Chernobyl* (C-70/88), the EP attacked the legality of a Council regulation that established permitted levels of radioactive contamination of food because this regulation had been adopted on the basis of an inappropriate legislative procedure. It should have been adopted under a procedure that would involve the EP more substantially. In this particular case, the Court rejected the Council's objection that the EP was not an eligible applicant in this regard and established for the first time that it would generally consider the Parliament able to bring such cases wherever its own prerogatives were at stake. There are many cases in which EU institutions accuse each other of adopting legal acts on a wrong treaty base and to strategically pick an inappropriate legal procedure just to maximize their institutional influence (McCown 2003; Jupille 2004). The Courts interpretation of the *Chernobyl* case laid the ground for this new category of semi-privileged applicants. Subsequently, the Maastricht Treaty formalized this category and explicitly extended this right to the ECB. The Treaty of Amsterdam and the Treaty of Lisbon followed by further extending this list to include the Court of Auditors and the Committee of the Regions.

Finally, Article 263(4) TFEU extends the right to initiate annulment proceedings to 'any natural or legal person'. This group of applicants is commonly referred to as non-privileged applicants or private applicants, a label that indicates the stricter conditions of admissibility that these actors face. Although the term 'private applicants' is often used as a synonym of non-privileged applicant, this category can also entail public authorities. In fact, regional governments, such as state governments or also municipalities, are an important part of this group of non-privileged actors.

The classification of regional governments, such as the German *Länder*, as non-privileged actors is quite consequential in this regard, as this keeps them from sending to the CJEU their own lawyers, who are not officially recognized at the CJEU bar. Unlike member states' governments, whose internal lawyers can plead before the CJEU, regions have to delegate their legal representation. This represents an additional hurdle when trying to initiate an action for annulment.

Overall, legal scholars have repeatedly described the conditions that non-privileged actors have to fulfil to be admitted to court with annulment actions to be 'notoriously strict' (Arnull 2001, 7) or even as an 'almost insurmountable barrier' (Barav 1974). And yet today, this group of applicants brings the majority of annulment actions to the Court's attention despite facing a relatively strict admissibility test. Nevertheless, the Court has been a bit more self-restrained when developing the standing rights of this applicant group then it has with respect to the EP and other EU institutions.[4] To a large extent, this conservative position is justified with reference to the role of the Article 267 TFEU preliminary reference proceedings. The Court has held that both procedures have to be seen in combination to understand the EU's system of judicial review. After all, in most cases, it should be sufficient for citizens to turn to national courts to enforce their rights and—where necessary—to press the national court to demand a preliminary ruling from the CJEU. In the context of such preliminary rulings, the CJEU can be asked to assess the validity of acts adopted by EU institutions. Only where this preliminary reference procedure is unavailable, should non-privileged actors have the chance to turn to the CJEU directly.

Consequently, actions for annulment are not available to non-privileged actors in case the contested EU legal act is not of direct concern to them. To the Court, this direct concern requirement means that the 'measure must directly affect the legal situation of the person concerned and its implementation must be purely automatic and result from Community rules alone without the application of other intermediate rules' (T-69/99). Therefore, non-privileged actors can have a hard time demonstrating that they are directly concerned by a European directive or by a decision addressed to a member state, for example. This does not mean, however, that non-privileged actors have never been able to successfully challenge such acts (e.g. C-386/96P or C-291/89).

In addition to having to demonstrate their direct concern, non-privileged applicants have to demonstrate that they are individually concerned by EU legal acts as well. What this means has essentially been developed in the Court's *Plaumann* ruling (C-25/62), where the Court held that 'persons other than those to whom a decision is addressed may only claim to be individually concerned if that decision affects them by reason of certain attributes which are peculiar to them or by reason of circumstances in which they are differentiated from all other persons and by virtue of these factors distinguishes them individually just as in the case of the person addressed'. One of the ironies of this interpretation is that particularly in those cases where the adverse effects of EU legal acts are rather widespread and affect many non-privileged actors at the same time, each of them will have a very hard time fulfilling the individual concern criterion and challenging the respective legal act before the Court (Moser and Sawyer 2008, 84f.).

Generally speaking, the relatively high hurdles that non-privileged actors must overcome to establish individual concern when trying to challenge regulations and directives initially formulated in *Plaumann* is upheld to this day. This does not mean, however, that non-privileged actors have never tried to challenge regulations and directives. They have done so and continue to do so despite being aware of the relatively low chance of having cases admitted to the Court. While the Court in *Codorniu v. Council* (C-309/89) had been interpreted by some legal scholars as a breakthrough for private actors' standing rights, subsequent case law quickly dissolved these kinds of hopes for easier access to the Court (Arnull 2001). Nevertheless, this case, in which a Spanish producer of Crémant challenged a Commission regulation that would only allow producers from France and Luxembourg to label their high-quality sparkling wine Crémant, helped to establish that non-privileged actors could in fact challenge true regulation and true directives (Arnull 2001, 80). However, later attempts to revise the so-called *Plaumann* test to assess the individual concern of directives and regulations have been rejected by the Court. In *UPA* (C-50/00), Advocate General Francis Jacobs had criticized the restrictive *Plaumann* test as inappropriate and proposed a less restrictive test for individual concern. The Court did not follow his opinion in this regard, however (Moser and Sawyer 2008, 85). Interestingly, when the French fishing company Jégo Quéré attacked a Commission directive that specified new minimum mesh sizes, the General Court handling the case at first instance tried to introduce a less restrictive reformulation of the *Plaumann* formula (T-177/01). When the Commission appealed against the Court's at the Court of Justice, however, the Court of Justice overruled this modification and reconfirmed its determination to stick to the *Plaumann* formula (Moser and Sawyer 2008, 90).

One important change of primary law that came with the Lisbon Treaty was an addition to Article 263(4) TFEU. Here, the member states explicitly stated that regulatory acts that do not entail implementation measures would be reviewable with the annulment procedure. This would get rid of the individual concern criterion, which has continued to be a substantial hurdle for private litigants to effectively have EU legal acts reviewed before the Court, at least as long as regulatory acts did not entail further implementing measures. Yet since the treaty abstained from defining what a regulatory act and implementing measures entailed specifically, it was—and still is—up to the Court to bring forward more specific definitions (Craig 2010). This is what the Court continues to do. In *Inuit* (C-583/11 P), for example, the Court established that it considered regulatory acts to be acts of general applicability (such as directives and regulations) that have not been adopted under the ordinary or special legislative procedure (Peers and Costa 2012). For acts adopted under these legislative procedures, non-privileged actors would thus still have to establish direct concern and individual concern to have the Court assess whether an annulment action is indeed founded. Moreover, in subsequent judgements, the Court upheld rather restrictive interpretations of what implementing measures entailed, sometimes even rejecting opinions by the respective advocate general (e.g. *T&L Sugars* [C-456/13 P]).

Conclusion

With this necessarily brief and selective overview over the legal background of actions for annulment, we have tried to highlight, among other things, that actions for annulment are not the only instrument through which the Court can be brought to review the legality of supranational actions. Yet quite importantly, they are the only instruments with which member states, other EU institutions, and even citizens, companies, or interest groups can *directly* invoke the Court. Moreover, the rules and interpretations guiding the conditions under which these different kinds of actors can successfully initiate actions for annulment have evolved considerably since the early days of the European project. Generally speaking, this road to Luxembourg has become broader and more accessible, allowing for the review of more legal acts by more types of actors. Typically, this evolution is seen to be driven by the judges at Luxembourg, who have helped to develop the annulment procedure through case law that has repeatedly led to the revision of primary law. Since the openness and shape of a legal system definitely influences the impact of this legal system on the resolution of political conflict, the political balance of power, and the general dynamic of policy processes (Hilson 2002; Andersen 2006; Wilson and Rodriguez Cordero 2006; Vanhala 2012), actions for annulment are likely to become even more important as a tool with which one can still leave a mark in an increasingly heterogeneous and fragmented European Union.

The legal evolution of actions for annulment has been influenced particularly strongly by annulment actions launched in areas where their admissibility was seen as highly questionable. It was those cases that required the Court to set the future course of this legal instrument. In this regard, the Court's interpretations have at times answered objective needs, for example, when the EP's legal acts were included in the list of supranational acts eligible for annulments (e.g. C-294/83, T-16/04, T-308/07). Such formal review of parliamentary acts was not needed as long as the powers of the EP remained merely symbolic. In this sense, the extension of annulments to comprise the EPs' acts was the logical consequence of the shifting balance of power in the supranational institutional order. A similar logic applied in those cases where the EP brought annulments against other institutions' actions to the Court (e.g. C-70/88, C-65/90, C-295/90). In the original treaty provision, the Parliament did not have the formal right to do so; the Court conferred this right, however, to the EP via its case law, and later, this change of legal doctrine found its way to into the treaty (McCown 2003).

While many legal scholars continue to question whether the rules that guide the admission of actions brought by non-privileged actors provide effective judicial protection (Eliantonio and Kas 2010; Kornezov 2014), the gradual extension of the scope of application of annulment actions, as well as the rising empirical importance of annulment actions over time, reflect the ever-greater powers delegated to the EU and its increasing internal sophistication. In itself, the evolution of annulments indicates the increasing maturity of the EU as a political system and supports our argument about the growing conflict potential in the EU multilevel system.

Nevertheless, the evolving rules on reviewable acts under, and eligible applicants for, actions for annulment influence the empirical patterns of annulment litigation. Semi-privileged actors, such as the ECB or the Court of Auditors, can only challenge those acts in order to defend their own prerogatives. Consequently, we see actions for annulments launched by these institutions where they do have prerogatives or where they claim to have prerogatives. Because of the relatively strict rules on admitting cases by companies, for example, many annulment actions initiated by these actors emerge in the context of competition and state aid law where these actors can often make a relatively strong case for being directly and individually concerned. And yet the sheer mass of actions for annulment in any one area does not necessarily determine the impact of actions for annulment in that area. On the contrary, areas with relatively few actions for annulment are areas where EU institutions only start to claim the right to act in legally binding ways. In those cases, the Court's assessment of that right is arguably quite influential for the future course of European integration.

Finally, in strictly legal terms, actions for annulment serve a rather clear legal purpose. They represent a legal attack on an EU institution that is claimed to have overstepped its mandate or at least has allegedly neglected procedural requirements. Consequently, the respective EU institution appears in Court as the defendant. From a legal standpoint, it is thus clear who the defendant is in this constellation. Interestingly, this is much less clear from a political perspective. After all, for member states, regional governments, and other subnational actors, the initiation of an annulment action can often be a measure of last resort to fend off legally binding interference by EU institutions that are perceived as illegitimate, inappropriate, politically inopportune, very costly, or all of the above. Politically, they try to defend their political realm against supranational interferences. Making use of the EU's legal system can be an important part of such a defence. Therefore, in the next chapter, we turn to these political motivations to initiate actions for annulment.

CASES CITED

See Table 3.1.

Table 3.1 Cases cited in this chapter

C-25/62	Judgement of 15 July 1963, *Plaumann v. Commission*, C-25/62, EU:C:1963:17
C-22/70	Judgement of 31 March 1971, *Commission v. Council*, C-22/70, EU:C:1971:32
C-138/79	Judgement of 29 October 1980, *Roquette v. Council*, C-138/79, EU:C:1980:249
C-295/90	Judgement of 7 July 1992, *Parliament v. Council*, C-295/90, EU:C:1992:294
C-60/81	Judgement of 11 November 1981, *IBM v. Commission*, C-60/81, EU:C:1981:264
C-294/83	Judgement of 23 April 1986, *Les Verts v. Parliament*, C-294/83, EU:C:166
C-70/88	Judgement of 22 May 1990, *Parliament v. Council*, C-70/88, EU:C:1990:217

(continued)

Table 3.1 (continued)

C-70/88	Judgement of 22 May 1990, *Parliament v. Council*, C-70/88, EU:C:1990:217
C-291/89	Judgement of 7 May 1991, *Interhotel v. Commission*, C-291/89, EU:C:1991:189
C-309/89	Judgement of 18 May 1994, *Codorniu v. Council*, C-309/89, EU:C:1994:197
C-65/90	Judgement of 16 July 1992, *Parliament v. Council*, C-65/90, EC:EU:C:1992:325
C-57/95	Judgement of 20 March 1997, *France v. Commission*, C-57/95, EU:C:1997:164
C-386/96P	Judgement of 5 May 1998, *Dreyfus v. Commission*, C-386/96P, EU:C:1998:193
C-50/00	Judgement of 25 July 2002, *UPA v. Council*, C-50/00, EU:C: 2002:462
C-583/11 P	Judgement of 3 October 2013, *Inuit v. Parliament and Council*, C-583/11P, EU:C:2013:625
C-456/13 P	Judgement of 28 April 2015, *T&L Sugars v. Commission*, C-456/13P, EU:C:2015:284
T-32/98; T-41/98	Judgement of 10 February 2000, *Nederlandse Antillen v. Commission*, Joined Cases T-32/98 and T-41/98, EU:T:2000:36
T-132/96; T-143/96	Judgement of 15 December 1999, *Saxony and VW v. Commission*, Joined Cases 132/96 and T-143/96, EU:T:1999:326
T-69/99	Judgement of 13 December 2000, *DSTV v. Commission*, T-69/99, EU:T:2000:302

NOTES

1. Article 263 TFEU reads as follows: 'The Court of Justice of the European Union shall review the legality of legislative acts, of acts of the Council, of the Commission and of the European Central Bank, other than recommendations and opinions, and of acts of the European Parliament and of the European Council intended to produce legal effects vis-à-vis third parties. It shall also review the legality of acts of bodies, offices or agencies of the Union intended to produce legal effects vis-à-vis third parties. It shall for this purpose have jurisdiction in actions brought by a Member State, the European Parliament, the Council or the Commission on grounds of lack of competence, infringement of an essential procedural requirement, infringement of the Treaties or of any rule of law relating to their application, or misuse of powers. The Court shall have jurisdiction under the same conditions in actions brought by the Court of Auditors, by the European Central Bank and by the Committee of the Regions for the purpose of protecting their prerogatives. Any natural or legal person may, under the conditions laid down in the first and second paragraphs, institute proceedings

against an act addressed to that person or which is of direct and individual concern to them, and against a regulatory act which is of direct concern to them and does not entail implementing measures. Acts setting up bodies, offices and agencies of the Union may lay down specific conditions and arrangements concerning actions brought by natural or legal persons against acts of these bodies, offices or agencies intended to produce legal effects in relation to them. The proceedings provided for in this Article shall be instituted within two months of the publication of the measure, or of its notification to the plaintiff, or, in the absence thereof, of the day on which it came to the knowledge of the latter, as the case may be'.
2. We have already discussed the *ERTA* judgements implied powers doctrine in Chapter 1 and will also touch on it in Chapter 5.
3. This terminology is not the terminology of the treaties. Yet the terms 'privileged applicant', 'semi-privileged applicant', and 'non-privileged applicant' are widely used in legal scholarship.
4. See above with the *ERTA* and *Chernobyl* cases, for example.

REFERENCES

Alter, K. J. (1998). Who are the "masters of the treaty"? European governments and the European Court of Justice. *International Organization, 52*(1), 121–147.

Andersen, E. A. (2006). *Out of the closets and into the courts: Legal opportunity structure and gay rights litigation*. Ann Arbor: University of Michigan Press.

Arnull, A. (2000). The action for annulment: A case of double standards? In D. O'Keefe (Ed.), *Judicial review in European Union law* (pp. 177–190). The Hague: Kluwer Law International.

Arnull, A. (2001). Private applicants and the action for annulment since CODORNIU. *Common Market Law Review, 38*, 7–52.

Arnull, A. (2006). *The European Union and its Court of Justice*. Oxford, UK: Oxford University Press.

Arnull, A. (2011). The principle of effective judicial protection in EU law: An unruly horse. *European Law Review, 1,* 51–70.

Barav, A. (1974). Direct and individual concern: An almost insurmountable barrier to the admissibility of individual appeal to the EEC court. *Common Market Law Review, 11*(2), 191–198.

Bellamy, C. (2010). An EU competition court: The continuing debate. In I. Kokkoris & I. Lianos (Eds.), *The reform of EC competition law: New challenges* (pp. 33–52). Alphen aan den Rijn, The Netherlands: Kluwer Law International.

Börzel, T. A. (2003). Guarding the treaty: The compliance strategies of the European Commission. In T. A. Börzel & R. A. Cichowski (Eds.), *The state of*

the European Union (6th ed., pp. 197–220). Oxford, UK: Oxford University Press.
Conant, L. J. (2006). Individuals, courts, and the development of European social rights. *Comparative Political Studies, 39*(1), 76–100.
Craig, P. (2010). *The Lisbon Treaty: Law, politics, and treaty reform*. Oxford, UK: Oxford University Press.
Craig, P., & de Búrca, G. (2011). *EU law: Text, cases, and materials*. Oxford, UK: Oxford University Press.
Eliantonio, M., & Kas, B. (2010). Private parties and the annulment procedure: Can the gap in the European system of judicial protection be closed? *Journal of Politics and Law, 3*(2), 2–121.
Fairhurst, J. (2010). *Law of the European Union*. London: Pearson Education.
Falkner, G. (2018). A causal loop? The Commissions new enforcement approach in the context of non-compliance with EU law even after CJEU judgments. *Journal of European Integration, 40,* 769–784.
Franchino, F. (2007). *The powers of the union: Delegation in the EU*. Cambridge, UK: Cambridge University Press.
Hartlapp, M. (2005). *Die Kontrolle der nationalen Rechtsdurchsetzung durch die Europäische Kommission*. Frankfurt: Campus Verlag.
Hartley, T. C. (2007). *The foundations of European Community law: An introduction to the constitutional and administrative law of the European Community*. Oxford, UK: Oxford University Press.
Hilson, C. (2002). New social movements: The role of legal opportunity. *Journal of European Public Policy, 9*(2), 238–255.
Horspool, M., & Humphreys, M. (2012). *European Union law*. Oxford, UK: Oxford University Press.
Jupille, J. (2004). *Procedural politics: Issues, influence, and institutional choice in the European Union*. Cambridge, UK: Cambridge University Press.
Kornezov, A. (2014). Locus standi of private parties in actions for annulment: Has the gap been closed? *The Cambridge Law Journal, 73*, 25–28.
McCown, M. (2003). The European Parliament before the bench: ECJ precedent and EP litigation strategies. *Journal of European Public Policy, 10*(6), 974–995.
Moser, P., & Sawyer, K. (Eds.). (2008). *Making community law: The legacy of Advocate General Jacobs at the European Court of Justice*. Cheltenham, UK: Edward Elgar.
Peers, S., & Costa, M. (2012). Court of Justice of the European Union (General Chamber), Judicial review of EU Acts after the Treaty of Lisbon; Order of 6 September 2011, Case T-18/10 *Inuit Tapiriit Kanatami and Others vs. Commission & Judgment* of 25 October 2011, Case T-262/10 *Microban vs. Commission*. *European Constitutional Law Review, 8*(1), 82–104.

Tallberg, J. (2002). Paths to compliance: Enforcement, management, and the European Union. *International Organization, 56*, 609–643.

Türk, A. (2009). *Judicial review in EU law*. Cheltenham, UK: Edward Elgar.

Vanhala, L. (2012). Legal opportunity structures and the paradox of legal mobilization by the environmental movement in the UK. *Law and Society Review, 46*(3), 523–556.

Wilson, B., & Rodriguez Cordero, J. C. (2006). Legal opportunity structures and social movements: The effects of institutional change on Costa Rican politics. *Comparative Political Studies, 39*(3), 325–351.

Open Access This chapter is licensed under the terms of the Creative Commons Attribution 4.0 International License (http://creativecommons.org/licenses/by/4.0/), which permits use, sharing, adaptation, distribution and reproduction in any medium or format, as long as you give appropriate credit to the original author(s) and the source, provide a link to the Creative Commons license and indicate if changes were made.

The images or other third party material in this chapter are included in the chapter's Creative Commons license, unless indicated otherwise in a credit line to the material. If material is not included in the chapter's Creative Commons license and your intended use is not permitted by statutory regulation or exceeds the permitted use, you will need to obtain permission directly from the copyright holder.

CHAPTER 4

Studying Annulment Actions

In the remainder of this book, we study the sequence through which annulment litigation affects multilevel politics. This sequence is composed of distinct, yet interlinked, analytical steps that feed into each other. We start by (1) analysing actors' motivations for turning a policy controversy into a judicial conflict. From there, we move on to investigate (2) litigant configurations that influence annulment proceedings, all the way to assessing (3) the judicial outcome and the political and institutional impact of annulment actions. Our focus on this whole sequence reflects our presumption that there are several different things to analyse in order to understand how the emergence of annulment litigation feeds back into the European Union (EU) multilevel system. We have to understand when and why different kinds of actors want to initiate annulment litigation; how this intention by different actors is reflected by the litigant configuration in court; and how this litigant configuration relates to judicial behaviour. Finally, we have to understand the institutional and political effects of judgements. Focusing on this whole sequence sets this book apart from much of the extant research on legal conflicts in the EU multilevel system, which has typically focused on these steps individually, without conceiving them as elements coming together in the form of a complex process. The research design applied in this study is thus innovative as it attempts to combine the analysis of single steps individually with a systematic argument about their interlinkages and their respective roles in the broader sequence through which litigation intervenes in multilevel governance.

© The Author(s) 2020
C. Adam et al., *Taking the EU to Court*,
Palgrave Studies in European Union Politics,
https://doi.org/10.1007/978-3-030-21629-0_4

In terms of data, this project brings together original quantitative data that aggregates information based on court documents on annulment actions as well as qualitative data collected through interviews with actors that took part in the studied processes and available documents. For each step of this study, we are thus able to combine quantitative analysis with in-depth analysis of concrete EU annulment conflicts. We also bring together a broad range of mostly new data sources, notably forty expert interviews with actors involved in annulment conflicts at the different stages of the EU multilevel system and a large-N original data set on all annulment actions in the EU multilevel system. Most of the annulment actions analysed in our case studies date from the last ten years. This relative recentness allows tracing processes that are still relatively fresh in the memories of interviewees. The data set, in contrast, allows us to assess long-term trends and to reach much further back in time. Specifically, it covers the whole period from the Treaties of Rome to the end of 2012. Specifically, we include annulment actions that obtained a judgement until the end of 2015. Note that once an annulment action is launched, it takes on average twenty-four months—at times substantially longer—until a judgement is taken. Thus, our quantitative analysis captures cases that have been launched until 2012 and concluded at the end of 2015. We can thus draw upon different quantitative and qualitative analysis techniques to shed light on the chain through which annulment conflicts intervene in the EU multilevel system. This chapter explains the logic behind the choice of our research strategy in more detail and justifies our case selection. Moreover, it provides all necessary information about the empirical material we collected. We hope that this chapter allows the reader to assess the empirical and systematic quality of our subsequent arguments and claims.

Research Strategy

So far, political science has paid little attention to annulment conflicts in the EU as an analytical category of its own. In fact, doing so begs the question of how the study of annulment actions can improve our understanding of EU multilevel politics. What are these annulment actions? To which theoretical concepts do they relate? Are they a case of supranational noncompliance and implementation conflict in the EU that could bring a new dimension to research on compliance and implementation? Will they help us to study this phenomenon of supranational noncompliance, or are actions for annulment only a tool of inter-institutional conflict and procedural politics, which help EU institutions struggle for legislative influence (Jupille 2004)? Do they speak to research on the strategic interaction between these institutions in the process of legislative bargaining, or are actions for annulment merely another channel through which the Court can influence the trajectory of European integration by means of judicial law making? Are they thus mainly a category of cases able to speak to scholars of judicial behaviour and European integration who have so far focussed primarily on the role of preliminary references?

Our tentative answer to all of these questions is yes. Actions for annulment are probably best viewed as a case of all of these things. Therefore, in order to understand their political role, all of these aspects have to be taken into account at the same time. Therefore, we take a more general approach and treat annulment actions as manifestations of conflict within the EU's multilevel system. These conflicts manifest themselves as accusations of noncompliance against EU institutions. Yet often, they result from conflicts over policy application between the respective supranational institution and national actors. As a result of these conflicts, the Court is activated and obtains a chance to develop the rules guiding policy making and decision competences within the multilevel system. All of these different aspects can be integrated by considering annulment actions as manifestations of conflicts within the multilevel system that are judicialised and thereby enabled to leave a permanent mark in that multilevel system. Therefore, it is essential to adopt a sequential analytical perspective that is able to integrate the individual steps within this rather complex chain of events that define the role and impact of annulment litigation. Because of the complexity of such an endeavour and the rather limited insights of prior research on the political role of annulments, such an effort is necessarily explorative to some extent.

With regard to the sequential causal chain linking litigation to multilevel governance, our research design is informed by the limited availability of data and theory that would allow tracing the conceptualized causal chain from the beginning to the end of an annulment cycle. Information on annulment conflicts seldom starts with the motivations underlying the conflict or ends with how rulings feed back into policy making. Given the absence of existing data covering all relevant steps of the chain, in combination with the lack of systematic theorizing about the operating causal mechanisms, our endeavour has an important exploratory dimension, which speaks for a deductive-inductive strategy carried out by a mixed methods approach. The analysis of the relevant steps in the annulment sequence (motivations to litigate, litigants' constellations, ruling outcomes, ruling impact) thus constitutes a heuristic attempt to order our research field and allow for applying theoretical insights from other discussions. Case study evidence exemplifies the working of hypothesized causality empirically while at the same time bringing to the fore additional explanatory factors and mechanisms. Furthermore, quantitative analysis allows probing the plausibility (or even testing their fit) of these factors and mechanisms on a larger number of cases.

In terms of analytical framework, we combine a focus on each of the steps in the sequential causal chain individually with a comprehensive and synthetic approach of their linkage throughout the multilevel system. This way, characteristics carved out in earlier steps become explanations for patterns in later steps of the annulment sequence. We thus emphasize the endogenous character of the way litigation emerges from and intervenes in multilevel policy conflicts. To be clear, the research design does not focus exclusively on these endogenous factors shaping annulment conflicts in the multilevel system. Rather, while our sequential argument works out this endogenous causality for each step, it comes as a complement to broader explanations that also include exogenous factors.

In sum, since the existing literature (on other forms of EU litigation than annulments) frequently addresses the use of litigation, litigants' constellations, outcomes, and impact of litigation as analytically separated issues, they do so with an exogenous explanatory approach. By linking these steps together into a wider causal chain, we develop a new explanatory approach for annulment litigation that is based on endogenous mechanisms.

Case Selection

There have been several thousand annulment rulings since the founding of the EU in 1957. From this universe of cases, a number of annulment rulings were selected for in-depth analysis. We selected these annulments in order to cover both vertical and horizontal conflict categories.

With respect to vertical conflicts, the case selection proceeded in two steps, aiming to cover the widest possible variety of types of multilevel policy conflicts. In the first step, we selected two countries from which to choose annulment cases, namely Spain and Germany. We chose these countries for three reasons. First, both Spain and Germany are among the member states that raise most annulment actions per year (Bauer and Hartlapp 2010). Second, both countries present different litigant profiles, as shown by the different extent to which they raise preliminary rulings before the Court of Justice of the European Union (CJEU); Germany raises many, Spain relatively few. Third, most annulment actions raised by Spain relate to financial sanctions in EU redistributive policies, mainly in agriculture and cohesion policies; such cases related to fiscal issues are relatively rare in Germany. In other words, because of such structural differences between both member states, we have reason to suspect that the nature of the conflicts underlying litigation might differ in those countries, too.

In the second step, we chose a series of annulment cases in each country. To select those individual annulment cases, we started by listing for both countries all annulment actions raised by national or regional governments between 2010 and 2015, coding them with regard to the type of policy field they belong to and the subject of the dispute. Many of the cases dealt with conflicts over EU redistributive policies, as mentioned above in agriculture and cohesion policies. This seems to be a relatively homogeneous category of cases that focuses almost exclusively on financial issues (Bauer and Hartlapp 2010). To assure variance across cases, we decided to treat all cases related to the use of EU funds as one analytical category instead of picking individual cases within this policy field. We then randomly selected six cases in Spain and six cases in Germany among the remaining cases that did *not* fall into the EU redistributive category.

The selection of our horizontal annulment cases for in-depth study had to be done differently. First, because the conflict involved EU institutions on both sides of the conflict, no different polity contexts (i.e. member states) could be selected. All horizontal conflicts, by our definition, originate in the political system of the EU. To select a broad range of annulment cases involving European institutions, we thus looked at the cross-sectoral distribution of the full sample of horizontal cases. Distribution across policy fields was assessed via the treaty article(s) referred to in the ruling. Treaty articles were grouped into broader policy areas with the help of an established codebook (Stone Sweet and Brunell 1999).[1] That meant, for example, that for external affairs, we selected all cases coded as dealing with external relations in the Stone Sweet and Brunell database (matter 412).[2] Cases dealing with common and foreign security policy (matter 384), development cooperation (matters 338 and 419), or integrated Mediterranean programmes (matter 423) were added. Where multiple treaty bases applied without corresponding to the same policy area systematic, the substance of the case was assessed in detail to identify the dominant policy field, and the case was then accordingly assigned to the correct category.

It turned out that the category of external affairs is the area with the highest number of horizontal annulment conflicts (forty-one cases representing 29% of all cases). The second most important area is staff regulation and institutional provisions (twenty-two cases, or 15%), followed by environment and energy as well as justice and home affairs (fourteen cases each, with the latter seeing a substantial hike in the last three years), agriculture and fisheries (eleven cases), community budget, state aid (eight cases each), and taxes (six cases). The number of horizontal annulment conflicts is negligible in all other policy fields (Hartlapp 2018). Based on this cross-policy distribution, we decided to focus on external affairs as the area with the highest overall number of annulment cases. Here, all cases have been studied systematically and in depth. In addition, horizontal cases from other policy areas have been added to the sample of cases studied in more depth where primary or secondary sources had highlighted that they are of particular interest, for example where interviewees mentioned them as particularly interesting or where a precedent was set. This helped us to gain in-depth insight into the most dynamic policy field while at the same time covering the politically relevant cases on other areas as well. In sum, our cases were selected to represent annulment conflicts that seem to be most typical from a bird's eye perspective while using the advantage of our research design to be open to include additional information and thus cases promising to enrich our understanding (see also Bauer and Knill 2014).

DATA

We built a data set covering all annulment actions that were launched since the founding of the European Community and received a judgement until the end of 2015. To this aim, we extracted all cases from the Stone Sweet and Brunell (2007) *Data Set on Actions under Article 230: 1954–2006*. We updated the selection done by our colleagues by retrieving the relevant information from *CURIA* and *EurLex*. All entries were double-checked and completed. We inserted in the emerging data base information on the date of litigation and ruling, claimant and defendant, the legal domain, or subject matter and decision type—thereby following and relying on Stone Sweet and Brunell's method. In addition, however, we added information on the title and substance of the case, the official number, actors intervening in the case, and information on who won or lost the case (here, cost transfer was used as indicator). In other words, we substantially enriched the Stone Sweet and Brunell database in terms of content and time line.

The database on which this book relies is substantially improved also with respect to data analysis done over the past years by us for various publications. First, we had selected only cases launched against the Commission (up until 2012); we later include actions against all EU institutions and not just against the Commission (until 2015). This includes the horizontal cases in which EU institutions also act as litigants. Additionally, this includes vertical cases in which the defendant is not the Commission (e.g. private/regional/member states v. Council/European Parliament [EP]/European Central Bank). This means that our analysis is no longer limited to accusations of noncompliance voiced against the Commission, but involves such actions raised against all EU institutions. Most importantly, however, we are able to assess the participant structure within these conflicts. We capture all litigants as well as all intervening parties for all of those cases. In our final database, every case refers to a factual court ruling. A ruling may combine court cases, and there can be more than one claimant to a case (joint cases). We treat joint cases as individual annulment conflicts as they result from the same underlying conflict. We include all cases initiated. Where cases were at some point found to be inadmissible, we record this as the respective judicial outcome of the conflict.

For the case studies, we meticulously analysed the text of the respective rulings and put it into context with other primary and secondary sources. Where access to primary documentation was restricted, we relied on expert interviews as the adequate approach to maximize the amount of available information for studying underlying motivations and assessments (e.g. Aberbach and Rockman 2002; Berry 2002). Our interviewees were usually high officials at the national level and EU level who themselves, in the capacity of their respective offices, took part in the decisions to litigate in the cases selected. Most of the time, our interviewees were state attorneys and officials from policy departments and legal services from the national and subnational ministries and EU institutions.

A total of forty semi-structured interviews were carried out between April 2009 and June 2016 in Berlin, Bilbao, Bonn, Brussels, Dresden, Madrid, Munich, and Santiago de Compostella (see the Annex for details). Three interview partners were Commission officials (labelled as COM_1, COM_2, COM_3), one interview partner worked in the legal service of the EP (EP_1), one interviewee came from the Council (CONS_1), nine interviewees worked for various German federal ministries (MIN_DE_1, etc.), nine interviewees were Spanish civil servants affiliated with various national ministries (MIN_ES_1, etc.), one interviewee worked for the regional ministry of Saxony (MIN_SA_1), one interviewee was from the regional ministry of Bavaria (MIN_BA_1), six interviewees were from various regional ministries of Galicia (MIN_GA_1, etc.), five interviews were led with lawyers working in private law firms (LAW_1, etc.) and four interviews with employees from private or public companies involved in annulment litigation (COMP_1, etc.).[3]

Each of the interviews followed a semi-structured guideline with open questions and lasted between thirty minutes and two hours.[4] The questions were constructed with a view to capturing process and preference information on the specific annulment cases as well as assessments of how specific the case at hand was—from the view of the interviewee—for EU annulment conflict more generally. In other words, we asked the interviewees to reconstruct the decision-making process of litigation and asked a series of questions aimed at uncovering the criteria and considerations that had driven the decision to litigate. All interviews were transcribed and deductively coded, which allowed systematic searches for specific issues covered throughout the argumentative chain; for example, to facilitate the interpretation of how the cases relate to motivations, we were interested in quotes that mentioned the objectives of going to court.

Besides collecting the interview material, we also traced information on the litigation process on the basis of published primary documents, most importantly the rulings and opinions available on *CURIA*. Apart from containing the CJEU's assessment of the situation, these documents typically describe the interaction between claimant and defendants in the conflict prior to litigation, as well as the core legal pleas brought forward. This information was complemented and validated by publicly available sources such as local, regional, and national press coverage and other media as well as position papers from the involved parties (when available).

Conclusion

To sum up, in this chapter, we presented the reasons behind our choices about how to study EU annulment conflicts empirically. The sequential approach, which we deem necessary to capture the political role of actions for annulment, requires us to look into a variety of issues spanning from multilevel policy conflicts to the feedback effect of litigation into policies and institutions of the EU multilevel system. Our attempt to do justice to the complexity of our research object finds expression in the research design that covers different steps in the process individually and their chain-like relationship. We believe a combination of quantitative data analysis and studying selected cases in depth to be the most appropriate strategy. The efforts to collect this quantitative and qualitative data have been immense. As a result of these efforts, the subsequent chapters can rely on substantial and original empirical data.

Notes

1. We updated the codebook by Stone Sweet and Brunell in order to cover new treaty bases (1999).
2. The mentioned matters 412, 338, 384, etc., are definitions taken from the codebook of Stone Sweet and Brunell (1999).
3. Please note that many of our interview partners were procedural and legal experts who spent much of their professional lives with annulments litigation. During the interviews, they added much to our understanding of various annulment cases.
4. Further details are provided in the Annex of this book.

References

Aberbach, J. D., & Rockman, B. A. (2002). Conducting and coding elite interviews. *Political Science and Politics, 35,* 673–676.
Bauer, M. W., & Hartlapp, M. (2010). Much ado about money and how to spend it! Analysing 40 years of annulment cases against the European Union Commission. *European Journal of Political Research, 49,* 202–222.
Bauer, M. W., & Knill, C. (2014). A conceptual framework for the comparative analysis of policy change: Measurement, explanation, and strategies of policy dismantling. *Journal of Comparative Policy Analysis: Research and Practice, 16*(3), 28–44.

Berry, J. M. (2002). Validity and reliability issues in elite interviewing. *Political Science and Politics, 35*, 679–682.

Hartlapp, M. (2018). Power shifts via the judicial arena: How annulments cases between EU institutions shape competence allocation. *Journal of Common Market Studies, 56*(6), 1429–1445.

Jupille, J. (2004). *Procedural politics: Issues, influence, and institutional choice in the European Union*. Cambridge, UK: Cambridge University Press.

Stone Sweet, A., & Brunell, T. L. (1999). *Data set on preliminary references in EC law*. San Domenico di Fiesole, Italy: Robert Schuman Centre, European University Institute.

Stone Sweet, A., & Brunell, T. L. (2007). *Data set on actions under Article 230: 1954–2006. NEWGOV Project*. San Domenico di Fiesole, Italy: Robert Schuman Centre, European University Institute.

Open Access This chapter is licensed under the terms of the Creative Commons Attribution 4.0 International License (http://creativecommons.org/licenses/by/4.0/), which permits use, sharing, adaptation, distribution and reproduction in any medium or format, as long as you give appropriate credit to the original author(s) and the source, provide a link to the Creative Commons license and indicate if changes were made.

The images or other third party material in this chapter are included in the chapter's Creative Commons license, unless indicated otherwise in a credit line to the material. If material is not included in the chapter's Creative Commons license and your intended use is not permitted by statutory regulation or exceeds the permitted use, you will need to obtain permission directly from the copyright holder.

CHAPTER 5

Motivations: When Conflict Leads to Litigation

What motivates political actors to engage in European Union annulment litigation? This is the main question studied in this chapter. Our starting point is the observation that it is not possible to reduce public actors' decisions to initiate annulment actions to the pure legal characteristics of the cases. Annulment actions do not automatically arise from specific legal circumstances. This is what we learn from the examples of annulments reported in the previous chapters. There is more to filing an annulment lawsuit then just a legal-technical quarrel. This *more* is the political context that surrounds a concrete decision to engage in annulment litigation.

While never contradicting the legal logic of annulment litigation, actors chose from the universe of potential annulment conflicts to engage in due to political reasons, which we conceive as material gains, institutional competences, ideology, or political trust. Consider in this context that annulment litigation is a defence against decisions made by an EU institution; such a supranational decision, if it remains unchallenged, constitutes a final point in a struggle about particular policy choices. In other words, if actors do *not* take up the fight—that is, if nobody litigates—the current interpretation of the supranational measure adopted prevails. It marks the institutional endpoint of a conflict, which can then have feedback effects. Actors obviously can choose *not* to engage in annulment conflict, but if their choice is to do so, it is the context of the struggle they go through in the multilevel policy

© The Author(s) 2020
C. Adam et al., *Taking the EU to Court*,
Palgrave Studies in European Union Politics,
https://doi.org/10.1007/978-3-030-21629-0_5

process—their priorities, perceived needs, and subsequently the utility they associate with potentially successful litigation—that tip them into active litigation.

It is thus important to uncover litigants' motivations behind the empirical decision to turn to court. To this aim, we first review the literature on judicial politics as well as the classical literature on actors' motivations. On this basis, we distinguish between four types of motivations that drive actors to initiate annulment lawsuits in EU Court: to maximize financial resources, institutional power, ideological and policy preferences, and political trust.

Second, based on extensive fieldwork carried out in Germany, Spain, and Brussels, this chapter assesses the relevance of these four motivations for launching annulment litigation empirically in selected cases (see also Chapter 4). Rather than classical ideal types in the Weberian sense, the four motivations are real types. Empirically, decisions to start an annulment case can be based upon several motivations simultaneously.[1] As we will show when analysing individual annulment cases, for almost all of them, a dominant motivation can be identified. We find, however, that not all motivations occur with equal frequency and that certain types of actors are associated more frequently with some motivations than with others.

First, financial gains are the most important motivation in quantitative terms, they underpin the bulk of annulment actions. Litigation is chosen when legal success would significantly improve the litigant's budget by either avoiding substantial expenses or maximizing revenue. Financial motives are important not only for private actors, such as companies having benefitted from state aid. They are also a crucial motivation for public actors, that is, member states and subnational authorities in the face of a Commission decision of financial correction in agriculture or cohesion policies. This type of motivation is generally associated with supranational decisions bearing little saliency, and often do not have much impact beyond the financial redistribution across levels—although they can also occasionally come with important policy change in the related sectoral policies, such as the common agricultural policy or cohesion policies.

Second, litigation is pursued when the Court's interpretation of unclear legal concepts may significantly improve the litigant's institutional and decision-making competences. This motivation is found almost exclusively among public actors, both national and European, to counter measures they perceive as a competence stretch threatening to reduce their own institutional power. This motivation is typically found with annulment actions that have important EU-wide repercussions, because they always bear a potential to alter the institutional status quo through a Court-led redefinition of competences within the EU.

With respect to the third motivation—ideology—litigation represents an opportunity to defend or promote an important ideological aspect or policy position by establishing or keeping a normative order. In terms of numbers, this motivation was not very significant. It was not found with that much frequency as the other three and we rather observed it occasionally. Interestingly, we found that this motivation tends to underpin conflicts in highly salient policy issues.

Finally, litigation can also be used as a political symbol to signal responsiveness and trustworthiness to the litigant's constituency and to important political partners. While overall less important empirically, a specificity of this motivation is the type of actor likely to initiate it. It matters for actors who are directly elected at the subnational, national, or supranational level, such as governments or, less frequently, the European Parliament (EP). Typically, the stakes underpinning this type of motivations are national or even local. So this type of action tends to have a significant distributive impact on national or local actors. While they can have EU-wide repercussions, this is not always the case.

The following analyses of empirical cases will demonstrate that annulment actions are regularly used for political purposes. They are inherently political tools employed as strategies in policy conflicts in the EU multilevel system. How the legal background mediates the political motivations to initiate annulment actions is thus a central puzzle to which this chapter now turns. In sum, the following pages shed light on the constellations, conditions, and mechanisms that bring actors to pursue their objectives with the help of annulment actions.

Conceptualizing Motivations for Litigation

Since Martin Shapiro's (1964) seminal introduction of a research agenda for political jurisprudence, the study of courts and litigation has escaped the narrow confines of legal scholarship. Since then, various social science disciplines have applied their concepts, theories, and methods to the study of judicial processes. This allowed grasping the non-legal dimension of judicial proceedings, such as actors' decisions to litigate and judges decision-making roles. The literature on judicial politics thus offers plenty of material that is potentially relevant for studying annulment actions. We have complemented this body of literature with insights from research on actors' motivations and preferences. This section presents a theoretically derived categorization of four types of motivations for litigation, extensive enough to do justice to extant research and yet parsimonious enough to be a useful tool in empirical research.

Material Gains

The first of these motivations is all about material—more precisely, financial—resources. Actors litigate because they hope to gain financial resources or avoid their loss. This motivation is particularly prominent for private litigators, as economic research on litigation has emphasized (Gould 1973; Posner 1973; Bebchuk 1984; Priest and Klein 1984). This literature typically investigates the conditions for the use of different conflict-resolution mechanisms by opposing parties, litigation being one, arbitration another. These works assess how a variety of factors (e.g. information asymmetry, judicial procedures, probability to win) affect the risk-benefit analysis made by litigants when deciding whether it is financially worthwhile to go to court. This literature thus assumes that litigation is driven primarily by financial considerations and leaves little room for other possible rationales regarding the use of litigation.

Wealth maximization is obviously of particular relevance for understanding the behaviour of private actors attempting to further their economic aims with the help of litigation. But public actors, too, care about their budgets. In contrast to the economic literature that focuses on individuals' material interest, for public actors, material motivations are typically studied in combination or alongside other motivational factors. Depending on the conceptualization of the role models of bureaucrats, individual material gains can be crucial to explaining public decisions (Downs 1967). Moreover, at an aggregate level, bureaucracies are often conceived as self-aggrandizing actors, searching to maximize their budget and expand their services (Niskanen 1971). This assumption also applies to governments whose capacity to act depends—inter alia—on the national budget. Given the political relevance of budgets, politicians are thus searching to maximize revenues (Brennan and Buchanan 1980) and to limit unnecessary or non-priority expenses.

Many decisions adopted in the EU multilevel system have a budgetary impact. Furthermore, as in any polity, EU budget decisions are subject to intense inter-institutional conflicts (Becker et al. 2017), which often lead to the use of judicial review, especially by the Council against decisions of the EP (Skiadas 2002). The Commission, too, may adopt decisions that affect member states' budgets in a negative way (Bauer and Becker 2014; Ege et al. 2018). The treaties and secondary law have delegated a series of sector—and issue-specific enforcement mechanisms to the Commission—other than the infringement procedure (Gil Ibañez 1998)—allowing the latter to impose financial sanctions on the member states. Judicial review may then be used by the member states to challenge these decisions (Bauer and Hartlapp 2010). We expect such a material motivation to be particularly relevant in EU policy areas where distributive instruments prevail or where regulatory instruments directly affect the allocation of resources. The maximization of material resources can explain annulment actions initiated by EU institutions or by the member states, where the litigant is willing to annul a decision that has a negative impact on its budget or to seek higher budgets, without necessarily being the only reason for engaging in annulments (as we shall see below). The motivational logic behind trying to protect or expand one's material resources, however, is simple: annulment actions motivated by financial resources aim at revoking a decision of EU institutions that has a negative impact on the litigant's budget. In short, the object to litigate is to receive a favourable decision about an actor's own material gains.

Institutional Competences

In his seminal work on the functioning of democracies, Downs (1957) argues that political actors are not interested in particular policies. Instead, they care about the privileges they derive from holding power. Thus, what motivates them is institutional power and positions. This motivation is likely to matter for annulment conflicts in the EU multilevel system, too. Litigation can be motivated by the intention to influence the distribution of institutional competences in a political system. We know that courts can have a profound impact on the structure of governance and politics, that is, on the distribution of power among political actors and their strategic behaviour and interactions. Stone Sweet's (1999) theory about the judicialization and the construction of governance and Jupille's (2007) argument about contested legislative procedures highlight the endogenous process through which the characteristics of a polity can be altered gradually and even profoundly through actors' recourses to litigation. Actors may thus resort to litigation in the hope to use the court's influence as a lever to alter the distribution of institutional competences to their advantage.

In federal states, courts have significant influence on the shape and evolution of the multilevel decision-making arrangement (Baier 2006). Hence, judicial review plays a particularly important role in federal countries. Comparative politics and legal scholarship understand it as a tool that allows protecting the constitutionally enshrined federal arrangements against attempts by the federal or regional governments to overstep each other's competences (Lijphart 1999; Baker and Young 2001; Ryan 2011). Courts' capacity to shape federal arrangements is particularly prominent in countries with a high number of veto players in the executive and legislative branches (Swenden 2006, 79). Being a highly fragmented polity, the EU appears particularly prone to judicial influence on the distribution of power between the supranational and national level. After all, the Court of Justice of the European Union (CJEU) has come to be seen as capable of transforming the relationship between the EU's and national legal orders in fundamentals ways for a long time (Burley and Mattli 1993; Stone Sweet and Brunell 1998).

Moreover, legal provisions—and particularly constitutional provisions—that define the distribution of competences are conventionally theorized as incomplete contracts (Farrell and Héritier 2007) that can be—or sometimes even need to be—clarified via litigation (Hadfield 1994). By inviting the judiciary to (re-)interpret the legal provisions specifying the distribution of competences on which a contested act was based, litigants might manage not only to dissolve the contested legal act, they might also be able to create an effective (legal) barrier that will keep the defending institution from adopting similar legal acts in the future. In this sense, litigation today can be initiated with the goal in mind of avoiding similar competence creep in the (far) future.

This motivation is likely to matter for two reasons, both related to systemic features of the EU. First, part of the EU's expansion of powers is the result of competence creep, in particular as provoked by the Commission (Pollack 1994; Weatherill 2004; Amaral and Neave 2009; Prechal 2010). Second, the high number of veto players involved in EU decision making makes it difficult for the member states to counteract, through the adoption of legislation or treaty change, the Commission's decisions once such a decision is taken (or those of other EU institutions). This turns the CJEU into an attractive venue for member states willing to put a hold on the Commission's extensive interpretation of the EU's competences (see Schmidt 1998, 173; Bauer and Hartlapp 2010). In line with this argument, Adam (2016, 158) argues that governments may use annulment actions 'for reasons that go beyond the desire to win a legal dispute […] and instead […] to bring more general questions concerning the design of institutions […] to the CJEU's attention', in the hope of exploiting the Court's judicial authority to alter the EU's institutionalized balance of power. In short, annulment actions are launched as an attempt to influence the distribution of institutional competences in the long term via inviting the CJEU to formulate a judicial interpretation of key legal concepts. We thus expect to see conflicts motivated by an interest in keeping or expanding competences, particularly in those policy areas and in those periods of time where competence allocation in the multilevel system changes or where competences are shared between institutions and levels. This motivation should be most relevant for public actors as their relationships and (future) checks and balances in a political system will be at stake. We refer to this kind of institutional motivation as the willingness to protect decision-making competences.

Ideology

Next to material gains and protecting institutional competences, a decision to litigate can also emerge from substantial policy interest. Going back to the early literature on political parties, Edmund Burke established the notion that groups of political actors are motivated by some principle in which they all agreed. The ideological orientation of a group can explain the positions chosen in line with such principles. Moreover, comparative politics research (De Swaan 1973; Müller and Strøm 1999) argues that the party political orientation of actors helps to explain why actors are seeking specific policies. Where this ideology is at odds with a process or instrument chosen, or where it does not fit the substance of an EU policy, conflict can emerge. In such a case, the active engagement in this conflict is driven by neither a material motivation nor an institutional motivation. Ideology can be a reason for actors to take decisions that are not in their material or institutional interest. Instead, values and norms about how things ought to be can be powerful drivers of agency.

In European integration research, the role of national interests has been heatedly debated ever since the early days of theorizing supranational institution building. Prominently, national positions are explained by particular policy interests, such as preferences for creating an internal market expressed by national economic elites (Moravcsik 1991). However, ideology is also an important explanation for European integration and for policies adopted in the EU system. Normative beliefs and deeply rooted values not only shape individual behaviour but may prevail at the level of collective actors or even entire nations, for example regarding nation-state identity, (Western liberal) values, and a shared understanding of human rights and the rule of law. Ideology motivates actors to propose and use EU instruments. Where this ideology is at odds with a process or instrument chosen or where it does not fit with the substance of an EU policy, conflict can emerge (Risse et al. 1999).

Policy actors may try to use litigation as a tool to advance their substantial policy goals. The extensive literature on the legal mobilization of social movements developed in the United States shows how litigation can serve ideologically driven actors (Scheingold 1974; McCann 1994). Similar results are found in the EU, where both gender rights activists and environmental organizations have used litigation strategies before the European Court of Justice as a mean to advance their policy agenda (Cichowski 2007). Yet this motivation for litigation is not exclusively reserved for social movements and non-governmental organizations. Ideology is also an important driver for national governments, the Council, the EP, and the European Commission. While it remains difficult to apply the notion of party families across all EU member states (Camia and Caramani 2012), the politicization of European integration has turned ideology into an important determinant of EU policy making (Hutter and Grande 2014; Hartlapp 2015; Rauh 2019). The early years of integration were characterized by a permissive consensus, where integration advanced without (public) contestation as an elite project (Hooghe and Marks 2009). This has started to change in the 1990s, and today, political contestation affects virtually all EU institutions. An increasingly critical public challenges specific EU policies as well as the overall direction of the integration process. There is more debate about desirable trajectories for European integration. Frequently, criticism and controversy follow party cleavages. The desire to defend policy design often motivates annulment actions against decisions of EU institutions that appear to come in the way of achieving ideological goals.

When a decision adopted by an EU institution clashes with a public actor's ideological preferences, we can imagine ideology motivating actors to raise an annulment action with a view to having the EU measure annulled. Such action may have, as a priority objective, the annulment of the contested EU measure.

Even more so, annulment actions may also serve long-term ideological goals reaching well beyond the case at hand. Indeed, litigation can be 'more than just litigation and courts' (Boutcher 2013), as is shown by the constitutive approach to legal mobilization by social movements (McCann 1994). Similar to what we discussed regarding a long-term institutional motivation, annulment litigation may also serve long-term ideological goals simply by subjecting legal concepts with ideologically important implications to judicial review. These ideologically important concepts become part of legal discourse. The prevailing legal interpretation turns the litigation on which it is based into a 'prophetic litigation' that 'often functions as an appeal to future generations' (Lobel 1995, 1347), 'to the brooding spirit of the law, to the intelligence of a future day, when a later decision may possibly correct the error into which the dissenting judge believes the court to have been betrayed' (Hughes 1928, 68). In other words, the contested case creates opportunities in the sense of Galanter's repeat players argument, according to which institutional actors often engage in litigation with the view of shaping courts' case law in the long run rather than in the tangible outcomes of specific cases (Galanter 1974). In the same line of reasoning, Granger's account of member states' participation to preliminary references trials emphasizes their willingness to weigh on the evolution of the Court's legal doctrine in the long run (Granger 2004). Ideology may thus motivate actions that can have, as a primary purpose, either the annulment of the contested EU measure or the promotion of a legal discourse supporting the litigants' normative order. In sum, annulment actions can be motivated by the goal to revoke EU measures that clash with the litigant's ideological preferences.

Political Trust

Scholarship on the strategies of social movements to mobilize against regulations argues that litigation, independent from the outcome of the trial, can increase social movements' credibility and public support (Lobel 1994; McCann 1998; NeJaime 2011). By initiating judicial proceedings, a social movement may attempt to change the public's perception about its action and to gain the public's trust, sympathy, and support. This mechanism can be an appealing way to signal trustworthiness to important constituencies for politicians and governments and should help to improve their chances for reelection (Müller and Strøm 1999). It is thus a form of legitimacy. Interestingly, in this case, the initiation of litigation is sufficient for gaining political trust and electoral support. The legal outcomes of judicial proceedings play only a secondary role, particularly when they materialize only after several years of proceedings.

Political trust, as we conceive it, is a highly valuable resource for office holders because it translates into citizens' support for their policies (Chanley et al. 2000; Davis and Silver 2004; Hetherington 2005; Rudolph and Evans 2005). Political trust also increases political actors' informal room for manoeuvre and thereby can smoother the functioning of the political system (Miller 1974; Coleman 1994; Gambetta 1998; Levi and Stoker 2000), as well as the chances for being reelected. It should thus not be surprising that political leaders eagerly invest continuous effort in maximizing political trust (Bourdieu 1991, 18).

Obviously, political trust is affected by many parameters, including the perceived quality of democratic institutions (Mishler and Rose 2001; Segovia Arancibia 2008), demographic variables (Christensen and Laegreid 2005; Macoubrie 2006), societal characteristics (Newton and Norris 1999), and exogenous events and the saliency of international issues (Chanley 2002; Hetherington and Rudolph 2008). Moreover, governmental performance (Citrin 1974; Hetherington 1998; Chanley et al. 2000; Van De Walle and Bouckaert 2003; Keele 2007), the alignment between the policies adopted and the public's preferences (Miller 1974), and leaders' personality (Citrin 1974; Citrin and Green 1986) affect levels of political trust.

As a matter of fact, it is less the objective governmental performance, responsiveness, and leadership per se than it is the public's *perception* of these aspects that affects political trust. Trust is a relational concept; to be trusted, trustees need to signal trustworthiness to their principals (Bacharach and Gambetta 2001). This is a sociological mechanism that applies in a wide variety of situations. Companies use third-party certification labels to signal trustworthiness (Aiken et al. 2004); bureaucracies design their public communication in order to improve their reputation—that is, the public's perception of their capacities and performance (Maor et al. 2013). Just as companies and bureaucracies do, politicians also need to convince their own audience, their constituency, of their trustworthiness.

While political trust as a relationship is important for any actor in a political system, electoral gains are particularly relevant where we can identify a constituency. This is the case for national governments as well as for the EP. They all need to take care of the image they send to their voters. Litigating against (other) EU institutions can be a way to signal trustworthiness to constituencies. Political parties can thereby demonstrate their willingness to "stand up and fight" for the rights and interests of their electorates. By litigating against legal acts that clash with public opinion, national governments, as well as members of the EP, can show their responsiveness to the public's concerns. Consequently, we speak of responsiveness and trustworthiness whenever the motivation to litigate is driven by the attempt to retain a good relationship with the public.

Table 5.1 depicts the four motivational logics for initiating an annulment action that we derive from our reading of the pertinent literature. The question, however, is whether these motivations drive empirical cases. It is thus to the analysis of annulment cases that we now turn.

Table 5.1 Overview of the four motivational logics for litigation

Motivations	Objective	How does litigation serve the actor's objective?
Material gains	Maximising returns or minimizing costs	Repealing a decision that has a negative impact on the litigant's budget
Institutional competences	Preserving political rights and ring-fencing the opponent's decision-making competences	Interpretation of competences and decision-making powers
Ideology	Promoting ideological or substantial policy preferences	Establishing or keeping normative orders
Political trust	Maintaining good relationships with addressees of a policy	Signalling responsiveness and trustworthiness to constituencies and partners

Source Own compilation

Empirical Analysis

We thus expect litigation to be driven by motivations to maximize material gains, to promote and protect one's ideological goals, to defend one's institutional competences, and to maximize political trust. Analytically, these motivations are clearly distinct. Empirically, however, it is challenging to objectively identify and distinguish these motivations. It is important to realize that these motivations are not mutually exclusive. For each case, we seek to identify the predominant motivation while also reflecting aspects of the other motivations. In addition, motivations are notoriously difficult to capture, as they cannot be directly observed. Motivations, understood as objectives an actor is seeking in the first place (and rather independently from other factors that render litigation more or less likely), can, however, be deduced indirectly from primary (interviews, rulings) and secondary sources.

The Legal Factor

The literature on the economics of litigation sees the chances of success in court as a crucial factor for deciding whether to litigate.[2] After all, it is the chances of success that strongly influence litigants' expected payoffs, no matter whether these are material or immaterial. We have asked our interviewees about the role of the legal factor, understood as the chances of judicial success, in their decisions. While it plays a central role for private actors, it is apparently not so crucial for public actors. Although the member states lose most vertical conflicts (i.e. 75% of the cases in which they litigate by themselves against single EU institutions), the legal merits of the case supporting the position of the member states do play a role. State attorneys and legal services of the EU institutions need a legal doubt, however small, in order to engage in litigation. When legal defeat in court is nearly certain—that is, when the application of the Court's case law will in all likelihood imply a rejection of the annulment action—these actors rather abstain from litigating. The reason is simple. State attorneys and legal services in the EU institutions want to preserve their reputation and credibility in Luxemburg, which means they are careful not to raise actions without adequate legal justification— and at least some chances of winning. By contrast, a legal doubt (even a small one) about how case law should apply to the case at hand suffices to legitimize judicial action; state attorneys are in such cases very keen to litigate (MIN_ES_4, MIN_ES_5). In this sense, a legal doubt on the case is a necessary condition for litigation, but it is not a sufficient one. We now examine, based on a carefully selected series of case studies, the role of material gains, institutional competences, ideology, and political trust in motivating public actors to raise annulment actions.

MATERIAL GAINS–DRIVEN MOTIVATION IN ANNULMENT LITIGATION

We claim that financial resources can play an important role in public actors' decisions to raise annulment actions. The underlying objective is to get the Court to declare void a decision that would have a negative impact on the litigant's budget. We find that this motivation is particularly important in vertical annulment conflicts, that is, in those cases initiated by (private) national or subnational litigants against EU institutions. Hence, this section essentially focuses on such vertical cases, although we also give an example of horizontal case (i.e. initiated by an EU institution) motivated by the litigant's willingness to maximize financial resources.

When member states litigate against EU institutions, many cases emerge in the context of agricultural policy and regional policy. Both the Common Agriculture Policy (CAP) and the regional policy are redistributive policies, which allocate funds to different types of beneficiaries across Europe. The application of these policies and their execution relies on the Commission's strong enforcement powers, which may adopt decisions of financial correction, where they find that EU funds are not spent according to EU law. When the sums spent under the CAP or the regional policy are advanced by the member states and reimbursed by the Commission at a later stage, by adopting a decision of financial correction, the Commission denies the transfer to the member states of the sums already issued. Annulment actions raised by the member states in both sectors typically target such Commission decisions of financial correction. This gives a first indication of the likely importance of material interests in member states' decisions to litigate against the Commission. To verify this, we asked national civil servants in Spain and Germany about the criteria they take into account when deciding to litigate for financial reasons.

In both countries, the regions or federal states manage the funds. As subnational actors have the responsibility to issue the funds according to EU law, they are also responsible in cases of detected non-compliance. In practice, this means that the region where funds have been misspent is the one to pay the financial correction back to the Commission. On the other hand, in the ruling *Regione Siciliana* (C 15/06), the Court made clear that it would not admit annulment actions over financial corrections from subnational authorities. It is very difficult for these subnational authorities to demonstrate the direct effect of supranational decisions. The Court found, for example, that the Commission's decision of financial corrections lacked a direct effect on the applicant region, which is an indispensable criterion for the region, treated as non-privileged applicant, to have their actions admitted by the Court (see Chapter 3). Hence, annulment actions against decisions of financial corrections should be raised by the member states on behalf of the regions concerned. Therefore, for matters related to the funds, while the regions bear the costs of the Commission's decisions, it is up to the member state to decide whether to litigate. Cooperation between regions and the central state is therefore necessary for litigation to take place.

The regions affected by financial corrections decisions usually want their member state to engage in litigation against the Commission. This material interest rationale for litigation is often paramount for the concerned regions (MIN_DE_5, MIN_ES_4). State-level actors, the central administration responsible for the funds, and the state attorneys are receptive to the region's interests and usually willing to cooperate with the regions on that matter. However, they also consider other criteria and balance them with the financial criteria when deciding whether to litigate or not, such as the legal merits of the case (MIN_DE_5, MIN_ES_4).

We found that financial considerations are driving many of the member states' decisions to litigate against the Commission. In the cases we studied, the higher the level of the financial correction, the more likely becomes a decision to litigate. State attorneys often have to arbitrate between several petitions for litigation. They must manage their workforce wisely, concentrating on those cases of greater significance. Hence, cases involving a high financial correction are more likely to lead to litigation than cases with low financial corrections (MIN_ES_4).

In Germany, the average amount of financial corrections imposed in the last few years in agriculture amounts to about ten million euros each year. Compared to the 6.5 billion euros spent in one year, this barely reaches 0.15% of the funds received. This is a particularly low level of financial corrections compared to other countries. In 2015, France was requested to return 1 billion euros for the period 2008–2012, which corresponds to about 2% of the forty billion received from the EU in the same period.[3] This explains why Germany has raised relatively few annulment actions in agriculture compared to other countries (MIN_DE_5).

In Germany, where financial corrections tend to be low, decisions to litigate depend much on the strength of their legal arguments. Given that the financial incentive is not high, German governments are more selective on the cases they bring to court and decide to go only when they have very strong arguments, that is, when they are nearly convinced that they are right and that they will win (MIN_DE_5). By contrast, in Spain, where financial corrections tend to be higher than in Germany, the financial incentive is higher, which reduces the importance of other criteria in the decision to litigate. In the face of a particularly high financial correction (e.g. several hundred million euros), state attorneys go to court anyway, doing their best to carve out of the case at least some legal issues in order to carry out the judicial battle.

The Potato Starch Case (T-557/13)

The only annulment action raised by Germany in the agriculture sector in the last eight years is the potato starch case. It illustrates the importance of both the financial and legal factors. The potato starch case is based on a misunderstanding between the Commission and German administrative authorities that arose from the way in which the EU regulation had been translated into the German language. The EU allows interventions to stabilize prices of agricultural products. The root of this disagreement was the question over the precise moment at which the German authorities can pay the direct financial aid to the producers. There is a minimal price—regulated by the EU—that applies to the potatoes sold by the potato producer who benefits from EU aids. To make sure the producer does not sell the potatoes below the minimal price, EU regulation stipulates that national authorities can only pay the aid once the producer has received this minimal price for potatoes. German authorities have allowed the application of this requirement in several instalments. The payment for the potatoes is issued in three instalments. The producer first receives 41% of the minimal price for the potatoes delivered; another two instalments complete the payment of the minimal price. Accordingly, the authorities granting the aid have paid 41% of the aid once the producer has received 41% of the minimal price, and so on. Arguably, this procedure is in line with the German version of the regulation. Nevertheless, based on the English version of the regulation, the auditors and the Commission claimed there was an irregularity. They argue that the aid can only be paid to the producer once the producer has received the full 100% of the minimal price for the potatoes produced and delivered. German civil servants, who insisted that the German language version of the regulation was different, rejected this interpretation. Despite the confusion over linguistic differences, the Commission decided to impose the financial correction of 6.3 million euros. This meant a substantial flow of money away from the coffers of the culprit *Länder*—in that particular case, Brandenburg. German state attorneys and civil servants were convinced that their interpretation was right; hence, they decided to litigate. In fact, Germany won this annulment against the Commission (MIN_DE_5).

Adjustment of Salaries and Pensions of Eurocrats (C-196/12, C-66/12, C-63/12)

Interests to maintain material benefits are at the heart of conflicts over salaries and work-related benefits running between the EU institutions themselves. At the EU level, the Council decides about the statute of European civil servants. Where direct material interests of the staff working in other institutions such as the EP, the Commission, or the European Investment Bank are negatively affected, they might go to court. Such conflicts already resulted in litigation in the 1970s through mid-1980s, as well as in the early 2000s. More recently, horizontal annulment cases related to such financial interests increased, especially in the wake of the financial crisis. Generally, an adaptation clause for the salaries and pensions of Eurocrats exists. Accordingly, the development of EU salaries links to the development of national wage indices in the EUROSTAT data, with a time lag due to technical requirements for working out the indices. 'And what happened—it was in the middle of the financial crisis—the calculations, which came from the years before, brought a result that was unacceptable for the member states. They said, you couldn't do that. We are asking for budget cuts' (EP_1). Neither

Commission nor Parliament staff wanted to accept this linkage, and their respective institutions decided to take the Council to court for refusal to adopt the Commission's proposal for salary adjustment. In fact, a number of related cases were successively opened (C-453/12, C-68/13), until the first case was settled in court.

In sum, these cases illustrate the importance of financial motivations when actors decide to file an annulment case against EU institutions—and even between EU institutions themselves. The evidence gleaned from the interviews also underlines that the legal merits of a case—how actors perceive their chances to succeed in court—are duly taken into consideration in the decision of public actors to engage in litigation or not.

INSTITUTIONAL COMPETENCES–DRIVEN MOTIVATION IN ANNULMENT LITIGATION

Annulment actions are also motivated by actors' willingness to maximize (or defend) their decision-making competences. They are driven by actors' institutional interests. Inviting the CJEU to intervene in such cases is a way to obtain an authoritative interpretation of the scope of the defendant's competences, with the hope to prevent competence creep into the litigant's institutional prerogative in the future. Thus, this motivation should be particularly relevant for public actors at the different levels of the EU multilevel governance system.

Our quantitative data highlights that institutional competences are an important motivation behind annulment actions. For example, we observe rises in the number of annulment cases shortly after treaty changes (see Fig. 5.1). After the adoption of new formal rules (marked by the vertical dotted lines), struggles over the interpretation of those rules follow (see also Farrell and Héritier 2007). To settle such conflicts, the actors involved call upon the judiciary to intervene. Such testing the ground and clawing back of competences explain the peaks of annulment litigation in the years following changes of the European treaties. Annulment actions tend to emerge after treaty changes alter the status quo of competence allocation in the EU. We turn now to some case studies that help illustrate the context of actors' strategies to preserve, defend, or obtain institutional competences with the help of annulment litigation.

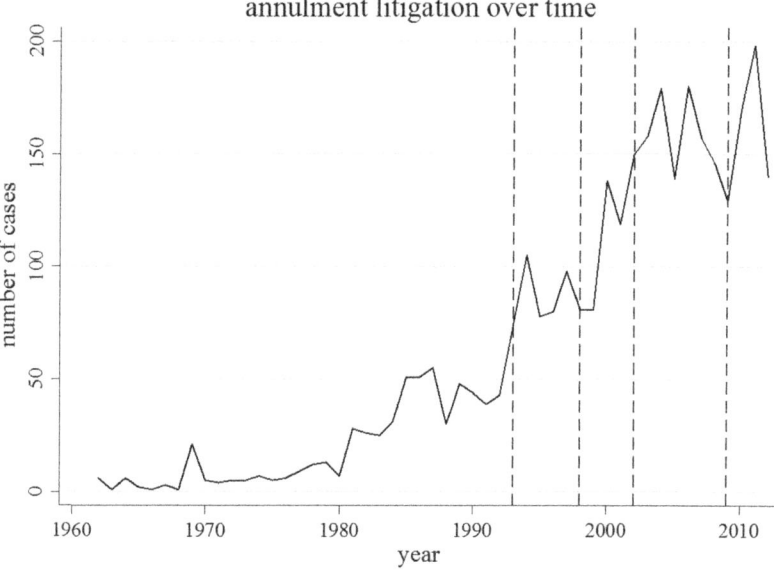

Fig. 5.1 Annulment actions and treaty changes (*Source* Figure based on own data. Dashed vertical lines indicate the year in which treaty changes came into effect [the Maastricht Treaty in 1993, the Amsterdam Treaty in 1998, the Nice Treaty in 2002, and the Lisbon Treaty in 2009])

The Renewable Energies Law Case (T-134/14 and T-47/15)

In cases T-134/14 and T-47/15 that dealt with the promotion of renewable energies in Germany, the motivation of the German government for challenging the Commission's decision derives from the willingness to protect its own institutional competences. The German renewable energy law subsidizes producers of alternative energies. The law guarantees that the electricity produced from renewable energies can be sold at a guaranteed price. The difference between the market price and the price effectively charged is sponsored by consumers. The law designed a financial circuit that transits between several actors (electricity companies, mainly network operators) and passes on the burden of the subsidy to all consumers of electricity. This implies that electricity prices in Germany are relatively high, which is a problem for those industries that consume a lot of electricity, the so-called energy-intensive

5 MOTIVATIONS: WHEN CONFLICT LEADS TO LITIGATION   101

consumers. To reduce the burden of these energy-intensive consumers, the renewable energy law puts up a compensation, which significantly reduces the intensive consumers' participation to the subsidy of renewable energies, compared to what they would pay if they were subjected to the normal regime. The Commission considered this advantage to energy-intensive users as constituting state aid, and Germany challenged this decision before the Court.

An important motivation for German state attorneys and the German administration was to place a limit on what they perceived as a competence creep on the side of the Commission (MIN_DE_6). The dispute was about the interpretation of the notion of state resources, which, according to EU competition law, must be involved in the aid scheme in order to qualify the scheme as illegal state aid. From the German perspective, no state resources were involved. This is because technically, the advantage enjoyed by the energy intensive users stemmed from a regulatory mechanism that passed the costs of the subsidies for renewable energies on to consumers. According to Germany, since the funds travelling in this circuit never transited through any kind of state fund, the criteria of state resources was not met. The Commission had a different perspective. Since the mechanism through which the subsidies are handed out to the final consumers is designed by the state, this is enough to consider that the mechanism constitutes state aid. This reasoning, contained in the controverted decision of the Commission, was new. As such, it represented a new threat for the member states, as its application would greatly broaden the scope of national measures that could be subject to EU state aid law, thereby limiting national room of manoeuvre.

To some extent, Germany's willingness to litigate was motivated by the intention to defend its legislative scheme and specific policy design (MIN_DE_6). Yet the concern with the growing scope of EU state aid law to the detriment of national autonomy has also played an important role in Germany's motivation to challenge the Commission (MIN_DE_6). While the case was examined by the Court, Germany prepared an updated version of its renewable energy law, which was negotiated with the Commission in terms of the design of the compensation mechanism for energy-intensive users. The Commission and Germany reached an agreement on a new national law that would enter into force in 2014. Therefore, Germany's necessity to defend the previous version of the renewable law before the Court faded away, so they could have simply withdrawn the case if their only goal was to protect their renewable energy approach. Very importantly, however, the state attorneys deliberately decided to continue to pursue the case. They wanted to have the Court decide on the interpretation of the notion of state resources, hoping to preserve their autonomy (at best) or to clarify the legal situation (at worst) (MIN_DE_6). This decision to continue litigation in order to reach a general clarification in terms of the Commission's powers to limit domestic policy, quite apart from the question of whether the concrete trigger of the case is still relevant or not, shows the general character of annulment litigation strategies. It is not only in defence of a particular policy for which annulment litigation is undertaken. Sometimes, litigation aims at settling the underlying legal issue, which might lead to similar struggles about institutional competences between national governments and the Commission in the future.

The Leipzig Halle Case (T-396/08) and the Dresden Airport Case (T-215/09)

Cases T-396/08 and T-215/09, which dealt with new runways at the Leipzig Halle and Dresden airports, provide other examples of litigation pursued in order to contain what is perceived as the Commission's competence creep in state aid. In the mid-2000s, the logistics company DHL considered moving its hub from Brussels to Leipzig. To attract DHL, Saxony's government committed itself to building a new runway at the Leipzig Halle airport with priority usage for the company; in case it would fail to do so, the regional government committed itself to compensating the company financially. Saxony notified this arrangement to the Commission in line with EU state aid law. While the agreement specified that DHL would only be compensated financially in case the runway would not be built, this arrangement with DHL could be state-aid relevant. The Commission, however, did not limit its examination of the dossier to the potential financial compensation for DHL. The Commission also assessed whether the building of a runway with priority usage was compatible with EU state aid law. The Commission argued that the building of this new runway by Saxony's government would constitute a state aid in favour of the Leipzig Halle airport. This came as a surprise to Saxony, as only the financial support of economic activities was traditionally perceived as state aid. In this sense, the *operation* of infrastructure like an airport had always been seen as an economic activity. Consequently, its support with public funds constituted state aid that would have to be declared to the Commission and checked for its compatibility with EU law. In contrast, the *construction* of infrastructure was traditionally not seen as an economic activity. Constructing infrastructure with public funds was thus not perceived as state aid and would thus not have to be examined by the Commission.

Although in this specific case, the Commission found that the building of the runway constituted state aid that was compatible with EU law and authorized the project, Saxony strongly opposed the decision. Most importantly, it did so because it would have significant implications for all future regional infrastructure projects. If one were to accept the Commission's approach towards regional infrastructure projects, all future projects would have to be passed by the Commission. Saxony feared that in the future, the Commission might not be so generous and would decide to cap or deny such projects. At the very least, the need to involve the Commission would definitely lead to a loss of control and time within such projects (MIN_SA_1). Consequently, in 2008, Saxony filed an annulment action against the Commission's decision. Germany's federal government supported Saxony as an intervener in court. In coordination with the Saxon government, the Leipzig Halle airport filed a separate action against the Commission.

A few months after initiating the annulment action over the runway at the Leipzig Halle airport, Saxony decided to also build a new runway at the Dresden airport. This was the perfect opportunity to further escalate this competence struggle with the Commission over the distribution of competences over state aid policy. Therefore, Saxony notified the Commission of the building of the new runway, yet it did so as a non-state-aid measure. Saxony anticipated that the Commission would reject this notification and qualify the runway again as state aid. This gave Saxony another chance to challenge the Commission's attempt to gain more control over regional infrastructure projects in court via annulment action in March 2009 (MIN_SA_1).

In March 2011, the General Court rejected Saxony's action over the Leipzig Halle runway. Since the Commission had authorized 100% of the aid, the measure lacked a direct legal effect on Saxony. Moreover, the Court backed the Commission's interpretation of the concept of economic activity in state aid law. Subsequently, the airport appealed the General Court's decision on the *Leipzig Halle* case and Saxony suspended the *Dresden* case (which was still pending) until the Court's decision on the appeal in the *Leipzig Halle* case. In December 2012, the

Court's final judgement confirmed the General Court's ruling in favour of the Commission and Saxony also withdrew the *Dresden* case. In light of this case law, there was no longer a realistic chance of winning this case. Both of these airport cases demonstrate rather well that annulment litigation is not always just about the specific policy decisions that these cases deal with legally. Annulment actions are also initiated in order to influence the distribution of competences in the long run. In this sense, annulments are employed strategically in the struggle between actors eager to protect or expand their decision-making powers.

Procedural Competences in Trade Negotiations (C-22/70 and C-425/13)

External affairs is a policy area that has seen many competence changes and competence conflicts over the last decade of EU integration. New offices have been created, such as the High Representative, and new organizations, including the European External Action Service with its hybrid organizational structure and mix of officials from national foreign services, the Commission, and EU diplomatic corps. While EU external trade policy has been strongly supranationalized, other, closely related issues, such as development aid, have not. In this context of evolving supranational competences, the European Commission, the Council, and even the EP are seeking to keep or expand their specific prerogatives. Early annulment rulings had established the principle of implied powers, which endowed the Commission with negotiation competences in all areas in which the community held internal competences, such as transport (cf. *ERTA* case C-22/70, see Chapters 1 and 3). Ultimately, this principle got promoted to EU primary law with the Nice Treaty (Cremona 2011). Despite such far reaching and lasting feedback effects in primary law, conflicts about competences continue in an area characterized by fuzzy and overlapping powers (MIN_DE_4). Issues of contention in more recent annulment actions have moved on to the questions of representation (role of the High Representative, C-387/00), as well as to procedural powers—that is, fine-tuning the broader competences set in the treaties, for example reporting rights during international negotiations or duration of negotiation mandates (C-425/13, COM_2). In this case, the Commission sought the annulment of a paragraph in a Council decision of 13 May 2013. The contended paragraph authorized the opening of negotiations that would link the EU emission allowances trading scheme with an emission-trading scheme in Australia. The Council decision was modelled on an earlier scheme for emission-allowance trading with another third country, Switzerland. Council competences for opening the negotiations were uncontested. Linking the negotiation mandate to existing schemes would, however, limit the room to manoeuvre in negotiations and was thus contested by the Commission, which insisted in its treaty-based right to negotiate international agreements that do not fall in the area of the Common Foreign and Security Policy without a more detailed Council mandate. From the Commission's perspective, an existing degree of independence was—illegally—challenged with which it can act in negotiations, in particularly vis-à-vis the Council and the EP.

The Selective Tax Benefits Cases (T-219/10, T-399/11)

The European Commission recently began examining national tax legislation to identify advantages that could result from specific tax provisions, with a view to applying state aid law. Indeed, tax advantages are only granted to some beneficiaries who comply with specific criteria. The extent to which these criteria imply a selective effect can be subject to debate. Yet selectivity is a key criterion in state aid law. Only those provisions that are selective can qualify as state aid.

After a first series of cases related to regional aid in the Basque country in the early 2000s, the Commission confirmed its interest in analysing national tax legislation from a state aid perspective. In the late 2000s, the Commission adopted decisions qualifying national tax provisions as illegal state aid, notably in Spain and Germany. This move surprised the member states, who saw tax legislation as measures of general applicability, deprived of selective effect (MIN_DE_6). Quite importantly, tax policy remains an area of member state sovereignty. EU policy making was characterized by conflict and stalemate. Several annulment actions followed against these decisions, some of them initiated by the member states who were keen to put a halt on the Commission's competence creep. The cases related to tax amortization in Spain are examples of such annulment actions.

There is a Spanish tax scheme that allows companies based in Spain that have acquired shares in a company established abroad to deduct from the basis of assessment for corporate tax in Spain part of the sum paid to acquire the share, corresponding to what is called the financial goodwill. The Commission examined this measure and concluded that insofar as it provides a fiscal advantage to those companies that invest abroad, the measure was selective. Hence, the Spanish tax scheme constituted state aid and the corresponding financial advantages granted should be recovered by the state.

Two companies affected, Autogrill and Banco Santander, brought annulment actions against the Commission's decisions (T-219/10, T-399/11) and won in first instance (the judgement was delivered in 2014). Unlike the Commission, the General Court considered that the derogation from the normal tax regime granted to companies investing abroad was not sufficient to find that the measure is selective. The selectivity criterion requires that the beneficiaries of the aid correspond to a category of undertakings that can be distinguished on account of their specific characteristics (e.g. location, sector, etc.). This was not the case here, as any company has the option of realizing an investment abroad.

The Commission appealed the judgements in 2015 (C-20/15 P, C-21/15 P). In the appeal, three countries decided to intervene in the case in support of the companies opposed to the Commission: Spain, Ireland, and Germany. Spain's motivation to intervene in the case was twofold. While Spain was interested in defending its legislation and tax scheme, its decision to intervene was also largely a result of its willingness to oppose the Commission's interpretation of the selectivity criteria and its extensive application to national tax regimes (MIN_ES_5). As for Germany, while the contested measure was a Spanish one, the German government felt concerned because the decision of the Commission threatened to broaden significantly the realm of application of EU state aid law, to the detriment of national autonomy in tax policy in general (MIN_DE_6). Germany's intervention had a clear and explicit purpose: Germany wanted to ring-fence the Commission in the area of tax law. The Court delivered its judgement in 2016, overturning the ruling of the General Court, thus confirming the Commission's broad understanding of the selectivity criteria. As for Ireland, enmeshed in a similar conflict with the Commissions about Irish tax law, as exemplified with the *Apple* case mentioned in Chapter 1, our document analysis indicates that their intervention in the case was also a result of their willingness to protect their institutional autonomy in the field of tax policy.

In sum, the four cases presented in this section illustrate, in various contexts and constellations, that protecting institutional competences is an important motivation for engaging in annulment actions.

Ideology-Driven Cases in Annulment Litigation

According to our conceptualization, actors' decisions to raise an annulment action can be motivated by ideology, that is, the willingness to promote ideological preferences. Ideological drivers are, for example, party political positions or liberal versus interventionist stances on policy designs. In our fieldwork, we regularly encountered ideological considerations leading to or backing up litigation strategies as one factor among others. We present three examples where policy and an ideological motivation were the main reason for launching annulment lawsuits.[4]

The EPSO and Patent Package Cases (T-148/13, T-149/13, T-191/13, C-274/11, C-147/13)

Spain challenged a decision of the European Personnel Selection Office (EPSO) to publish the call for recruiting staff in EU institutions because it did not include Spanish as a working language. They argued that this constituted discrimination because the language requirements for the competition were lower for those applicants whose mother tongue was either French, German, or English. This action reflects a constant policy line of Spain: fighting to have Spanish recognized as a working language in all EU organizations (MIN_ES_2, MIN_ES_5). Therefore, whenever there is an opportunity to manifest this position before the Court on the subject, the Spanish government goes for it (MIN_ES_2).

The same explanation applies to a series of annulment actions initiated by Spain against the adoption of a European unitary patent package (adopted by the member states in 2012). The translation arrangements for the unitary patent would be discriminatory towards individuals whose mother tongue is neither French, German, nor English because the patents would be granted in French, German, or English only. The Court rejected Spain's actions in 2015.

Italy has an interest similar to Spain's on this topic. Just like Spain, Italian authorities regularly resist decisions of the EU that privilege the three working languages of the EU (French, English, and German) to the detriment of other languages. Just like Spain, the Italian government takes annulment actions against EU institutions in the attempt to promote Italian (C-295/11; T-443/16), as was the case in the negotiation of the European Patent package (Van Zimmeren et al. 2015).

Passenger Rights (C-317/04 and C-318/04)

In the aftermath of the 9/11 terrorist attacks, the United States tightened legal requirements for air carriers flying to or over the United States. Accordingly, now passenger name records would have to be communicated to the United States Department of Homeland Security, the Bureau of Customs, and Border Protection US. Aware of the potential clash between this provision and European rules on data privacy, the Commission negotiated an international agreement that led to Commission Decision 2004/535/EC[5] and Council Decision 2004/496/EC.[6]

These internationally negotiated rules, however, collided with the EP's views on data privacy. For nearly a decade, and particularly since the adoption of the first EU data privacy directive, civil liberty rights had been high on the Parliament's agenda (Long and Quek 2002; Newman 2008). From the viewpoint of the EP, the agreements signed with the United States were not merely a setback. The Parliament considered this agreement to be a blunt violation of fundamental individual rights (COM_2). Consequently, the Parliament launched two closely related annulment cases against the Commission (C-318/04) and against the Council (C-317/04). Leaving victorious in both legal actions, the EP was able to defend a policy position that it has since developed further, a prominent example of which was its negotiation of a framework for the processing of personal data with the General Data Protection Regulation.[7] Given the Parliament's strong preferences for data privacy and its objective to present itself as a defender of civil liberty rights, securing values on civil liberty enshrined in existing policies and preparing the ground for future instruments is a core motivation to go to court. Annulment actions are one important instrument to do so.

The Private Pension Market Case (C-57/95)[8]

This conflict between France and the Commission has roots that reach back to the year 1991, when the Commission submitted to the Council a proposal for a Council directive relating to the freedom of management and investment of funds held by institutions for retirement provision. This proposal represented the first attempt to effectively harmonize the European market for pension funds. While the basic freedoms ensured within the internal market that was to be completed by 1992 was also seen—at least by the Commission—to extend to pension funds delivering financial services, these were at that point in time still subjected exclusively to highly diverse national regulation.

The Commission's proposal for a Council directive did not try to abolish the national diversity of pension systems and abstained from forcing member states to allow for the national establishment of pension funds. Yet the proposal nevertheless contained several requirements. Specifically, member states would no longer be allowed to constrain national actors to use the services of pension funds established in other member states (European Commission 1991, Article 3). Furthermore, the proposal defined several principles guiding the investment practice s of pension funds (European Commission 1991, Article 4). In this context, it emphasized, among other things, that member states should no longer prohibit pension funds from investing in foreign securities. Pension funds would thus have a right to choose their investments within the internal market freely.

While the matter was undisputed among actors at the supranational level, the proposal was highly controversial among the member states in the Council, with France being one of its main opponents. Consequently, the Commission decided to withdraw the proposal in 1994. France opposed the proposal not only because it challenged the French approach towards private pension funds, but also—and mainly—because it challenged the French approach towards regulating investments by institutions for retirement provision. While France was one of the few member states that traditionally defined detailed quantitative investment restrictions, the Commission's proposal rather included qualitative concepts. It specified that assets should be sufficiently diversified, avoid major accumulations of risk, and restrict investment in the sponsoring undertaking (i.e. the company for which the pension fund works to ensure the pensions of its workers) to a prudent level. Instead of relying on strict quantified obligations, this regulatory approach reflects a precautionary principle (or prudent-person rule) that was typically applied in Ireland, the United Kingdom, and the Netherlands but ran counter to the French approach. In 1998, the financial institution Deutsche Bank still diagnosed an ongoing clash of regulatory cultures with respect to investment rules for institutions of retirement provision. The debate between proponents of quantitative restrictions on investment and proponents of the prudent-person rule was at the heart of this conflict (Deutsch 1998; Haverland 2007).

The Commission, however, did not give up on its intention of laying the foundation for pension fund reform. On the contrary, the Commission simply decided to pursue this objective by different means. Specifically, the Commission quickly moved to publish its interpretation of relevant Community law with respect to rights and obligations of pension funds in the Official Journal. In fact, the *Communication on the Freedom of Management and Investment*[9] of funds held by institutions for retirement provision was purposefully published on 17 December 1994, not even two weeks after the proposal for a directive had been withdrawn. Moreover, the connection between the proposed directive and the *Communication* was not only their temporal proximity. The two texts were also rather similar in content (Hartlapp 2008; Adam 2016).

Thus, unsurprisingly, France quickly decided to initiate an action for annulment against the *Communication*. The motives driving France to litigate were the same as their motives to prevent the adoption of the directive proposed by the Commission. In the backdrop of the clash of regulatory cultures, the French government wanted to preserve their regulatory approach. They were thus seeking to keep the policy in line with the precautionary principle.

This section presented annulment cases dealing with recruitment practices, the EU's patent package, data privacy, passenger rights, and private pension market reform. These cases illustrate that seeking policies on ideological grounds plays a crucial role in public actors' decisions to engage in annulment litigation.

Political Trust–Driven Annulment Cases

Seeking to improve, restore, or protect political trust is a common driver of annulment conflicts, especially in multilevel conflicts that pit member states against EU institutions. Where supranational actions clash with public opinion in certain countries or regions, standing up to Brussels can be politically opportune no matter whether legal actions will be successful. Obviously, this motivation of building political trust is particularly important to actors that seek (re-)election. We distinguish three situations in which political trust motivates annulment actions by national governments. National governments may challenge EU institutions to gain trust from citizens, from subnational territorial authorities, or from companies. We illustrate the empirical relevance of these constellations below.

Toy Safety Case (T-198-12)

The German case on toy safety illustrates how governments may litigate against the Commission to gain the trust of an important constituency. After a series of problems with toy safety in the mid-1990s, the Commission decided to revise the old EU toy safety regulatory regime established in 1988. The scientific report that the Commission used as a basis to work on the regulatory reform was controversial among the academic community. Based on studies other than those used by the Commission, Germany contested the limit values for lead and other toxins recommended by the Commission, arguing they were too high to guarantee children's health. In other words, Germany considered the Commission's approach to be too lenient and unable to effectively protect child health. Nevertheless, Germany's input was ignored, and a new directive on toy safety was adopted in 2009. This directive was based on the limits for toxic substances as proposed by the Commission.

Once the directive came in force, the obligation to transpose it clashed with the pressure felt by the German government to respond to public opinion concerns. After all, even before the adoption of the directive, the German government had publicly communicated its concerns about the high limits proposed by the Commission. The German Parliament, along with consumer protection groups, scrutinized the topic rather closely. With the directive adopted, all eyes were on Ilse Aigner, Germany's federal minister for consumer protection, to see what she was going to do in order to secure the highest possible protection for German children (MIN_DE_9).

Minister Aigner had two options at the time: Germany could either launch an annulment action against the directive, or it could delay the transposition to negotiate lower limits within comitology. Since Germany disagreed with only about 10% of the directive's content, Aigner chose the second option. Over time, however, the German government realized that it would not be able to meet its objectives via comitology and technical ex post negotiations, as the concessions made by the Commission to raise the regulatory requirements were still far below German's safety standards. Having missed the chance to litigate against the directive and having failed to negotiate an appropriate compromise, Germany turned to its right—guaranteed by the treaties—to deviate from EU safety standards in case this was deemed necessary to ensure a higher level of health protection. Germany thus made a formal request to the Commission for the authorization to introduce stricter limits on toxins in toys than those defined by EU law. Yet in response to the request, the Commission only accepted deviation from EU levels for some toxins but not for others. Here, Germany would still have to comply with EU standards.

Germany's government was divided over this issue. There was disagreement between the Ministry for Consumer Protection and the Ministry for Economic Affairs, and the issue escalated up to the highest political level, the German federal cabinet. The Ministry for Economic Affairs opposed litigation against the Commission's decision for fear that diverging from EU-wide standards could have a negative impact on German toy industry. On the other hand, Minister Aigner was under great pressure to follow-up on her public commitment to do all she could to 'protect German children', even if that meant going to Luxembourg. Aigner won this dispute, and Germany decided to litigate against the Commission. Even though the German government lost this legal conflict in the first instance and its subsequent appeal, it did not lose this conflict politically. The public accepted the sentence and did not punish its leaders, as the blame was successfully shifted to the Commission and the Court. Aigner could be seen as having done her best in 'standing up to Brussels' for a good cause (MIN_DE_9).

The Molluscs Case (T-204/11)

In all cases related to funds in agriculture and cohesion policies, political trust between the state and its regions plays a central role in the decision to litigate. We explained above that many of these cases were essentially based on financial motivations. Yet when negative financial effects rest on the shoulders of an actor not able to litigate itself, this actor relies on a privileged litigant, such as a member state government, to litigate in its behalf. In Spain, for example, the regions are responsible for carrying financial sanctions imposed by the Commission for inappropriate spending of agriculture funds and cohesion funds. Yet the Court has established a very restrictive approach towards the regions' ability to challenge such financial corrections decisions by the Commission. Therefore, they depend on the national government to endorse their interests and litigate on their behalf. Only when the federal government's budget is affected by such corrections does it have a clear financial motivation to litigate. But what is its motivation to litigate if mostly regional budgets are affected? Our interviews suggest that, particularly in Spain, the principle of constitutional loyalty plays an important role in this regard. Maintaining smooth and cooperative relationships with its respective regions or states is of paramount importance for a central government. It is a way to improve or protect the relationship with a specific region. Annulment litigation in this sense is a way to build political trust.

One case that illustrates the relevance of this motivation is the molluscs case. In 2011, the Commission adopted a regulation to change the methodology used for the detection of toxins in bivalve molluscs such as clams and oysters. While the detection of toxins had relied on trials on mice, analyses would now have to rely on chemical procedures. Galicia, a coastal region in northern Spain whose economy relies heavily on the fishing sector (especially on molluscs), opposed this regulation. In particular, this opposition resulted from the fact that this chemical method was much more expensive for the Galician administration and for Galician shell fishermen. Having to switch to this method was portrayed and perceived as a catastrophe for Galicia. Equipped with scientific evidence that questioned the new method, Galicia tried to litigate against the regulation before the CJEU. However, being aware that the restrictive standing rights of regions would likely prevent such an action from being admitted, Galicia decided to turn to the central state for support (MIN_GA_5).

In Spain, this petition is made informally via the day-to-day communication between the relevant ministries of both governmental levels. If the relevant central ministry then endorses the region's interests, it makes a formal petition to the central monitoring commission, which is led by state attorneys. This monitoring commission effectively decides whether Spain will take the matter to court. While this is usually a rather smooth process, the strong clash of interests between Galicia and the national agriculture and health ministries resulted in a rockier process in this particular case. First of all, a Spanish laboratory affiliated with the Spanish national agency for food safety had played a central role in the development of the new chemical methodology adopted at the EU level. Naturally, they defended the advantages of this method (MIN_GA_5). Second, in an informal deal with the European Commission in comitology, Spanish representatives had committed *not* to challenge the regulation before the Court. In exchange, the European Commission agreed to prolong the transition period until the new method became obligatory. The competent ministries at the central level were therefore strongly opposed to litigate, and for this reason, they refused to endorse Galicia's petition before the monitoring commission (MIN_ES_1).

Galicia thus followed the formal procedure to make their petition to the monitoring commission, which is carried out through the intermediation of the Conference for Issues Related to the European Union (CARUE), the commission for the coordination between the central state and the regions about EU issues. Galician representatives were duly invited to present their views before the monitoring commission, which led to a lively technical debate between experts from Galicia and the Spanish food safety agency (MIN_GA_5). Within the monitoring commission, composed of the state attorneys and all central ministries, decisions to litigate are adopted under unanimity. This obviously implies that when one or several ministries oppose the judicial action, there is no litigation. Surprisingly, despite the clear opposition of the central ministries for health and agriculture, the monitoring commission decided to support Galicia.

While the central state acknowledged the deep impact of the regulation on Galician producers and the good legal and technical arguments in favour of an annulment action, these conditions cannot normally justify overcoming the opposition of a central ministry. The decisive factor for this surprising decision was the willingness of the central state to signal a cooperative attitude and good will towards Spanish regions in matters related to interventions before the CJEU. Previously, the CARUE process yielded little support for Spanish regions, as many petitions raised by the regions were rejected. This fuelled substantial resentment, as the regions felt their interests were not duly taken into account, even in such matters for which they held the formal competence according to the Spanish constitution. With its decision to litigate over the method used to test Galician shellfish for toxins, the Spanish central government decided to send a positive signal to the regions to show that their concerns were heard and supported (MIN_ES_1). Once the decision to litigate was taken, Spanish state attorneys and Galician officials worked in close collaboration to defend the case, which they eventually lost, however.

BMW Case (T-671/14)

Finally, the *BMW* case exemplifies the situation where governments use judicial actions to maintain good relationships with certain companies. The German region Saxony wanted to have BMW, the German carmaker, establish its new plant for electric cars in Leipzig and promised the company an aid of forty-nine million euros if they did so. They justified this measure by the EU regime for regional aids, exclusively applicable to Europe's poorer regions. Under the regional aid regime, poor regions only have to notify the Commission of aid that exceeds 22.5 million euros (below this threshold, a block exemption applies; such smaller aids are automatically legal and exempted from notification obligation). Since Saxony wanted to give 49 million to BMW, they however had to notify the Commission of the aid. Before being able to authorize the aid, the Commission assessed whether the aid was in fact necessary to attract the new plant. To do so, it asked BMW to demonstrate that it would have been cheaper for them to set up shop elsewhere. BMW was able to show a document that evaluated that building the new plant in Bavaria was seventeen million euros cheaper than in Saxony without the aid. While this justified Saxony's need to grant aid to attract a new employer to this poorer region, the Commission used this evidence to evaluate the forty-nine million as excessive aid. It concluded that the aid granted by Saxony could not exceed seventeen million euros. Alternatively, it could take advantage of the block exemption regime and give up to 22.5 million euros in aid if they withdrew their notification completely.

Saxony left it up to BMW to decide what to do. The company, which had seventeen million euros in aid guaranteed, preferred to not withdraw the notification and to sue the Commission's decision (the alternative would have been withdrawing the notification and taking advantage of the block exemption to give 22.5 million euros to BMW). Saxony wanted to show support for BMW as they had promised the aid before the intervention of the Commission. It was important for Saxony to signal that the regional government was a reliable partner standing by its financial promises (MIN_SA_1). However, given that Saxony had lost several previous state aid cases—as in the *Leipzig Halle* case presented above—the regional authorities shied away from a direct annulment appeal. Instead, Saxony decided to join BMW's action as intervener before the Court and contracted first-rank law firms in order to bring additional legal expertise to the case in close coordination with the actions of BMW (MIN_SA_1).[10]

The cases presented in this section illustrate the importance of what we conceive of as political trust for public actors when deciding to raise an annulment case. Especially in cases where the national litigant is unlikely to win (given the objective assessment of the legal situation), raising an annulment action can be a strategy for securing political trust from the electorate, from institutional partners (like regions or subnational authorities), and from big companies—no matter what the final outcome of the legal case is going to be.

Conclusion

Annulment litigation is about politics. Annulment actions are likely to be used when political considerations blend in. Understanding the use of judicial review thus requires going beyond a purely legalistic view of judicial conflicts, particularly since litigation is costly. Actors thus litigate only after some calculation about the potential costs and benefits; this calculation is done on various levels and with complex aims of the litigating actors. Formally winning a case is sometimes only one objective among others, and occasionally, it is not at all the major driver for litigation.

This is not to say that legal factors are irrelevant. They do play a role in actors' decision to engage in litigation rather than trying to exert influence in the political arena. In addition, they structure choices between different legal channels. Legal options provide the opportunity structure in which actors' concrete political calculations take place. However, in contrast to the literature on the economics of litigation (Gould 1973; Posner 1973), which emphasizes the probability of winning as the essential element in litigants' risk-benefit analysis about their decision to litigate, the expectation to win is often only secondary in annulment cases—at least for public actors. The more annulment litigation is pursued for symbolic reasons—that is, as a signal to domestic constituents—the less important success in court becomes to litigants (Adam et al. 2015). Not to be misunderstood; annulment litigants do genuinely seek judicial success. But in terms of the legal merits of the case, the minimum requirements for justifying litigation are rather low. The important analytical consequence of this being so is that the explanatory power of legal factors on public actors' decision to litigate is limited.

Based on a new conceptualization of actor motivations, this chapter has identified four possible types of motivations that lay behind engaging in annulment litigation. Litigation can be chosen (1) in order to maximize material gains (or minimize financial costs), (2) to preserve political decision rights and to ring-fence the opponent's decision-making competences, (3) to promote ideological and policy preferences, and (4) to signal trustworthiness to addressees of a policy. Not all of these motivations appeared equally frequent. Ideology, for example, found fewer echoes in our cases. Yet all motivations clearly constitute particular types that provide distinct analytical levers to understand annulment actions in the EU multilevel system. What is more, we saw that specific groups of actors are more likely to litigate based on one particular motivation: financial gains are frequently important for private and subnational governments. Signalling trustworthiness and responsiveness, in turn, are objectives of actors that face electoral competition at the subnational, national, or supranational level. Moreover, the motivation to keep or expand institutional competences matters most for public actors that want to protect their role in public decision taking. Finally, ideology matters most for strongly politicized actors, such as social movements (private litigants) or public actors for which demonstrating that they hold a certain position according to party politics is important in preventing loss of legitimacy for their representational role.

We illustrated the four types of motivations in a number of empirical cases. These cases generally represent one dominant motivation type; only a couple of cases show evidence of motivations coexisting with the predominant one. The applicability of our typology appears thus to be on solid empirical grounds. It backs the conclusion that annulment actions are examples of how multilevel policy conflicts in the EU translate into judicial conflicts when the financial, institutional, ideological, or legitimacy stakes are sufficiently high in the eyes of the actors to justify the dedication of administrative resources to litigation. Before this result, the next chapter analyses the factors that make different litigant configurations more or less likely to occur.

Cases Cited

See Table 5.2.

Table 5.2 Cases cited in this chapter

C-317/04; C-318/04	Judgment of 30 May 2006, *Parliament v. Council*, Joined Cases C-317/04 and C-318/04, EU:C:2006: 346
C-274/11	Judgment of 16 April 2013, *Spain v. Council*, C-274/11, EU:C:2013: 240
C-295/11	Order of 13 October 2011, *Italy v. Council*, C-295/11, EU:C:2011: 660
C-20/15 P	Judgment of 21 December 2016, *Commission v. World Duty Free Group*, C-20/15 P, EU:C:2016: 981
C-21/15 P	Order of 6 October 2015, *Commission v. Banco Santander*, C-21/15 P, EU:C:2015: 674;676
T-396/08	Judgment of 8 July 2010, *Sachsen and Sachsen-Anhalt v. Commission*, T-396/08, EU:T:2010: 297
T-215/09	Order of 18 March 2013, *Sachsen v. Commission*, T-215/09, EU:T:2013: 132
T-219/10	Judgment of 7 November 2014, *Autogrill España v. Commission*, T-219/10, EU:T:2014: 939
T-204/11	Judgment of 11 February 2015, *Spain v. Commission*, T-204/11, EU:T:2015: 91
T-399/11	Judgment of 5 December 2014, *Banco Santander v. Commission*, T-399/11, EU:T:2014: 938
T-198-12	Judgment of 14 May 2014, *Germany v. Commission*, T-198/12, EU:T:2014: 251
T-148/13	Order of 15 October 2013, *Spain v. Commission*, T-148/13, EU:T:2013: 564
T-149/13	Order of 15 October 2013, *Spain v. Commission*, T-149/13, EU:T:2013: 561
T-191/13 T-124/13	Application of 5 April 2013, *Italy and Spain v. Commission*, Joined Cases T-124/13 and T-149/13, Official Journal 389, 23.11.2015, pp. 29–30
C-147/13	Judgment of 5 May 2015, *Spain v. Council*, C-147/13, EU:C:2015: 299
T-557/13	Judgment of 24 September 2015, *Germany v. Commission*, T-557/13, EU:T:2015: 682
T-134/14	Order of 8 June 2015, *Germany v. Commission*, T-134/14, EU:T:2015: 392
T-47/15	Judgment of 10 May 2016, *Germany v. Commission*, T-47/15, EU:T:2016: 281
T-443/16	*Application of 9 August 2016, Italy v. Commission*, Official Journal C 371, 10.10.2016, pp. 21–22
T-671/14	Judgment of 12 September 2017, *BMW v. Commission*, T-671/14, EU:T:2017: 599

NOTES

1. In other words, while we expect to find cases explained by, for example, both motivation 1 and motivation 2, we do not expect to find cases explained by one motivation that would be a hybrid between motivation 1 and 2. In our conception, whereas our motivations can coexist in a single annulment case, they could not be mixed into hybrid types.
2. For example, Eisenberg (1990).
3. Le Figaro, *La France va devoir rendre un milliard d'euros d'aides agricoles* (27 January 2015), accessed 22 January 2017.
4. In addition, the annulment action initiated over pension market reform in France described by Adam (2016) can also be read as evidence for the relevance of ideological motivations.
5. 2004/535/EC:Commission Decision of 14 May 2004 on the adequate protection of personal data contained in the Passenger Name Record of air passengers transferred to the United States' Bureau of Customs and Border Protection (notified under document number C[2004] 1914), Official Journal L 235, 6.7.2004, pp. 11–22.
6. 2004/496/EC:Council Decision of 17 May 2004 on the conclusion of an Agreement between the European Community and the United States of America on the processing and transfer of PNR data by Air Carriers to the *United States Department* of Homeland Security, Bureau of Customs and Border Protection, Official Journal L 183, 20.5.2004, p. 83.
7. Regulation (EU) 2016/679 of the European Parliament and of the Council of 27 April 2016 on the protection of natural persons with regard to the processing of personal data and on the free movement of such data, and repealing Directive 95/46/EC (General Data Protection Regulation), Official Journal L 119, 4.5.2016, pp. 1–88.
8. A more detailed description of this case can be found in Adam (2016).
9. COMMISSION, E. C. 1994. Commission Communication on the Freedom of Management and Investment of Funds held by Institutions for Retirement Provision (94/C 360/08). *Official Journal of the European Communities*, 1994, pp. 7–11.
10. At the time of writing, the case was still pending.

REFERENCES

Adam, C. (2016). *The politics of judicial review: Supranational administrative acts and judicialized compliance conflict in the EU*. Basingstoke, UK: Palgrave Macmillan.

Adam, C., Bauer, M. W., & Hartlapp, M. (2015). It's not always about winning: Domestic politics and legal success in EU annulment litigation. *Journal of Common Market Studies, 53*(2), 185–200.

Aiken, K. D., Liu, B. S., Mackoy, R. D., & Osland, G. E. (2004). Building internet trust: Signalling through trustmarks. *International Journal of Internet Marketing and Advertising*, 1(3), 251–267.

Amaral, D. A., & Neave, D. G. (2009). On Bologna, weasels and creeping competence. In A. Amaral, G. Neave, C. Musselin, & P. Maassen (Eds.), *European integration and the governance of higher education and research* (pp. 281–299). Dordrecht, The Netherlands: Springer.

Bacharach, M., & Gambetta, D. (2001). Trust in signs. In K. Cook (Ed.), *Trust in society* (pp. 148–184). New York: Sage.

Baier, G. (2006). *Courts and federalism: Judicial doctrine in the United States, Australia, and Canada*. Vancouver, BC: University of British Columbia Press.

Baker, L. A., & Young, E. A. (2001). Federalism and the double standard of judicial review. *Duke Law Journal*, 51(1), 75–164.

Bauer, M. W., & Becker, S. (2014). The unexpected winner of the crisis: The European Commissions strengthened role in economic governance. *Journal of European Integration*, 36(3), 213–229.

Bauer, M. W., & Hartlapp, M. (2010). Much ado about money and how to spend it! Analysing 40 years of annulment cases against the European Union Commission. *European Journal of Political Research*, 49, 202–222.

Bebchuk, L. A. (1984). Litigation and settlement under imperfect information. *The RAND Journal of Economics*, 15(3), 404–415.

Becker, S., Bauer, M. W., & De Feo, A. (Eds.). (2017). *The new politics of the European Union budget*. Nomos Publisher: Baden-Baden, Germany: Nomos (Series Studies on the European Union).

Bourdieu, P. (1991). La représentation politique. Elements pour une théorie du champ politique. *Actes de Recherche En Sciences Sociales*, 36–37, 3–24.

Boutcher, S. A. (2013). Law and social movements: It's more than just litigation and courts. *Blog Post*. https://mobilizingideas.wordpress.com/2013/02/18/law-and-social-movements-its-more-than-just-litigation-and-courts/. Accessed 9 March 2017.

Brennan, G., & Buchanan, J. M. (1980). *The power to tax: Analytic foundations of a fiscal constitution*. Cambridge, UK: Cambridge University Press.

Burley, A.-M., & Mattli, W. (1993). Europe before the court: A political theory of legal integration. *International Organization*, 47(1), 41–76.

Camia, V., & Caramani, D. (2012). Family meetings: Ideological convergence within party families across Europe, 1945–2009. *Comparative European Politics*, 10(1), 48–85.

Chanley, V. A. (2002). Trust in government in the aftermath of 9/11: Determinants and consequences. *Political Psychology*, 23(3), 469–483.

Chanley, V. A., Rudolph, T. J., & Rahn, W. M. (2000). The origins and consequences of public trust in government: A time series analysis. *Public Opinion Quarterly*, 64(3), 239–256.

Christensen, T., & Laegreid, P. (2005). Trust in government: The relative importance of service satisfaction, political factors, and demography. *Public Performance and Management Review, 28*(4), 487–511.
Cichowski, R. A. (2007). *The European court and civil society*. Cambridge, UK: Cambridge University Press.
Citrin, J. (1974). Comment: The political relevance of trust in government. *American Political Science Review, 68*(3), 973–988.
Citrin, J., & Green, D. P. (1986). Presidential leadership and the resurgence of trust in government. *British Journal of Political Science, 16*(4), 431–453.
Coleman, J. S. (1994). *Foundations of social theory*. Cambridge, MA: Harvard University Press.
Cremona, M. (2011). External relations and external competences of the European Union: The emergence of an integrated policy. In P. Craig & G. de Burca (Eds.), *The Evolution of EU Law* (pp. 217–268). Oxford, UK: Oxford University Press.
Davis, D. W., & Silver, B. D. (2004). Civil liberties vs. security: Public opinion in the context of the terrorist attacks on America. *American Journal of Political Science, 48*(1), 28–46.
De Swaan, A. (1973). *Coalition theories of democracy*. New York: Harper and Row.
Deutsch, K. G. (1998). Aktuelle Themen: Perspektiven einer EU-Richtlinie zu Pensionsfonds. *Deutsche Bank Research Bulletin, 103*, 1–10.
Downs, A. (1957). *An economic theory of democracy*. New York: Harper and Row.
Downs, A. (1967). *Inside bureaucracy*. Santa Monica, CA: RAND.
Ege, J., Bauer, M. W., & Becker, S. (2018). *The European Commission in turbulent times: Assessing organizational change and policy impact*. Baden-Baden, Germany: Nomos.
Eisenberg, T. (1990). Testing the selection effect: A new theoretical framework with empirical tests. *The Journal of Legal Studies, 19*, 337–358.
Farrell, H., & Héritier, A. (2007). Contested competences in the European Union. *West European Politics, 30*(2), 227–243.
Galanter, M. (1974). Why the "haves" come out ahead: Speculations on the limits of legal change. *Law and Society Review, 9*(1), 95–160.
Gambetta, D. (1998). *Trust: Making and breaking cooperative relations*. Hoboken, NJ: Blackwell.
Gil Ibañez, A. (1998). *Commission tools for the supervision and enforcement of EC Law other than Article 169 EC Treaty: An attempt at systematization* (Jean Monnet Working Papers No. 12/98).
Gould, J. P. (1973). The economics of legal conflicts. *Journal of Legal Studies, 2*(2), 279–300.
Granger, M. (2004). When governments go to Luxembourg…: The influence of governments on the European Court of Justice. *European Law Review, 29*, 1–31.

Hadfield, G. K. (1994). Judicial competence and the interpretation of incomplete contracts. *The Journal of Legal Studies, 23*(1), 159–184.
Hartlapp, M. (2008). Intra-Kommissionsdynamik im policy-making. EU-Politiken angesichts des demographischen Wandels. *Politische Vierteljahresschrift 40* (PVS-Sonderheft 2007/2), 139–160.
Hartlapp, M. (2015). Politicization of the European Commission. When, how and with what impact? In M. W. Bauer & J. Trondal (Eds.), *The Palgrave handbook of the European administrative system* (pp. 145–160). Basingstoke, UK: Palgrave.
Haverland, M. (2007). When the welfare state meets the regulatory state: EU occupational pension policy. *Journal of European Public Policy, 14*(6), 886–904.
Hetherington, M. J. (1998). The political relevance of political trust. *American Political Science Review, 92*(4), 791–808.
Hetherington, M. J. (2005). *Why trust matters: Declining political trust and the demise of American liberalism.* Princeton, NJ: Princeton University Press.
Hetherington, M. J., & Rudolph, T. J. (2008). Priming, performance, and the dynamics of political trust. *The Journal of Politics, 70*(2), 498–512.
Hooghe, L., & Marks, G. (2009). A postfunctionalist theory of European integration: From permissive consensus to constraining. *British Journal of Political Science, 39*(1), 1–23.
Hughes, C. E. (1928). *The Supreme Court of the United States: Its foundation, methods and achievements.* Washington, DC: Beard Books.
Hutter, S., & Grande, E. (2014). Politicizing Europe in the national electoral arena: A comparative analysis of five West European countries, 1970–2010. *Journal of Common Market Studies, 52*(5), 1002–1018.
Jupille, J. (2007). Contested procedures: Ambiguities, interstices and EU institutional change. *West European Politics, 30*(2), 301–320.
Keele, L. (2007). Social capital and the dynamics of trust in government. *American Journal of Political Science, 51*(2), 241–254.
Levi, M., & Stoker, L. (2000). Political trust and trustworthiness. *Annual Review of Political Science, 3*(1), 475–507.
Lijphart, A. (1999). *Patterns of democracy: Government forms and performance in thirty-six countries.* New Haven, CT: Yale University Press.
Lobel, J. (1994). Losers fools and prophets: Justice as struggle. *Cornell Law Review, 80,* 1331–1421.
Lobel, J. (1995). Losers fools and prophets: Justice as struggle. *Cornell Law Review, 80,* 1331–1421.
Long, W. J., & Quek, M. P. (2002). Personal data privacy protection in an age of globalization: The US-EU safe harbor compromise. *Journal of European Public Policy, 9,* 325–344.
Macoubrie, J. (2006). Nanotechnology: Public concerns, reasoning, and trust in government. *Public Understanding of Science, 15*(2), 221–241.

Maor, M., Gilad, S., & Bloom, P. B.-N. (2013). Organizational reputation, regulatory talk, and strategic silence. *Journal of Public Administration Research and Theory, 23*(3), 581–608.

McCann, M. W. (1994). *Rights at work: Pay equity reform and the politics of legal mobilization.* Chicago: University of Chicago Press.

McCann, M. W. (1998). How does law matter for social movements? In B. G. Garth & A. Sarat (Eds.), *How does law matter?* Evanston, IL: Northwestern University Press.

Miller, A. H. (1974). Political issues and trust in government: 1964–1970. *The American Political Science Review, 68*(3), 951–972.

Mishler, W., & Rose, R. (2001). What are the origins of political trust? Testing institutional and cultural theories in post-communist societies. *Comparative Political Studies, 34*(1), 30–62.

Moravcsik, A. (1991). Negotiating the single European act: National interests and conventional statecraft in the European Community. *International Organization, 45*(1), 9–56.

Müller, W. C., & Strøm, K. (1999). *Policy, office, or votes? How political parties in Western Europe make hard decisions.* Cambridge, UK: Cambridge University Press.

NeJaime, D. (2011). Winning through losing. *Iowa Law Review, 96*, 941–1012.

Newman, A. L. (2008). Building transnational civil liberties: Transgovernmental entrepreneurs and the European data privacy directive. *International Organization, 62*(1), 103–130. https://doi.org/10.1017/S0020818308080041.

Newton, K., & Norris, P. (1999). *Confidence in public institutions: Faith, culture or performance?* Presented at the American Political Science Association, Atlanta, GA.

Niskanen, W. A. (1971). *Bureaucracy and representative government.* Chicago: Transaction Publishers.

Pollack, M. A. (1994). Creeping competence: The expanding agenda of the European Community. *Journal of Public Policy, 14*(2), 95–145.

Posner, R. A. (1973). An economic approach to legal procedure and judicial administration. *Journal of Legal Studies, 2*(2), 399–458.

Prechal, S. (2010). Competence creep and general principles of law. *Review of European Administrative Law, 3*(1), 5–22.

Priest, G. L., & Klein, B. (1984). The selection of disputes for litigation. *The Journal of Legal Studies, 13*(1), 1–55.

Rauh, C. (2019). EU politicization and policy initiatives of the European Commission: The case of consumer policy. *Journal of European Public Policy, 26*(3), 1–22.

Risse, T., Engelmann-Martin, D., Knope, H.-J., & Roscher, K. (1999). To euro or not to euro? The EMU and identity politics in the European Union. *European Journal of International Relations, 5*(2), 147–187.

Rudolph, T. J., & Evans, J. (2005). Political trust, ideology, and public support for government spending. *American Journal of Political Science*, *49*(3), 660–671.
Ryan, E. (2011). Negotiating federalism. *Boston College Law Review*, *52*(1), 1–136.
Scheingold, S. (1974). *The politics of rights: Lawyers, public policy, and social change*. New Haven, CT: Yale University Press.
Schmidt, S. K. (1998). Commission activism: Subsuming telecommunications and electricity under European competition law. *Journal of European Public Policy*, *5*(1), 169–184.
Segovia Arancibia, C. (2008). *Political trust in Latin America*. Ph.D. thesis, University of Michigan.
Shapiro, M. (1964). Political jurisprudence. *Kentucky Law Journal*, *52*, 294–345.
Skiadas, D. V. (2002). *Judicial review of the budgetary authority during the enactment of the European Unions Budget* (SSRN Scholarly Paper No. ID 302757). Rochester, NY: Social Science Research Network.
Stone Sweet, A. (1999). Judicialization and the construction of governance. *Comparative Political Studies*, *32*(2), 147–184.
Stone Sweet, A., & Brunell, T. L. (1998). Constructing a supranational constitution: Dispute resolution and governance in the European Community. *American Political Science Review*, *92*(1), 63–81.
Swenden, W. (2006). *Federalism and regionalism in Western Europe: A comparative and thematic analysis*. Basingstoke: Palgrave.
Van De Walle, S., & Bouckaert, G. (2003). Public service performance and trust in government: The problem of causality. *International Journal of Public Administration*, *26*(8–9), 891–913.
van Zimmeren, E., Mathieu, E., & Verhoest, K. (2015). The interaction between agencies, networks and the European Commission in emerging regulatory constellations: A comparative analysis of the European telecom sector and the European patent system. In E. Ongaro (Ed.), *Multi-level governance: The missing linkages* (pp. 125–162). Bingley, UK: Emerald.
Weatherill, S. (2004). Competence creep and competence control. *Yearbook of European Law*, *23*(1), 1–55.

Open Access This chapter is licensed under the terms of the Creative Commons Attribution 4.0 International License (http://creativecommons.org/licenses/by/4.0/), which permits use, sharing, adaptation, distribution and reproduction in any medium or format, as long as you give appropriate credit to the original author(s) and the source, provide a link to the Creative Commons license and indicate if changes were made.

The images or other third party material in this chapter are included in the chapter's Creative Commons license, unless indicated otherwise in a credit line to the material. If material is not included in the chapter's Creative Commons license and your intended use is not permitted by statutory regulation or exceeds the permitted use, you will need to obtain permission directly from the copyright holder.

CHAPTER 6

Litigant Configurations: Turbulence and the Emergence of Complex Configurations

Scholars describe policy processes in the European Union (EU) as multileveled, networked, and fluid. As such, they typically involve a wide range of different actors, located at different governmental levels, whose interactions can feature cooperation but also conflict. Generally, political disputes over policy issues mobilize a fair number of actors from within the multilevel system whose relative positions, rivalries, and alliances come to form what we conceive as a policy conflict configuration. The emerging policy positions tend to be supported by several actors that may even unite into a coalition. Hence, far from being limited to a face-off between two actors, policy conflicts typically involve numerous stakeholders. While policy conflicts involve a large number of actors, the great majority of judicial conflicts do not. Most often, legal conflicts include only two parties: the applicant and the defendant. This is also true for EU annulment actions. Most of the conflicts discussed in Chapter 5 represent such a simple applicant-defendant configuration, as, for example, when Germany brought the Commission to court because of the Commission's interference with the German renewable energy law (T-134/14).

Even when more actors effectively have a stake in particular cases, the resulting litigant configuration in court does not always reflect that. This indicates that a filtering process from societal conflict to legal dispute must be at work (Glenn 1999). Two important structural aspects—in the sense of legal opportunity structures, as discussed in Chapter 3—work as

© The Author(s) 2020
C. Adam et al., *Taking the EU to Court*,
Palgrave Studies in European Union Politics,
https://doi.org/10.1007/978-3-030-21629-0_6

enabling or constraining factors in this filtering process: actors' standing rights and their legal and financial resources. Simply put, not all interested actors are allowed to take on an active role before court even when they want to. Furthermore, not all actors are able or willing to invest the financial or legal resources necessary to take part in court proceedings, particularly when there are options for a free ride on the decision of other actors to go to court. Yet despite these factors discouraging interested actors from joining annulment cases, we do observe a substantial number of complex litigant configurations. In fact, while simple litigant configurations represent the majority of annulment cases, complex litigant configurations, in which additional litigants or defendants join cases, are far too frequent to be regarded as mere exceptions. Before this background, we set out to study simple and complex litigant configurations in this chapter. We will show that emerging conflict configurations can be linked to the motivations outlined in Chapter 5. The financial litigation motivation coins conflicts between member state governments and EU institutions and between national companies and the Commission. The institutional power motivation generally drives conflicts between member state governments and the EU, as well as between EU institutions among themselves. The ideological motivation is found in vertical conflicts between member states or non-governmental organizations and EU institutions, as well as among EU institutions. The political trust motivations generally underpin annulment actions, intervening as a two-level game where a national or regional government judicialises a conflict with an EU institution to send a positive signal to their constituency at home.

The specific link we explore in this chapter is the nexus between institutional turbulence and the emergence of complex litigant configurations. We propose in this regard that the emergence of complex litigant configurations is causally linked to institutional turbulence. Institutions are in turbulence when existing institutional arrangements are in flux, are new, or become unsettled. Annulment litigation that emerges in this context often involves more than just two actors. This is because the status quo ante of the turbulence represents a negotiated temporary equilibrium situation that tends to involve a substantial number of stakeholders. This temporary equilibrium comprises a financial dimension, an ideological dimension, an institutional or competence-related dimension, and a political or electoral dimension. Therefore, threats to disrupt the status quo hold the potential to trigger litigation decisions driven by

6 LITIGANT CONFIGURATIONS: TURBULENCE AND THE EMERGENCE ... 129

all four motivations we described in Chapter 5. Moreover, institutional turbulence reduces legal certainty—an observation that can hardly be overestimated. In consequence, such turbulence makes the prospects of judicial success higher for potential litigants. Legal conflicts that involve fundamental struggles over the status quo that take place at such critical institutional and policy junctures are thus most likely cases that attract not only one but several actors and therefore reflect a more complex litigant configuration.

Engaging with Complexity

In the previous chapter, we addressed the decisions of individual public actors to litigate. Now, we take a more macro-level perspective and focus on what we conceive of as litigation configurations. In annulment litigation, a diverse set of actors from various territorial levels can take part in lawsuits. We think of the possible combinations as configurations or constellations.

While litigant configurations differ enormously across annulment cases, we generally distinguish between simple and complex configurations based on the number of participants that take part in the case. Simply put, cases that involve only one applicant and one defendant are considered simple configurations. All other cases are complex configurations. Obviously, this is a simple distinction that lumps together various different alliances and cleavages. The following paragraphs intend to do justice to the various different constellations that make up the group of complex litigant configurations. With this, we hope to demonstrate that the distinction is conceptually and theoretically fruitful and empirically relevant.

In line with the distinction drawn between simple and complex conflicts (cf. Chapter 2), we speak about complex litigant configurations when at least three actors take an active role in the annulment litigation. One of these actors, the defendant, does not consciously choose to be involved; it has to defend itself as soon as a litigant decides to challenge one of its decisions. The crucial actor actually deciding to start a litigation is the applicant for an action for annulment. Additional parties can intervene either in favour of the applicant or in favour of the defendant. Actors on the applicant's side can also decide to raise an additional annulment action against that same EU measure that is already in force. Typically, the Court joins these cases under the umbrella of one proceeding and one judgement that binds together such cases against the same EU measure. Such joint cases thus reflect a complex litigant configuration.

Figure 6.1 provides an overview of the absolute number of annulment cases with a complex litigant configuration and of the share of complex cases (based on the total number of annulment cases). In total, we find 936 complex litigant configurations. Complex configurations reached a temporary peak relative to the absolute number of annulments in the mid-1990s. In absolute terms, the highest number of cases with complex litigant configurations emerged around a decade later, in the mid-2000s.

We discuss litigant configurations for vertical and horizontal conflicts separately. In the context of vertical annulment conflicts, we observe 828 complex litigant configurations. This amounts to about 26% of all vertical cases (see Table 6.1). Simple vertical constellations mostly include conflicts between individual private actors on the claimant side and the Commission or the Council on the defendant side. Yet they also often include individual member states litigating against the Commission.

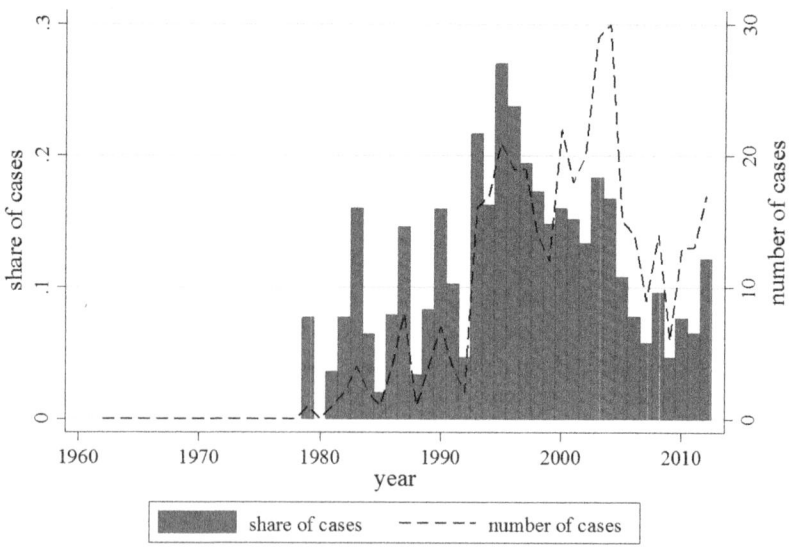

Fig. 6.1 Complex litigant configurations over time (*Source* Own data)

The specific litigant arrangement in such vertical complex litigant configurations is quite diverse. Table 6.2 explicitly describes the five most frequent actor configurations that lead us to classify cases as complex vertical configurations. It is important to highlight that these configurations are not mutually exclusive as they refer to either the claimant or the defendant side. In 452 cases, we observe that several private actors joined forces on the claimant side of a conflict against the defending EU institution. In 158 cases, private actors and the Commission fought on the same side—the defendant side—of the conflict. Yet the Commission is supported as a defendant not only by private actors but also sometimes by one or several member state governments. We count 145 such constellations. As claimants, member states and private actors align in 155 cases and several member states align in 81 cases. While these configurations represent configurations that are rather numerous, another 155 cases remain; these belong to other complex litigant configurations, not explicitly referenced here. In any case, the purpose of this section is to provide a condensed insight into the complexity and diversity of actor configurations in annulment conflict rather than to provide a detailed data report.

Turning to horizontal annulment conflicts, it is important to note that in relative terms, complex litigant configurations are more frequent here. While we classify only twenty-six horizontal conflicts as cases with simple litigant configurations, 108 of these cases feature a complex

Table 6.1 Simple and complex cases in vertical conflicts (1957–2012)

Type of legal conflict	Frequency
Simple vertical conflicts	2254
Complex vertical conflicts	828

Source Own data

Table 6.2 Most frequent complex actors' configurations in vertical conflicts (1957–2012)

Complex configurations	Frequency
Private + Private	452
Commission + Private (defendants)	158
Commission + MS (defendants)	145
MS + Private	155
MS + MS	81
Other configurations	155

Source Own data. MS = member state

configuration. This amounts to about 81% of all horizontal cases. Complex configurations are thus the norm rather than the exception for horizontal conflicts (see Table 6.3).

Most often, these complex horizontal configurations consist of the cases in which the Council and one or several member states join forces (on either side of the conflict). We find this configuration forty-nine times. In thirty-one cases, the Commission and member states fought on the same side, while the Commission and the European Parliament (EP) did so seventeen times. Again, we include a catch-the-rest category for other configurations that turn fifteen cases into complex cases. It is important to highlight that, as for vertical constellations, these horizontal configurations are not mutually exclusive. So one annulment conflict can feature, for example, the Commission and the EP on one side and the Council and member states on the other side. Similarly, the same annulment conflict can feature the Council and some member states on one side versus the Commission and other member states on the other side (Table 6.4).

Overall, we see that in relative terms, complex litigant configurations are more frequent in the context of horizontal conflicts than in vertical conflicts. However, even among vertical conflicts, complex configurations can hardly be treated as a phenomenon of marginal empirical relevance. Complex litigant configurations come in many forms and emerge in different contexts. While it is difficult to determine precisely whether a specific case will give rise to a complex litigant configuration, we argue that the emergence of complex configurations is far from random.

Table 6.3 Simple and complex cases in horizontal conflicts (1957–2012)

Type of legal conflict	Frequency
Simple horizontal conflicts	26
Complex horizontal conflicts	108

Source Own data

Table 6.4 The Council and the Commission in complex configurations (1957–2012)

Complex configuration	Frequency
Council + MS	49
Commission + MS	31
Commission + EP	17
Other configurations	15

Source Own data. MS = member state

Theorizing Complex Litigant Configurations

Unfortunately, extant research has so far not provided much insight regarding the factors that shape litigant configurations. Typically, litigant configurations are treated as exogenous factors that potentially influence judicial decisions. Legal scholars do so when studying *amicus curiae*[1] briefs before national courts to learn about supporters and their arguments in court. The question in this context is whether litigants supported by (legally) powerful *amici* have a greater chance of success; although the empirical validity of this assumption is debated (Sheehan et al. 1992).

Political scientists take a similar approach when they analyse how litigant configurations correlate with Court of Justice of the European Union (CJEU) decisions to assess the Court's independence (e.g. Carrubba et al. 2008, 2012; Larsson and Naurin 2016). Again, this approach starts with different litigant configurations as exogenous factors. On this basis, scholars assess how the Court responds to them. Does the Court tailor its rulings to the political power that backs up either side of the dispute or is it immune to such political pressures? This way of using litigant configurations does not explicitly theorize the emergence of different litigant configurations. And yet it rests on the assumption that actors participate because they have a stake in the legal conflict they join. This is why they reveal their preferences to the Court. While we are far from challenging this assumption, we try in this chapter—and throughout this book more generally—to complement and qualify the underlying assumption in several regards.

First, Chapter 5 has laid out that there are different motivations for taking an active role in court proceedings. Winning the imminent legal case is not always important for this decision. While some actors might have a financial stake in a case, the same case might be of electoral relevance to other actors. Ideological or policy goals, institutional competence-related stakes, material or financial stakes, political trust, and electoral stakes can all cause actors to take an active role in court proceedings. In fact, we assume that motivations are particularly heterogeneous in conflicts characterized by complex constellations. It seems overly rigid to assume that all parties involved share the same motivation. This flows from our argumentation above. Developing the different motivations, we highlighted that frequently, a specific motivation is typical for one category of actors but not for another. For example, we expect private actors to be motivated by material gains in most cases. Political trust, in the form of electoral gains, in turn, is likely to motivate actors that compete for votes at the ballot box. As the tables above show, complex conflicts regularly involve different types of actors and constellations. Thus, they are likely to comprise different motivations for conflicts and objectives when going to court, too.

Second, it would be a mistake, however, to exclusively focus on these motivations and overlook the legal merits of the case. This might be obvious to legal scholars. Rather strikingly, however, this constraint seems too often to escape the eye of political scientists. Social movement research has highlighted that legal claims cannot be based on just any argument when going to court. After all, bad and clearly invalid legal arguments will maximize the chances of legal defeat that can seriously hurt actors' long-term interests. Rather, available precedent or statutory basis on which the case can be argued is crucial (Andersen 2005). Here, analytically, the legal stock is a structural factor that influences litigation decisions (Vanhala 2011). However, the impact of this is typically discussed within extant research at the level of single cases rather than as a systematic factor. In the aforementioned studies that focus on the correlation between actor configurations and CJEU decisions (e.g. Carrubba et al. 2008, 2012), analyses do not control for the legal merits of a case or plea. Obviously, this would be rather difficult to do. But without doing so, we cannot account for the empirical fact that certain cases are more likely to be won in court than others merely because of the different legal merits of the cases. Yet what if the legal merits of a case should tend to spur different kinds of litigant configurations? Would we not always run the risk of mistaking correlations between litigant configurations and legal outcomes for causal impacts of litigant configurations on judicial behaviour?

As Chapter 5 on motivations has laid out extensively, very different motivations can bring actors to litigate. At the same time, our interviews highlighted that actors systematically consider the legal merits of a case. Before a decision to go to court is taken, they make an analysis of the situation by considering whether 'we have a chance to succeed "yes/no", or to what extend do we technically speaking recommend to [go to court] "yes/no"' (EP_1, cf. also COM_1, CONS_1, MIN_DE_1, MIN_ES_4, MIN_ES_5). Thus, while actors might be motivated differently, they are always constrained or enabled by the legal merits of a case. In a logical extension from the arguments presented in Chapter 5 on the motivations of individual actors, complex litigant configurations are thus the result of several actors having a stake in the case and perceiving the legal situation—at the very least—to be sufficiently unclear as to be willing to go to court.

Obviously, this general condition can and does arise in various contexts. It is, however, most likely to emerge in situations that we choose to describe as situations of institutional turbulence. With this emphasis of turbulence, we make use of a concept from the context of organizational research. Here, turbulence is used to describe situations when organizations are facing changes that 'are nontrivial, rapid, and discontinuous' (Cameron et al. 1987, 225). Often, the term turbulence is also used to describe situations of uncertainty (Burns and Stalker 1961) or as a direct consequence of organizational change (Cameron et al. 1987; Ansell et al. 2017; Trondal and Bauer 2017).

Turbulence thus refers to a situational context that lacks clarity, routine, and certainty. These situations are likely to threaten established policy paradigms, legal interpretations, implementation practices, competence distributions, political alliances, or resource allocations. Situations of institutional turbulence are situations that apply beyond individual interests. They alter the setting for many actors at a given point in time; in other words, the situation provides supranational, national, or subnational actors with ideas about why annulments might further their—possibly differing—stakes. When this is the case, many different actors are likely to have a particular stake in overturning or consolidating the legality of a specific legal act. Institutional turbulence can thus be the result of treaty or policy changes. Historical institutionalists describe situations that can fundamentally alter the path of law and public policy as critical junctures (Hall and Taylor 1996). Institutional turbulence is a typical result when such path changes are adopted. They represent a divergence from the status quo by changing interpretations, introducing new legal concepts for the first time, abolishing old rules, or changing the competence structure.

Supranational acts can be the source of institutional turbulence. We find several different empirical manifestations of which we highlight the three most obvious in the following. First, a treaty change clearly represents a time of substantial institutional turbulence. Assuming that with the entering into force of a treaty change, all uncertainties would vanish neglects that treaties consist of rather abstract terms and rules that require further interpretation to come to life. Treaties are always incomplete contracts. Second, treaty change is not the only trigger of institutional turbulence; sector specific policy reforms, typically shifting the underlying logic of a number of different policy instruments and practices, can also be at the origin of turbulences. Such reforms sometimes even come in the form of soft law (Terpan 2015). The adoption of a new state aid action plan, new guidelines on merger control, or new rules on funding the common agricultural policy can represent similar threats or disruptions of the status quo, which in turn will generate critics and proponents and will come with a non-negligible amount of legal vulnerability that can be exploited in court. Third, even individual decisions create institutional turbulences. Consider a Commission decision that changes the standards for assessing particular issues, as was the case when the Commission declared illegal state aid to ProSiebenSat1 and the RTL Group, two private broadcasting companies.[2] That decision, meant as a particular intervention, turned out to be a critical juncture in the Commission's way of assessing the legality of state aid.[3]

We argue that supranational acts causing situations of institutional turbulence are particularly likely to lead to complex litigation patterns. These situations are likely to both yield high stakes for several actors and to create sufficient legal uncertainty to encourage these different actors to try their luck in court. First, whenever the status quo is disrupted, protest and support by several actors, which act upon different motivations, are likely to emerge. The status quo represents equilibrium on several dimensions simultaneously; it consists of a situation of stability on the financial, institutional, ideological, and political fronts. Consequently, disrupting the status quo implies bringing about important changes on most (if not all) of these dimensions simultaneously. While some actors may be reactive to a disruption in a financial situation, others might rather be sensitive to the institutional or political dimension of the disruption. Hence, institutional disruption is likely to affect different types of actors, each of whose reasons for considering raising annulment actions may be different. Likewise, institutional disruption opens an opportunity for other actors (the losers of the status quo that is being disrupted) that may want to intervene in support of the defendant to prevent a return to the status quo ante. Here again, several dimensions (financial, institutional, ideological, political) are at stake simultaneously. Hence, such situations are particularly likely to see the engagement of different types of actors, creating a multi-actor defending front before the Court.

Furthermore, institutional turbulence creates legal uncertainty. When a supranational act is aligned with the corresponding policy or institutional path, its legality has typically already stood the test of time and the review by courts. Schmidt (2012) refers to this as the path dependency of case law. Following a functionalist argument, she shows that litigants transfer legal arguments from one case to the next or even from one policy area to the next. This creates a positive feedback loop that paves the trajectory of case law. Legal certainty in such contexts of continuity is relatively high. Put differently, in stable situations, a case is more likely to be clear-cut, and an actor can more easily assess its chance of succeeding by simply applying path dependent reasoning. By contrast, institutional turbulence on these various levels creates legal uncertainty. When a supranational act represents a critical juncture in policy or institutional terms, the result of its adjudication by the Court is an open question. If the supranational act is exploring new territory, the existing legal stock does not allow predicting with relative certainty how the Court will assess it. Chances of success are thus significantly higher for litigants against supranational acts disrupting the status quo than against supranational acts reinforcing an existing policy or institutional path that has been previously adjudicated by the Court. Higher chances of success should therefore, logically, attract a higher number of litigants, which, in turn, makes complex litigant configurations a more likely outcome.

Complex Litigant Patterns in the Face of Institutional Turbulence

To assess the plausibility of this link between institutional turbulence and the emergence of complex litigant patterns, we proceed in several steps. In the context of an initial correlational analysis, we start from the emergence of institutional turbulence in the form of treaty reforms and assess the relative frequency of complex litigant configurations. In a second step, we turn to qualitative case analyses. Here, we start from the observation of complex litigant configurations and try to trace them back to instances of institutional turbulence.

In our conceptualization, treaty changes represent instances of substantial institutional turbulence. By adjusting the distribution of competences within the EU system, or better within the EU's different policy systems, they essentially change the rules according to which actors interact: treaty changes thus alter the games that actors play. As such, treaty changes create the opportunity to alter established routines of interactions and change the substance of public policy. Elsewhere, we have described this mechanism in more detail (Bauer and Hartlapp 2010). The argument is that the modification of treaty provisions invites supranational actors to engage in attempts to actively stretch their competences, since the amendment of existing treaty provisions or the adoption of new rules often results in formal compromises and ambiguous wording, giving rise to legal uncertainty. Presuming the interest of the Commission and other EU institutions for that matter, 'to extend its powers, it might be inclined to use these situations of legal flux for testing out supranational room for manoeuvre (Bauer and Hartlapp 2010). These are moments of institutional turbulence, where old equilibria arrangements—in terms of resource allocation, competence allocation, ideology, etc.—are substantially threatened without having settled on any new specific equilibrium. 'The concrete balancing of interests and legal interpretations invites a tug-of-war' (Bauer and Hartlapp 2010, 209). Rather than strictly setting a new path for policy development, treaty modifications thus represent critical institutional and policy junctures. The trajectory that policies will take from there will be subject to conflict.

As we have laid out in detail in Chapter 5, there are different motivations for initiating annulment litigation against such attempts to shape new institutional or policy trajectories. The motivation to protect decision-making competences is just one of them. Trying to avoid a certain policy trajectory implied by supranational legal acts taken at such critical junctures can also be ideologically, financially, or electorally motivated, where political trust depends on entering into conflict. This is why situations of institutional turbulence that represent critical policy junctures are most likely situations for complex litigant configurations to occur. In combination with the legal flux (Bauer and Hartlapp 2010), which is a typical feature at critical junctures after larger institutional or policy modifications, many actors might be motivated not only to litigate. They are also likely to perceive the legal situation as sufficiently unclear to allow for litigation. Legal defeat against the EU institution in these situations does not seem to be inevitable. Consequently, the probability that several actors will engage in annulment litigation and will not shy away from the Court, because the matter is too important—again, financially, ideologically, electorally, or in terms of competences—and is not legally discouraging per se, creates a most likely situation for complex litigant configurations to emerge.

One of the consequences of this effect of institutional modification is that we see a significantly elevated share of complex litigant configurations in the year in which treaty changes enter into force as compared to all other years. Table 6.5 presents the results of an independent-samples t-test to compare the share of complex litigant configurations of all annulment conflicts per year in which the case was launched, between years in which treaty changes went into effect and years without such an event. For years with treaty modifications entering into force, we observe an average of 15% of annulment conflicts featuring a complex litigant configuration where we observe only an average of around 7% for years without such events. This difference is statistically significant at the 5% level. All treaty modifications from the Single European Act, the Maastricht Treaty, the Amsterdam Treaty, the Nice Treaty, to the Lisbon Treaty are included as treaty modifications. Instead of using the year of ratification, we use the year of entering into force to capture their effects.

While these results help to support our argument, we do not want to rely solely on this group comparison. On the one hand, the rather large difference in means is partly the result of the fact that complex litigant configurations were absent or very rare before the 1980s, a time for which we included no (major) treaty modifications. While this does correspond to our general argument, the average shares between both groups move much closer together if we exclude the years before the 1980s for the purposes of a robustness check. With 15% versus 10%, the treaty modification years still display a higher share of complex litigant configurations. However, the standard deviation is somewhat higher and

Table 6.5 T-test on the relative frequency of complex litigant configurations in years with and without treaty changes

	Year without treaty change		*Year* with treaty change		
	Mean	SD	Mean	SD	T-test
Share of complex annulment cases	0.07	0.01	0.15	0.03	−2.27*

Note *$p<0.05$; $N=51$; the share of complex cases is measures as a fraction between a minimum of 0 and a maximum of 1
Source Own data

thus the difference does not quite make it over the typically accepted threshold for statistical significance. Therefore, we seek to substantiate our argument through case study evidence that allows tracing the causality underlying this correlation of treaty change and complex constellations in a more nuanced way.

The annulment case *Commission v. Council* (C-114/12) serves as a first illustration. Here we see how treaty changes create institutional turbulence that leads to attempts to stretch and specify new competences and ultimately promote complex litigant configurations. One of the many modifications that came with the Treaty of Lisbon was a clarification of the EU's competences in external affairs. The treaty added Article 3(2) to the Treaty on the Functioning of the European Union (TFEU). This article stipulates that the EU has exclusive competence to conclude an international agreement where 'its conclusion is provided for in a legislative act of the Union or is necessary to enable the Union to exercise its internal competence, or in so far as its conclusion may affect common rules or alter their scope' (Woods and Peers 2014).

While Article 3(2) TFEU seemed to strengthen the EU's competences to conclude international agreements, it remained to be seen how this provision would affect the actual conclusion of such agreements in practice. This became clear in 2011 when the Council of Europe set out to update regulations on neighbouring rights for broadcasting organizations and was looking for negotiation partners in the EU. While the Commission submitted a decision proposal to the Council that would delegate the negotiation of this agreement to the Commission, member states in the Council were rather reluctant to delegate this task fully. Instead, they adopted a decision that would authorize the Commission 'to participate, on behalf of the Union, in the negotiations for a Convention of the Council of Europe'. At the same time, however, they declared that 'the member states should participate on their own behalf' (CJEU 2014, para. 32). While this latter provision was clearly confined to 'matters that arise in the course of the negotiations that fall within their competence' (CJEU 2014, para. 32), the overall approach of trying to establish a shared role in the negotiations can be interpreted as a quite restrictive application of Article 3(2) TFEU. Even more so, in an attempt to limit the Commission's freedom in these negotiations, the decision foresaw that 'to ensuring the unity of the external representation of the Union, the Member States and the Commission should cooperate closely during the negotiation process' (CJEU 2014, para. 32).

After all, neighbouring rights had become a sensitive political issue in several member states. Generally, neighbouring rights are similar to copyright laws in that they regulate how much broadcasting organizations have to pay for playing music. Yet instead of regulating how much money copyright holders obtain, they regulate how much money music labels, producers, and performers get. Such neighbouring rights have gained a special place in the Commission's Digital Single Market Strategy. News publishers have found it increasingly difficult to collect revenue for the content they create. Print subscriptions have been going down and advertising income has followed suit. While many news publishers put a lot of hope in online advertising revenue from their websites, so called news aggregators such as *Google News* have become a serious threat since they collect and gather snippets of content from publisher's websites and draw a lot of consumer traffic without paying for displaying the content provided.

Different member states eventually took different steps to approach this issue. In 2012, Belgium, for example, settled with Google in a bilateral agreement. According to this agreement, Belgium abstained from passing legislation that would force Google to pay for services to publishers in exchange for a commitment by Google to partner with publishers and help them to increase their revenues via 'implementing *Google+* social tools, including video Hangouts, on news sites, and launching official YouTube channels' (Geerts 2012; Rosati 2016). France quickly followed to strike a very similar deal in 2013, in which Google agreed to create a sixty million euros Digital Publishing Innovation Fund and reinforce its previous commitments in France, such as the Google Cultural Institute in Paris (Rosati 2016). Germany, in contrast, took a more adversarial approach by adopting a law that would allow publishers to charge Google for using their content (Rosati 2016).

The Council's (partial) delegation to negotiate an agreement on these and other related issues of cross-border publishing and broadcasting preceded these national responses. Member states had not yet adopted these approaches but were still in the process of formulating national responses. Therefore, they were reluctant to have the Commission tie their hands regarding national broadcasting policies by setting an unwanted legal frame in the negotiations with the Council of Europe. The Commission, however, strongly opposed this reluctance on the side of the member states and demanded full responsibility and competence. The resulting annulment conflict initiated by the Commission against the Council's decisions to secure a strong place for member state governments in these negotiations represented the 'first case in which the Court interpreted Article 3(2) TFEU added by the Treaty of Lisbon' (Woods and Peers 2014). While the Lisbon Treaty modified the rules, there remained substantial conflict between member states in the Council and the Commission over how this would affect the game—particularly in this specific situation. This first Court ruling on this newly added article thus represented a critical juncture in terms of clarifying (1) future competences in the negotiation of international agreements and (2) in terms of the specific negotiation of neighbouring rights for broadcasters.

In line with the arguments presented above, and in awareness of the relevance of such critical junctures, several member states joined the case—all in support of the defending Council—as did the EP in support of the applying Commission. Specifically, the eventual litigant configuration included the EP and the Commission on one side, and the Council and the German, Dutch, Polish, Czech, and United Kingdom governments on the other side. Since this was the first time the Court had to interpret the specific meaning of Article 3(2) TFEU, it seems fair to say that the Court's eventual decision was far from obvious. Particularly contested was the question of whether this specific international agreement fell under Article 3(2) TFEU at all. The defendants contested the claim that existing EU legislation even covered the substance of the agreement. While several EU directives—such as the Council's Satellite and Cable Directive No. 93/83/EEC[4]—dealt with cross-border publishing, they were formulated with respect to specific technologies and created uncertainties with respect to the applicability for internet-based services (Woods and Peers 2014). Overall, the case thus nicely illustrates the link between treaty changes, institutional turbulence in specific policy sectors, and the resulting incentives for many actors to take an active role in annulment litigation at such critical policy junctures. In this case, the EP as well as several member state governments were motivated by the struggle over the future competence distribution and encouraged to litigate by the uncertainty characterizing the legal situation.

Obviously, however, treaty modifications are only one potential source of institutional turbulence in different policy fields. This plausibility probe thus only relates to one aspect of our argument. While treaty changes do represent large disruptions of the status quo and do imply subsequent struggles over the materialization of these treaty changes in specific alterations of existing policies, institutional turbulence manifests itself in smaller scale and more regular actions, too.

The Expanded Tobacco Case (T-170/03)

Manifestations of the mechanism at a smaller scale can be illustrated with the help of case T-170/03 dealing with expanded tobacco products. In this particular case, the established policy equilibrium was not dissolved through a treaty modification. Instead, the Commission created institutional turbulence by considering modifying the application of Council Directive 95/59/EC on Manufactured Tobacco.[5] Whereas the Commission had traditionally classified expanded tobacco as 'manufactured tobacco other than smoking tobacco',[6] it decided within its comitology system to reclassify expanded tobacco and henceforth treat it as smoking tobacco, in line with Article 5(1) of the Council Directive 95/59/EC on Manufactured Tobacco.

Tobacco refers to a processed form of tobacco. The producer British American Tobacco compared this process with the process for making puffed rice snack food; specifically, the process to make dry ice expanded tobacco 'involves permeating the tobacco leaf structure with liquid carbon dioxide before warming. The resulting carbon dioxide gas forces the tobacco to expand' (British American Tobacco 2014). Expanded tobacco has become a popular product among producers and customers because it helps both groups save costs. Essentially, it allows producers to buy fewer tobacco leaves for the same number of rolled cigarettes. Furthermore, when sold as roll-your-own tobacco, its greater volume at lighter weight produces a tax advantage for customers, who are able to roll just as many cigarettes (due to greater volume) with a lighter pack of tobacco, which is taxed (typically to a substantial part) based on its weight (Canadian Coalition for Action on Tobacco 2004). Because of these characteristics, expanded tobacco has carried the hopes of the tobacco industry, which hoped that 'by offering customers expanded tobacco in our cut filler products, we will continue to grow our business in the face of continuing governmental regulations and higher excise taxes' (Miller 2013).

This reclassification essentially meant two things. First, it meant that expanded tobacco was now subject to excise duties (CJEU 2001, para. 8). According to Commission Regulation (EEC) No. 3311/86, expanded tobacco was considered unsuitable for smoking without further industrial processing. In Article 11(d) of Directive 95/59/EC, the Commission explicitly excluded tobacco products from excise duties 'if it was reworked by the producer'. Now expanded tobacco would be treated under the category of smoking tobacco subject to excise taxes.

Second, as a result of this classification, the transporting and trading of expanded tobacco was now subject to stricter administrative requirements. These requirements were specified in Article 18(1) of Council Directive 92/12/EEC.[7] Most importantly, any shipment of expanded tobacco would now always include an enclosed document. The directive did not specify this document any further and merely stated that this could be an administrative or commercial document and that the Excise Duties Committee would specify its form and content. Generally speaking, the system was, however, the paper-based precursor to today's Electronic Excise Movement and Control System, which is now able in real-time to monitor the movement of products for which excise taxes still have to be paid.

As one of the main exporters of expanded tobacco from the United Kingdom to other EU member states, the private company British American Tobacco requested to see the minutes of the respective comitology deliberations underlying this reclassification. When the Commission denied this access to the respective internal document, British American Tobacco initiated an action for annulment against the Commission (T-170/03 but also T-111/00). Essentially, the company claimed that denying this request violated the common code of conduct concerning public access to internal documents adopted in 1993.[8] For the company, it would be essential to know exactly which member state delegates argued for and against the reclassification and why. This knowledge would facilitate its interactions with national customs authorities, which were necessary to minimize the administrative burden and legal uncertainty associated with expanded tobacco exports. While excise duties were harmonized to some degree among member states, 'there remain significant differences in the treatment of expanded tobacco by the various customs authorities of the member states, and this causes the applicant difficulty' (CJEU 2001, para. 27). Therefore, it would be essential to know exactly the positions of the respective member states on how they would handle expanded tobacco under the national excise duty regime.

In fact, the differential and complex handling of expanded tobacco as a specific tobacco product continues to be an issue to this day. In 2012, a study conducted by Ramboll Management and Europe Economics still discussed the administrative burden involved in the movement of expanded tobacco as an intermediary product that is hard to verify between member states (Pedersen et al. 2012, 171). In terms of the motivations for engaging in the respective conflict, it seems clear that British American Tobacco as exporter of the respective good was driven by financial concerns resulting from the subjection to excise duties and from the administrative burden that came with it in different national contexts.

Importantly, however, this conflict also triggered litigation by other actors for different motivations. Specifically, the governments of Denmark and Sweden, as well as the European Data Protection Supervisor, joined British American Tobacco. The case thus clearly comprises a more complex litigant structure than a bilateral face-off between British American Tobacco and the Commission. Our argument about the tendency of institutional turbulence to engage actors with very different motivations is clearly supported by the participation of governments and EU institutions that are motivated differently to engage in litigation.

In the case of Denmark and Sweden, litigation was most likely by the implied clash between the Commission's practice to deny access to documents and the Scandinavian culture of transparency. In Scandinavia's culture of open government, transparency through public access to documents is a fundamental right of citizens that improves the political system's accountability and is part of these countries' constitutional, political, and cultural heritage (Grønbech-Jensen 1998). There have regularly been judicial conflicts between private actors and EU institutions about transparency and public access to EU documents where Scandinavian countries joined the dispute in favour of the litigant (e.g. T-84/03, T-174/95, T-14/98, T-111/07, T-250/08, T-362/08, T-436/09, or T-306/12). Against the background of strong national policies and a culture that favours transparency, the involvement of Denmark and Sweden in the annulment case is clearly the result of an ideological motivation for litigation.

Similarly, the active role of these governments is also due to these countries' history as outspoken critics of the EU's tobacco policy approach, which differentiates strongly between tobacco products. Sweden in particular has been willing to lobby at the EU level for the abolition of the ban on *snus*, a moist powder tobacco that is placed under the upper lip and enjoys a high popularity in Sweden. Sweden even negotiated an opt-out from the *snus* ban when joining the EU.

Without the opt-out, the referendum on EU integration would probably not have passed (Haydon 2012). To avoid distortions, all tobacco products—smoking and non-smoking tobacco—should be treated equally in the internal market, the Swedish government argued, according to *Tobacco Tactics*, a platform provided by the Tobacco Control Research Group at the University of Bath, which monitors the tobacco industry and charts its influence on public health, scientific research, and policy regulation (Tobacco Tactics 2017). Treating non-smoking tobacco more strictly than smoking tobacco was not seen to be fair or proportionate. Whether in this case, Scandinavian litigation was motivated by the willingness to send a signal of political trust worthiness to (*snus*-affine) electorates and Swedish Match (one of the world's largest producers of smokeless tobacco products), or by a willingness to voice Scandinavia's ideological preferences for transparent bureaucracy, their involvement in the conflict supports our point. Status quo disruption, even at the scale of comitology regulation, can trigger reactions from different kinds of actors based on different kinds of motivations, ultimately leading to complex judicial configurations.

While it seems fair to argue that Denmark and Sweden had motives that went beyond a mere financial interest in the case, this claim becomes even clearer for the participation of the European data protection supervisor. While the role of this actor is generally to ensure EU's institutions compliance with the processing of individual information and data protection rights of EU citizens, it also joined the case on the side of British American Tobacco. Essentially, the Commission justified the denial of the document request with a reference to the need to protect the identity of member state delegations in order to ensure frank and open discussions in committee. In the attempt to still flesh out his role, the European Data Protection Supervisor joined this case to have the Court confirm its general stake not only when personal data are processed but in all cases that involve data processing (Hofmann et al. 2011, 744). Its motivation was thus related to an attempt to establish the scope of his competences.

Overall, the case illustrates (1) how institutional turbulence can be created by challenges to the policy status quo of a minor magnitude than treaty modifications, and (2) that at such critical policy junctures, conflicts often attract multiple actors for different motivations because the multidimensional character of the challenged equilibrium creates multiple incentives to litigate.

Spanish Coal Case (T-57/11)

That multidimensional motivations trigger complex litigant configurations becomes even clearer in case T-57/11 that dealt with Spanish coal subsidies. The conflict in the Spanish coal and energy sector emerged when the Spanish government decided in 2010 to protect domestic coal producers with subsidies for power plants using domestic as opposed to imported coal. The measure was adopted by the Socialist government in response to enduring protests by mine workers in Castile and León over unpaid wages (Abend 2010). While this measure strongly benefited power plants based on coal in the region of Castile and León, the regional government of Galicia opposed the subsidy since power plants in this area mainly ran on imported coal, gas, and oil. Consequently, the Galician government saw its power plants as falling victim to discrimination by this subsidy.

While the Spanish subsidy had challenged the status quo arrangements in local energy industries, the Commission consolidated this threat with its decision to authorize the subsidy as compatible with the internal market. The measure represented a clear change in Spain's energy policy. While Spain had been called a poster child for clean energy by Greenpeace, the environmental interest group decried that 'this success story is now under threat' as the 'Spanish government is retroactively changing the rules and cutting back on support for renewables' while at the same time increasing subsidies for its domestic coal industry (Simons 2014).

It is thus relatively easy to see that the resulting institutional turbulence comprised multiple dimensions. First, the Spanish measure, together with the Commission's decision to authorize it, comprised a clear financial dimension, since power plants feared for their revenue, and an environmental (ideological) dimension, since environmental interest groups decried the renewed subsidies for the coal sector. Furthermore, the measure was a threat to the Galician energy sector for benefitting the region of Castile and León as its competitor. There, the population and the mayors of the cities related to the Galician energy sector were very concerned and expected the Galician government to react in order to protect the local economy and Galician workers (MIN_GA_3).

These additional motivations were clearly reflected by the complexity of the litigant structure, which included, in this case, the Commission and the government of Spain, two private operators of coal-operated power plants, the regional government of Castile and León, and the Spanish National Association of Mining Companies on the defendant side. On the applicant side, the private power plant operator Castelnou Energia SL, which felt that the subsidy distorted competition in the energy sector, was supported by the environmental interest groupGreenpeace in its attack on the Commission's authorization (Abend 2010). The Galician government attempted to join the conflict in support of Castelnou Energia SL, but the General Court rejected its demand because Galicia, as a non-privileged applicant, was lacking legitimacy to litigate against the Commission's authorization (MIN_GA_3, LAW_1).

This conflict emerged in response to a change in EU policy that altered the path of national energy policy and put the Spanish energy policy at a critical juncture. This triggered responses by actors acting upon multiple motivations. Specifically, the case entailed a fair amount of legal uncertainty that encouraged different actors to join the case. This legal uncertainty resulted not only from the unusual form in which the subsidy was granted. While a simple subsidy payment would have had little prospect of sustaining a legal challenge, the Spanish government introduced an obligation to produce energy for power plants using Spanish coal to ensure a stable electricity supply and reduce Spain's dependence on energy imports. Consequently, the Spanish government justified the subsidy by referring to exemptions allowed by EU competition policy for services of general economic interest, which the power plants would provide. In exchange for this service of general economic interest, power plants would receive a financial compensation. More importantly, since no legislation or case law existed on this specific question, the Court's position was rather unclear as to how far the Commission would have to go in examining state aid. Would it be enough to examine its compatibility with state aid rules? Or would its coherence with other EU policies, such as climate change legislation and electricity market legislation, have to be taken into consideration as well (Cisnal de Ugarte and Di Masi 2016, 21)? One clear indicator for the high level of uncertainty connected to the legal case was the great interest with which the legal community observed the proceedings. The Court's position on the inherent connection between state aid law and EU environmental law was seen to be unclear and was awaited with some excitement. Would state aid measures that did not pursue environmental objectives have to take EU rules on the protection of the environment into account anyways? No matter what the Court's answer would be, this answer would represent a critical juncture in the EU's state aid law (Cisnal de Ugarte and Di Masi 2016, 21).

Conclusion

While litigant configurations are typically treated as exogenous factors that are merely analysed for their impacts on judicial decisions, in this chapter we explored the conditions under which different litigant configurations emerge. While we highlighted the variety of litigant configurations in the context of annulment litigation, we proposed that a distinction between simple (1 v. 1) configurations and complex configurations (all other constellations) represents an analytically rather powerful difference. This chapter constitutes a first step towards supporting this claim by highlighting that such complex litigant configurations (of whatever form) emerge more often in situations of institutional turbulence.

Obviously, legal standing rights of non-privileged actor types can be effective obstacles for the emergence of complex litigant configurations. Nevertheless, we observe an empirically non-trivial number of such complex litigant configurations; particularly in times of institutional turbulence. Institutional turbulence shakes up established equilibria and thereby increases the stakes for policy conflicts for a wide variety of actors. Simply put, the question of how conflicts in such a situation of turbulence are resolved is very important for financial, ideological, power-related, and political trust reasons. Thereby, turbulence increases the chances of complex litigant configurations because court rulings have greater implications on more diverse respects on a greater number of actors. Moreover, turbulence comes with legal uncertainty. After all, the Court has not had the chance to interpret the new rules that created the turbulence in the first place. This acts as a further incentive to not shy away from annulment litigation. These empirical conditions that promote the emergence of annulment conflicts with complex litigant configurations also affects patterns of legal outcomes of court proceedings. We assess these in the Chapter 7.

Cases Cited

See Table 6.6.

Table 6.6 Cases cited in this chapter

C-114/12	Judgment of 4 September 2014, *Commission v. Council*, C-114/12, EU:C:2014:2151
T-111/00	Judgment of 10 October 2001, *British American Tobacco v. Commission*, T-111/00, EU:T:2001:250
T-84/03	Judgment of 23 November 2004, *Turco v. Council*, T-84/03, EU:T:2004:339
T-170/03	Order of 6 September 2010, *British American Tobacco v. Commission*, EU:T:2010:348
T-174/95	Judgment of 17 June 1998, *Tidningen Journalisten v. Council*, EU:T:1998:127
T-14/98	Judgment of 19 July 1999, *Hautala v. Council*, T-14/98, EU:T:1999:157
T-111/07	Judgment of 7 July 2010, *Agrofert Holding v. Commission*, T-111/07, EU:T:2010:285
T-250/08	Judgment of 24 May 2011, *Batchelor v. Commission*, T-250/08, EU:T:2011:236
T-362/08	Judgment of 13 January 2011, *IFAW v. Commission*, T-362/08, EU:T:2011:6
T-436/09	Judgment of 26 October 2011, *Dufour v. ECB*, T-436/09, EU:T:2010:89
T-57/11	Judgment of 3 December 2014, *Castelnou Energia v. Commission*, T-57/11, EU:T:2014:1021
T-306/12	Judgment of 25 September 2014, *Spirlea v. Commission*, T-306/12, EU:T:2014:816

Notes

1. The *amici curiae* concept refers to a professional person or organization that is not a party to a particular litigation but that has the permission of the Court to advise it in respect to some matter of law that directly affects the case in question.
2. Commission decision of 9 November 2005 on the state aid that the Federal Republic of Germany has implemented for the introduction of digital terrestrial television (DVB-T) in Berlin-Brandenburg (notified under document number C [2005] 3903). *Official Journal of the European Communities*, 2006 (L 200), p. 14.
3. Specifically, the Commission based its decision on the concept of market failure, a practice it announced in its *State Aid Action Plan* and became subjectable to judicial review when it was used in a regular state aid decision (Adam 2016).
4. Council Directive 93/83/EEC of 27 September 1993 on the coordination of certain rules concerning copyright and rights related to copyright applicable to satellite broadcasting and cable retransmission, Official Journal L 248, 6.10.1993, pp. 15–21.

5. Council Directive 93/83/EEC of 27 September 1993 on the coordination of certain rules concerning copyright and rights related to copyright applicable to satellite broadcasting and cable retransmission, Official Journal L 248, 6.10.1993, pp. 15–21.
6. Commission Regulation (EEC) No. 3311/86.
7. Council Directive 92/12/EEC of 25 February 1992 on the general arrangements for products subject to excise duty and on the holding, movement and monitoring of such products, Official Journal L 76, 23.3.1992, pp. 1–13.
8. On 6 December 1993, the Commission and the Council approved a common code of conduct concerning public access to Council and Commission documents (OJ 1993 L 340, p. 41, hereinafter 'the code of conduct').

REFERENCES

Abend, L. (2010). Spain's coal miners fight for the right to keep digging. *Time.* http://content.time.com/time/world/article/0,8599,2020555,00.html. Accessed 22 August 2017.
Adam, C. (2016). *The politics of judicial review: Supranational administrative acts and judicialized compliance conflict in the EU.* Basingstoke, UK: Palgrave Macmillan.
Andersen, E. A. (2005). *Out of the closets and into the courts legal opportunity structure and gay rights litigation.* Ann Arbor: The University of Michigan Press.
Ansell, C. K., Trondal, J., & Øgård, M. (Eds.). (2017). *Governance in turbulent times.* Oxford, UK: Oxford University Press.
Bauer, M. W., & Hartlapp, M. (2010). Much ado about money and how to spend it! Analysing 40 years of annulment cases against the European Union Commission. *European Journal of Political Research, 49,* 202–222.
British American Tobacco. (2014). *Science-tobacco blend.* http://www.bat-science.com/groupms/sites/BAT_9GVJXS.nsf/vwPagesWebLive/DO7AXG65. Accessed 22 August 2017.
Burns, T., & Stalker, G. M. (1961). *The management of innovation.* London: Tavistock.
Cameron, K. S., Kim, M. U., & Whetten, D. A. (1987). Organizational effects of decline and turbulence. *Administrative Science Quarterly, 32*(2), 222–240.
Canadian Coalition for Action on Tobacco. (2004). *A win-win: Enhancing public health and public revenue—Recommendations to increase tobacco taxes submitted to the minister of finance.* http://www.smoke-free.ca/pdf_1/2004taxreport.pdf. Accessed 7 December 2017.
Carrubba, C. J., Gabel, M., & Hankla, C. (2008). Judicial behavior under political constraints: Evidence from the European Court of Justice. *American Political Science Review, 102*(4), 435–452.

Carrubba, C. J., Gabel, M., & Hankla, C. (2012). Understanding the role of the European Court of Justice in European integration. *American Political Science Review, 106*(1), 214–224.

Cisnal De Ugarte, S., & Di Masi, L. (2016). The European antitrust review 2016. *Crowell.* https://www.crowell.com/files/European-Union-Energy.pdf. Accessed 22 August 2017.

Court of Justice of the European Union. (2001). Judgment of the Court of First Instance of 10 October 2001 on *British American Tobacco International Investments Ltd. v. Commission* in Case T-111/00. *European Court Reports 2001*(II), 02997.

Court of Justice of the European Union. (2014). Judgment of the Court of 4 September 2014 in *European Commission v. Council of the European Union* Case C-114/12. *Official Journal of the European Union 57,* C 395.

Geerts, T. (2012). Partnering with Belgian news publishers. *Google Europe Blog.* https://europe.googleblog.com/2012/12/partnering-with-belgian-news-publishers.html. Accessed 22 August 2017.

Glenn, H. (1999). *Paths to justice: What people do and think about going to law.* Oxford, UK: Hart Publishing.

Grønbech-Jensen, C. (1998). The Scandinavian tradition of open government and the European Union: Problems of compatibility? *Journal of European Public Policy, 5*(1), 185–199.

Hall, P. A., & Taylor, R. C. R. (1996). Political science and the three new institutionalisms. *Political Studies, 44,* 936–957.

Haydon, P. (2012, October 29). In Sweden, smokers have another option—Snus. *The Guardian.* https://www.theguardian.com/commentisfree/2012/oct/29/sweden-smokers-option-snus.

Hofmann, H. C. H., Rowe, G. C., & Türk, A. H. (2011). *Administrative law and policy of the European Union.* Oxford, UK: Oxford University Press.

Larsson, O., & Naurin, D. (2016). Judicial independence and political uncertainty: Assessing the effect of legislative override on the European Court of Justice. *International Organization, 70*(2), 377–408.

Miller, D. (2013). TRP starts DIET plant. *Tobacco Reporter.* http://www.tobaccoreporter.com/2013/08/trp-starts-diet-plant/. Accessed 7 December 2017.

Pedersen, H. S., Floristean, A., Iseppi, L., Dawkins, R., Smith, C., Morup, C., et al. (2012). *Study on the measuring and reducing of administrative costs for economic operators and tax authorities and obtaining in parallel a higher level of compliance and security in imposing excise duties on tobacco products.* http://ec.europa.eu/smart-regulation/evaluation/search/download.do?documentId=11702485. Accessed 7 December 2017.

Rosati, E. (2016). Neighbouring rights for publishers: Are national (possible) EU initiatives lawful? *International Review of Intellectual Property and Competition Law, 47*(5), 569–594.

Schmidt, S. K. (2012). Who cares about nationality? The path-dependent case law of the ECJ from goods to citizens. *Journal of European Public Policy*, *19*(1), 8–24. https://doi.org/10.1080/13501763.2012.632122.

Sheehan, R. S., Mishler, W., & Songer, D. R. (1992). Ideology, status, and the differential success of direct parties before the Supreme Court. *American Political Science Review*, *86*(2), 464–471. https://doi.org/10.2307/1964234.

Simons, D. (2014). Should the European Commission wear green goggles more often? Greenpeace International. http://www.greenpeace.org/international/en/news/Blogs/makingwaves/Castelnou-Energia-v-Commission/blog/50868/. Accessed 22 August 2017.

Terpan, F. (2015). Soft law in the European Union—The changing nature of EU Law. *European Law Journal*, *21*(1), 68–96. https://doi.org/10.1111/eulj.12090.

Tobacco Tactics. (2017). *Snus: EU ban on snus sales*. University of Bath. http://www.tobaccotactics.org/index.php/Snus:_EU_Ban_on_Snus_Sales. Accessed 22 August 2017.

Trondal, J., & Bauer, M. W. (2017). Conceptualizing the European multilevel administrative order: Capturing variation in the European administrative system. *European Political Science Review*, *9*(1), 73–94.

Vanhala, L. (2011). *Making rights a reality? Disability rights activists and legal mobilization*. Cambridge, UK: Cambridge University Press.

Woods, L., & Peers, S. (2014). Copyright: Anything left of member states external competence? *EU Law Analysis*. http://eulawanalysis.blogspot.de/2014/09/copyright-anything-left-of-member.html. Accessed 22 August 2017.

Open Access This chapter is licensed under the terms of the Creative Commons Attribution 4.0 International License (http://creativecommons.org/licenses/by/4.0/), which permits use, sharing, adaptation, distribution and reproduction in any medium or format, as long as you give appropriate credit to the original author(s) and the source, provide a link to the Creative Commons license and indicate if changes were made.

The images or other third party material in this chapter are included in the chapter's Creative Commons license, unless indicated otherwise in a credit line to the material. If material is not included in the chapter's Creative Commons license and your intended use is not permitted by statutory regulation or exceeds the permitted use, you will need to obtain permission directly from the copyright holder.

CHAPTER 7

Litigant Success: How Litigant Configurations Relate to Legal Outcomes

This chapter analyses how complex litigant configurations relate to legal success and policy and institutional outcomes. In the first section, the chapter revisits the literature on litigant constellations by carving out the relevant approaches and interpretations. This will provide orientation for analysing empirical patterns of complex constellations as identified by our statistical exploration. In the second section, we spell out our argument based on an endogenous conception of litigant configuration and legal uncertainty, which provides an innovative explanation to the relationship between complex litigants' configuration and judicial success. In a third section, we identify an additional causal mechanism driving the relation between complex litigants' configurations, legal uncertainty, and judicial success based on the heterogeneity of legal arguments presented to the Court. We then analyse empirical patterns of litigant's configuration and judicial success, which give support to our argument about the endogenous relationship between legal uncertainty, litigants' configuration, and judicial success. Finally, we close the sequence linking policy conflict to litigation, to litigants' configurations, and to ruling outcome by turning to the distributive effects of annulments rulings on policy stakeholders. Taking into account the objective that motivated the litigant to turn to court in the first place, we find that, although winning—the achievement of the litigant's primary objective—is generally associated with judicial success, in many cases, winning and judicial success are disconnected.

© The Author(s) 2020
C. Adam et al., *Taking the EU to Court*,
Palgrave Studies in European Union Politics,
https://doi.org/10.1007/978-3-030-21629-0_7

Litigant Configurations and Judicial Success: What We Know

With the increasing empirical relevance of courts and litigation described under the well-known labels of judicialisation and legalisation, judicial behaviour has increasingly come under the focus of social science research (see Chapter 2). In this regard, the relationship between litigant configurations and the content of court rulings has become an area of particular scholarly interest.

From a strict legalistic perspective, litigant configurations should not be an important influence on judicial decisions. Instead, decisions should be based on the legal merits of the case, not on the question of who presents the case. Consequently, any observed covariance between litigant configurations and legal outcomes should be purely coincidental. From this perspective, any aggregate-level variation of legal success might simply be the product of chance, untouched by the structural characteristics of member state litigants and their strategic interactions with the Court. Instead, what matters is the plain meaning of the legal texts, the intention with which the legal texts were written, existing case law, and precedents that determine judicial decisions (Segal and Spaeth 2002, 48). While court decisions can have political consequences and litigation, as we have also argued throughout this book, can be politically motivated, rulings as such are apolitical decisions; for the legitimacy of court decisions, a lot depends on whether the decisions are perceived as politically neutral. Regarding the Court of Justice of the European Union (CJEU), it thus comes as no surprise that legalist approaches deny 'the existence of ideological and socio-political influences on the Court's jurisdiction' (Burley and Mattli 1993, 45). From this perspective, any pro-integration bias of the Court results directly from treaty asymmetries (Scharpf 2002, 2007), and CJEU case law might reflect the 'inevitable working out of the correct implications of the constitutional text' (Shapiro 1980, 538).

Such legalistic conceptions have been heavily criticized by proponents of an attitudinal model of judicial decision making. This attitudinal model proposes that legalistic considerations 'serve only to rationalize the Court's decisions and to cloak the reality of the Court's decision-making process' (Segal and Spaeth 2002, 53). Rulings do not emerge automatically from existing law. No matter which legal method of interpretation one uses, rulings are always based on interpretations of the law. This process of the interpretation of more-or-less (un-)clear words, phrases, situations, and potential precedents adds the attitudes and ideological predispositions of judges to the equation (Segal and Spaeth 2002, 86–97; for the CJEU, see Höpner 2011; Vauchez 2012). Based on this understanding of judicial decision making, potential litigants—and researchers, for that matter—try to predict court decisions based on the ideological predispositions of judges. For the CJEU, this has proved particularly difficult because of the non-transparent decision-making process of the Court, where positions of individual judges cannot be identified. Abstracting from the attitudes of individual judges, researchers have assumed the Court to be generally very favourable of European integration. Otherwise, the argument goes, the Court's drive towards legal integration could not be explained. While this reasoning is hard to reject, recent attempts to open the black box of CJEU decision making have revealed that CJEU judges do not necessarily have uniform preferences regarding the development of the European Union (EU)'s body of law (Malecki 2012).

A third prominent theoretical perspective on judicial decision making is commonly summarized under the label of strategic approaches to judicial decision making. While this perspective does not deny that judges might hold relevant policy-related and institutional preferences, it emphasizes that judges are hardly able to act freely on those preferences. Instead, judges are constrained by the anticipated reactions to their rulings. As a result, decisions reflect strategic interactions between judges, within courts, between the court and the litigant, and between courts and public opinion (Segal and Spaeth 2002, 100).

In the EU context, this perspective supports intergovernmentalist accounts of European integration. As such, intergovernmentalist scholars have emphasized the strategic relationship between the CJEU and member state governments. Garrett et al. (1998) provide a formalized and strategic model of the relationship between member state governments and the CJEU in which the authors claim that the Court is a strategic actor that works to protect its institutional authority (Garrett et al. 1998, 174). This authority rests on both the perception of the Court's impartiality and integrity and on its ability to adopt rulings that are not overruled by subsequent legislation and are obeyed. More recently, Larsson and Naurin (2016) have demonstrated a strong correlation between the CJEU's rulings and the political signals it receives from member states. Ultimately, in both studies, the authors argue that CJEU decisions reflect strategic assessment (Garrett et al. 1998; Larsson and Naurin 2016).

In contrast to this strategic approach to judicial behaviour, the general litigation literature coined by US scholars has highlighted other reasons for which certain actors will be more successful in court than others. In this literature, the question about who has success in court has been on the research agenda since the 1980s. Concerning litigant groups, the evidence is quite clear-cut. Governments and public actors come out first, followed by businesses and other organized interests, while individuals only reach the lowest success rates in comparison with the other groups (Farole 1999). Usually, litigant success is associated with arguments about judicial constraint or litigants' capacity. In a comparative study of social activists' ability to succeed in court, Epp (1998) emphasizes economic resources available to the claimant as the most important support factor (for similar results on EU preliminary rulings, see Tridimas and Tridimas 2004). This purely economic factor partly overlaps with Galanter's (1974, 97; similar McGuire 1995; Haire et al. 1999) prominent repeat-player argument. Accordingly, resource rich claimants can afford to appear in court regularly and thereby gain the experience necessary to increase their chance of success in court. The relevance of capacity is also emphasized by studies analysing governmental litigation in the context of the World Trade Organization's system of dispute resolution. Only governments with a high degree of executive effectiveness are found to be able to navigate the complex procedures, learn effectively from experience, and keep up with the constantly changing body of case law (Kim 2008; Davis and Bermeo 2009).

Authors that consider ideological closeness to the Court as the more relevant strategic factor oppose such arguments, which stress (economic) characteristics of claimants. In a much cited study on federal or state courts in the United States, Sheehan et al. (1992) find that across different litigant groups, the ideological complexion of courts was more important to explain success than other factors. More recently, Skiple et al. (2016) also found substantial explanatory power of Supreme Court judges' ideological orientation—via appointment mechanisms—to matter for outcomes on economic conflicts.

At a more general level, judicial constraints can systematically affect litigant success. Studies along this line adopt a principal-agent perspective and assess whether national governments are able to effectively constrain the CJEU, which tries to avoid non-compliance and legislative overriding of its rulings. From this perspective, active participation in judicial proceedings by more powerful member states is likely to constrain the

Court in its rulings because threats of legislative override and non-compliance with rulings from that side are more credible (Garrett and Weingast 1993; Carrubba et al. 2008). Given that more powerful states are seen to be less susceptible to the reputational costs resulting from non-compliant behaviour, the probability of winning, that is the probability with which the European Court of Justice should be found to agree with the litigant government, increases with this government's degree of political power.

With regard to multiple litigants, it has been argued that a threat of legislative override is reduced where member states appear to be divided over the legal question. In the EU context, which regularly demands high degrees of consensus or even unanimity in the Council, voting jointly becomes less likely in such cases. Whether or not there is empirical support for these theoretical propositions remains heatedly debated, however (Carrubba et al. 2008, 2012; Stone Sweet and Brunell 2012).

But the ratchet effect created by the arithmetics of decision making in the Council is not the only aspect heatedly discussed within this controversy. Some authors claim that the model is based on a misconception of the CJEU as an agent of the member states when it should really be considered to be a trustee (Stone Sweet and Brunell 2013). The trustee role, the argument goes, is distinctly different from the role of an agent and is characterized by three different aspects, '(1) the court is recognized as the authoritative interpreter of the regime's law, which it applies to resolve disputes concerning state compliance; (2) the court's jurisdiction, with regard to state compliance, is compulsory; and (3) it is virtually impossible, in practice, for contracting states to reverse the court's important rulings on treaty law' (Stone Sweet and Brunell 2013, 62). As trustee, the Court's decisions would rather reflect a logic of majoritarian activism. This means that it tries to produce rulings that reflect standard practices in many member states and are characterized by a high level of state consensus (Stone Sweet and Brunell 2013). This brief literature review can hardly do justice to the vast existing and emerging literature on the CJEU, let alone on judicial behaviour. Nevertheless, it hopefully serves to highlight that there is a controversial debate over the ability of powerful political actors to influence judicial decision making. While legalistic, attitudinal, and neo-functional approaches to CJEU decision making refute this claim, adherents of the strategic model argue that litigant configurations are an important influence on judicial behaviour. Accordingly, strategic models of court behaviour argue that when many powerful member states support a specific legal argument, the Court becomes more inclined to follow this argument than when many powerful member state governments oppose this particular argument. Therefore, the threat of member state non-compliance or legislative override is conceptualized with the help of member state's political power and the number of member states supporting or opposing particular arguments. This approach yields so called net-weighted observations (Carrubba et al. 2008, 2012), which basically counts the number of legal observations of member state governments on either side of the legal argument and weights this number by the political power of the respective member state. Neo-functionalist accounts have heavily criticized this approach (e.g. Burley and Mattli 1993). Neo-functionalist accounts of European integration through law argue that the CJEU has—with the help of private litigants—promoted European integration well beyond the preferences of member state governments. Most importantly, the critique against strategic models of the CJEU emphasizes that because of the high number of member states and the heterogeneity of their preferences, any sort of threat of legislative override is hardly ever credible. Therefore, this threat should not be measured on a continuous scale. Only when the vast majority of member states were clearly opposed to a particular legal interpretation would this threat be credible. In all other cases, the threat would be absent (Stone Sweet and Brunell 2012).

LITIGANT CONFIGURATIONS AND ENDOGENEITY: A NEW APPROACH

We use this chapter to highlight one further problem inherent in the empirical evaluation of strategic models of court behaviour that strongly rely on observed litigant configurations. Essentially, authors such as Carrubba et al. (2008) treat litigant configurations as factors that are exogenous influences on judicial decision making. The emergence of different litigant configurations is not explicitly theorized within such models. Empirical evaluations of these models thus rely on the assumption that cases that include many powerful actors are not systematically different in any relevant way from cases that do not include powerful actors, except for the different participant configurations. Therefore, a correlational relationship between litigant configurations and patterns of legal success can be interpreted as supporting the theoretically assumed causal relationship between these variables. We believe, however, that patterns of correlation between litigant configurations and legal success are better understood when litigant configurations are endogenized within the analysis and conceived in relation to the nature of the conflict. We argue that it is not necessarily the litigant configuration that produces certain rulings. The causal chain is much longer. As we have argued in the previous chapter, different litigant configurations emerge—to a substantial extent—as a result of different characteristics of the underlying situation. More specifically, we have argued that complex litigant structures tend to emerge in situations of institutional turbulence. Such institutional turbulences often trigger active litigation by several actors who not only have a stake in the outcome of conflicts but, importantly, also perceive the legal situation to be sufficiently unclear—the legal merits of the case being open to different interpretations—as to consider it worthwhile joining the case.

As seen in Chapters 5 and 6, actors are typically more likely to engage in costly litigation where the chances of legal success are substantial, which is the case in situations of greater legal uncertainty. Success rates in annulment actions are rather low (around 25% across all cases and litigant configurations). Situations of greater legal uncertainty, that is, when issues disputed before the Court are not clearly predetermined by previous case law, should translate into a higher success rate, close to 50%. Greater legal uncertainty thus typically means higher chances of success for potential applicants and thus a higher likelihood to see complex litigant configurations as a result of additional actors joining the case in favour of the applicant.

This is particularly obvious for private actors who generally litigate out of financial motivations and where the chance of success is a critical element of the risk-benefit analysis underpinning the decision to litigate. Yet legal uncertainty is also an important factor to public actors, such as national governments. As repeat players before the Court (Galanter 1974; McGuire 1995), they are unwilling to risk their reputation as serious partners in the legal discourse regarding EU law and European integration by pushing conflicts without legal merits. Besides, litigation before the CJEU consumes key human resources that need to be managed wisely (state attorney units are typically relatively small), which requires prioritization among possible cases where the legal uncertainty criterion does play a role. Member states or other public authorities are thus rather likely to launch annulment cases or join them in support of an applicant where chances of success are higher, that is, in situations of greater legal uncertainty.

Interestingly, the same should be true for actors potentially interested in joining the case in support of the defending EU institution. In situations of great legal certainty (i.e. great predictability of the court ruling), the necessity to intervene in support of the defending institution does not appear as important. As the defending EU institution is more likely to win anyway, the actors interested in the success of the defendant adopt a free-rider approach and refrain from investing resources into the conflict. By contrast, if the chances of the defending institution are lower, an actor interested in the defeat of the action might perceive its intervention in the case as being potentially able to tip the scales and help to obtain a favourable ruling. The incentive to join the case is thus higher. Hence, situations of legal uncertainty are also more likely to see at least one actor intervening in support of the defending EU institution than situations of high legal predictability.

All this is not to say that complex litigant configurations will never emerge in cases with a marginal degree of legal uncertainty and consequently an expected ruling. Yet the emergence of complex litigant configurations in this context is less likely as compared to the emergence of simple litigant configurations. Put differently, if conflicts with little legal uncertainty—that is, when the outcome of court rulings is rather predictable—do lead to annulment litigation at all, they tend to lead to simple rather than complex litigant configurations.

In sum, we argue that treating litigant configurations as exogenous factors is problematic when trying to analyse their impact on judicial behaviour. It is not necessarily the litigant configuration that produces certain rulings. Instead, it is specific characteristics of the underlying conflict situation that promotes specific litigant configurations and triggers respective rulings. Accordingly, any correlation between litigant configurations and legal outcomes is not necessarily the result of the litigant configurations' causal effect. Instead, the correlation is a reflection of the different character of underlying cases.

In an earlier study, we have made a similar point (Adam et al. 2015). While we found correlational evidence supporting arguments of judicial constraint, we emphasized that the characteristics of the litigant inform us not only about the abilities of this litigant to constrain or influence the Court in its decision making. Instead, the characteristics and motivations of the litigant tell us something about the kind of cases the litigant will bring to the Court's attention. In this particular context, we argued with the help of case studies and regression analysis that member state governments, which face strong subnational governments with a high degree of authority, are more likely to initiate annulment litigation against the European Commission for other reasons than trying to win the legal case. Instead, annulment litigation for those governments is often part of a two-level game. Adverse rulings might not harm them politically and in fact might even have positive electoral effects. This is particularly the case where such adverse rulings can be used as normative levers legitimizing domestic reform processes. These characteristics and motivations help us understand why national governments facing strong regional governments are substantially less successful in winning annulment cases than national governments operating within centralized political environments. They do not possess a lower level of legal expertise and they are not necessarily less likely to constrain the Court politically. Instead, they are somewhat more often inclined to initiate litigation in cases with only meagre chances of success in a legal sense, because they more often choose cases for their political rather than legal merits.

In this chapter, we make a similar argument. Yet it is not only the characteristics of litigants that contain information about the kind of cases litigants bring to the Court's attention. More generally, litigant configurations in specific cases contain information of the underlying conflict situations that the Court has to settle. Building directly on the arguments presented in the previous chapter (see Chapter 6), complex configurations tend to arise more often in contexts in which court behaviour is difficult to predict and less certain, that is, in situations of greater legal uncertainty. This is subsequently reflected by the Court's rulings fluctuating around a 50:50 chance of winning or losing in complex configurations, whereas annulment actions with a simple litigant configuration (simple applicant constellation v. simple defendant constellation) succeed in only about one in four cases.

LITIGANT CONFIGURATIONS AND LEGAL REASONING

In line with Chapter 6, we argue that success rates for cases with complex litigant configurations should be around 50% because these configurations tend to emerge in situations of lower legal certainty. In this section, we put forward an additional mechanism through which complex litigant configurations not only emerge in situations of higher legal uncertainty, but even contribute to increasing the legal uncertainty of the case under consideration. It is in this sense that we argue that litigant configurations can have a causal impact on court rulings. This is a second reason that we expect chances of legal success in cases with complex litigant configurations to be closer to 50% than in cases with simple litigant configurations.

Since the Court has to engage with the arguments brought forward by the litigants, the merits of the different legal arguments advanced by the parties are important. In this regard, complex litigant configurations seem not only to be reflective of the legal stock of a case but also to potentially affect the diversity of arguments presented in court. Therefore, since complex litigant configurations tend to increase rather than decrease the heterogeneity of legal perspectives presented to the Court, court decisions in these situations are again more difficult to predict.

While the legal merits of a case are obviously important, so are the arguments that build on this legal stock and their presentation in court. It requires adequate pleas and reasoning to present these arguments in a way that will convince the Court. Thus, participation by different litigants is anything but merely symbolic. On the contrary, our interviews indicate that the belief of being able to influence the Court's decision making with the help of convincing legal arguments is an important factor that brings public actors to participate in annulment litigation. The logic of an intervener's plea is to support arguments by adding new ways of reasoning and 'to place emphasis on a point that is particularly important' (COM_1, own translation; similarly COM_2; MIN_D_4; COMP_2; MIN_GA_2). In contrast, interviewees attributed little relevance to legal constraints on the Court. They argued that the Court is rarely impressed by the political weight that member states put behind certain demands or arguments. An interviewee's explanation that in horizontal annulments, high numbers of interveners are indicators of an uncertain defendant, supports this view. 'All the time the Council has a problem, there are large numbers of member state interveners—but this does not impress the Court' (COM_1, own translation). Instead, interveners matter because even when formally limited in the length of their pleas, they are able to add legal arguments, information, and nuances to the debate and thereby provide the Court with a wider array of pieces to choose from. What is more, they avail themselves of more time to do so, since their pleas can be submitted after the case is launched before the Court. This is important because—as we outlined in Chapter 3—actions for annulment are subject to a tight time line and can be filed only within two months after a legal act is published. In this sense, more actors means more legal perspectives. To be clear, it is not the number of issues discussed in court that increases, but rather the number of different perspectives on a somewhat fixed number of legal questions (formally no additional aspect can be raised by interveners).

Of course, we cannot predict the diversity of legal arguments presented to the Court simply based on the complexity of litigant configurations. In our interviews, we have questioned litigants about their judicial strategies in cases involving other litigants on their side of the conflict. The answers indicate that the diversity of arguments is often reflected in complex configurations—but not always. This has a lot to do with the efforts of coordination between different litigants.

Across the multiple possible complex constellations of litigants, we found quite different efforts to coordinate. Public claimants often organized along existing networks of national legal experts, where member state officials are sometimes approached directly by mail to draw attention to an upcoming or submitted case and a related request for a friendly intervention (MIN_D_4). Coordination by phone or email assures that substantial support is forthcoming. Moreover, such cooperation avoids 'being in front of the Court and saying different things' (EP_1).[1]

Finally, we came across cases where a given EU measure was being challenged in parallel by several applicants who never entered in contact with each other. This seems to be more likely for private actors who frequently do not avail themselves of the same inter- and transnational networks. In the renewable energy case (cases T-134/14 and T-47/15 presented in Chapter 5), the EU measure was attacked by fifty-one companies. One team of lawyers defended the interests of about ten of these companies. The legal arguments for these ten companies were de facto very similar to the legal arguments of law firms defending the remaining companies. However, the respective lawyers had no contact whatsoever with the lawyers defending the remaining forty-one companies involved in the conflict (LAW_5).

It is important to note that such strategic interaction before or during the process does not necessarily create convergence of positions and arguments. We found cases where litigants exchanged information on their respective cases and legal strategy that did not lead to an alignment of substantial arguments. In the milk quality case (T-683/15), the Commission attacked a Bavarian practice whereby investigations of the quality checks in the milk industry were paid by a fund of the Bavarian state. While the dairy industry pays into the fund, the fund itself is a public instrument. The Commission thought that companies themselves must pay the investigations and that the involvement of the Bavarian fund constituted illegal state aid. Both the Bavarian government and the association of Bavarian milk producers raised an annulment action against the Commission's decision. They exchanged information, but they put different arguments at the core of their reasoning. On the one hand, the association claimed, in line with existing CJEU case law, that the measure could not be classified as state aid, because no state resources were involved. The Bavarian government, on the other hand, was not convinced that they could win based on this argument. Instead, they argued that the scheme had already been in place before EU state aid law became applicable, thus falling into the category of the so-called existing aid, which is subject to a specific and less restrictive procedure. When the Commission finds an existing state aid to be in breach of EU state aid rules, it cannot ask the member state to recover the aid granted but rather asks it to put an end to the measure. In this case, while the dairy industry association claimed that the contested measure was not state aid, the Bavarian government acknowledged that it was state aid, arguing instead that it was a particular kind of state aid (MIN_BA_1). Here, we have two legal arguments that are contradictory. This is not necessarily a bad thing for the litigant, however, since it offers two alternative legal perspectives to the Court. If one does not convince the judges, the other may.

By contrast, the *BMW* case (T-671/14) is an example of a high level of substantial argumentative alignment among litigants. In that case, BMW raised an annulment action against a decision of the Commission that declared illegal aid by the German state of Saxony for BMW, which was meant to encourage the creation of a new factory in their region as contrary to EU state aid law (see discussion in Chapter 5). The Saxon government intervened in support of an action raised by BMW. Saxony hired expensive lawyers in order to bring additional argumentation to the Court. While BMW and Saxony had different lawyers, there was a lot of coordination among them. Both teams of lawyers shared all the information on the cases, met in Berlin, and developed strong ties. Every argumentation was exchanged and checked by the other claimant. While they had slightly different views—some points were more important for Saxony, some more for BMW—they did not disagree on the points put forward by the other party. The common argumentative strategy was to present to the Court a convincing story, with complementary legal narratives contributing to the same common interest (MIN_SA_1).

Complex litigant configurations enhance rather than reduce the diversity of legal arguments provided. If the arguments presented to the Court are to have any effect on the rulings, then a greater variety of legal arguments should, in principle, make rulings less predictable. In any conflict, a greater variety of legal interpretations provides the Court with more possibilities to diverge from its preestablished legal interpretations. In other words, independent of the legal stock preceding a given case, where a complex litigant configuration brings about a higher diversity of legal arguments, this increases the Court's capacity to diverge from the preexisting case law. Thereby, complex litigant configurations can add to the level of legal uncertainty: where more complex litigant configurations bring more heterogeneous legal arguments as well as varying perspectives to legal cases, CJEU rulings are again more difficult to predict than for simple litigant configurations with just one applicant and one defendant.

Empirical Patterns of Litigant Configurations and Legal Success

We now turn to empirical evidence on success in annulment cases. When going to Court, litigants seek a decision on a particular conflict. The Court can decide that the applicant is inadmissible and consequently reject making any decision. Typically, this is the case where the grounds raised are invalid. In all other cases that are not dropped or withdrawn, a judgement will eventually be made on the conflict. The plaintiff can be successful or lose the claim. We coded legal success based on the eventual decision of the Court taken at the end of the respective proceedings and clearly stated at the very end of the text of its judgements. Specifically, we consider applicants to have been successful whenever the Court completely or partially annuls the contested legal act. All other outcomes are treated as unsuccessful cases. Figure 7.1 depicts the share of successful annulment litigation over time.

Figure 7.1 shows that on average, the success rate lies somewhere between 18 and 35%. The volatility of success rates was higher in the

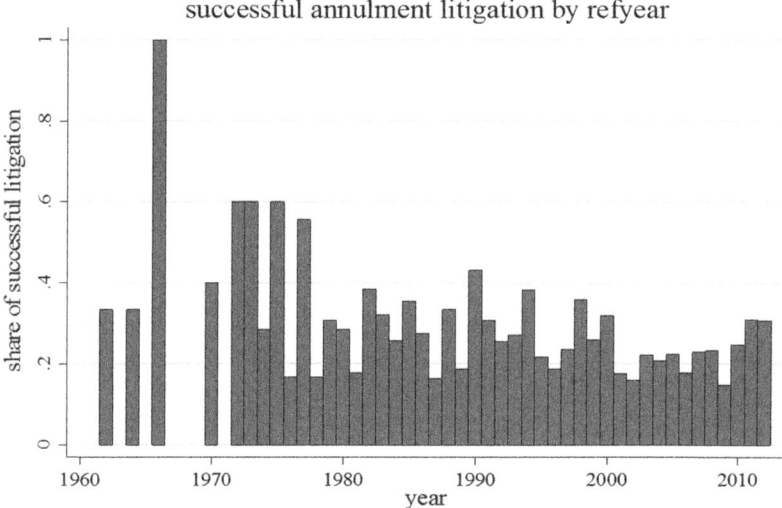

Fig. 7.1 Success rate over time (*Note* Successful annulments are counted by the year of their referral to the Court. Absolute numbers include cases that were found inadmissible by the Court, cases that were dropped later on, or cases where a ruling became obsolete during the time of proceedings)

early years of integration. Note, however, that in these early years, overall numbers of annulments were substantially lower and therefore one single ruling influences the overall success rate substantially. Nevertheless, success in court seems to have been somewhat more likely for plaintiffs in the early decades than it is today. Despite highs and lows between single years, the overall trend has been rather stable since the number of annulments has started to increase in the 1980s.

With this picture in mind, we now return to the constrained court argument put forward in the debate. In essence, this argument considers success to be a function of the threat for legislative override. In contrast, we posit that success is a function of the characteristics of the conflict situation from which legal cases emerge. If we look at the patterns of litigant success for different litigant configurations, we find further support for our argument. To see how, consider Fig. 7.2 in light of strategic approaches to judicial decision making; in situations in which the Court settles conflicts with private applicants on the one side and an EU institution on the other side, political constraint should play hardly any role in

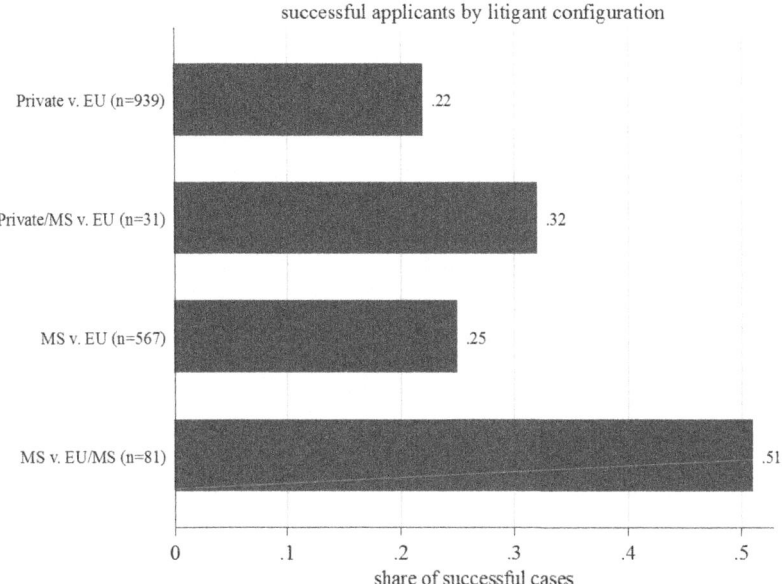

Fig. 7.2 Litigant success by litigant configuration (*Source* Own compilation)

the Court's decision-making process. In these situations with simple litigant configurations ($n=939$), we observe that EU institutions lose only 22% of cases. Alternatively, to put it the other way around, private litigants win 22% of cases against EU institutions. If we compare this success rate to the success rate in which an EU institution faces challenges from private actors and from at least one member state government at the same time, the Court should—if anything—be more constrained and thus more sensitive towards the applicant's concerns. In fact, the higher success rate for the applicants in this complex litigant configuration of 32% appears at the first glance to support this proposition. Yet considering our argument about endogeneity of litigant constellations, we should not jump to quick conclusions. First of all, an analysis of variance (ANOVA)[2] that tests for significant differences in the mean success rate between the four different litigant groups, displayed in Fig. 7.2, indicates that the success rates of the first two groups (private v. EU and private/MS v. EU) are not significantly different from each other.

Second, and maybe more importantly, the other success patterns do not really fit the constrained court narrative. This may result from the fact that the constrained court narrative remains theoretically underspecified by failing to explicitly theorize the emergence of different litigant constellations. To begin with, it is difficult to see why such a constrained court would be less responsive to applicants when these applicants are just member state governments (25%) as opposed to member state governments combined with private actors (32%)—as the latter cannot threaten legislative override (see Fig. 7.2).

Similarly, and perhaps even more interestingly, we find that when litigating against an EU institution, a member state has more chances to succeed when the defending EU institution is supported by another member state. This finding is completely at odds with the expectations of the strategic approach, which would predict a lower success rate when a defending EU institution is supported by a member state. Instead, we observe that member state applicants are much more likely to succeed in court when they face a defence alliance consisting of the contested EU institution and at least one other member state, compared to an EU institution acting on its own; this cannot be brought in line with the argument about court constraint, either.

We conduct a one-way ANOVA to determine whether these nominal differences in success rates are statistically significant (see Table 7.1). The differences between the first three groups are not statistically significant. We do find, however, that the success rate of group four (MS v. EU/

Table 7.1 Pairwise comparison of configuration-specific differences in success rates

Group	Name	Mean	Std	Sig. of diff. (Group A–B)	Sig. of diff. (Group B–C)	Sig. of diff. (Group C–D)
A	Private v. EU	0.22	0.41	0.62		
B	Private/MS v. EU	0.32	0.47		0.82	
C	MS v. EU	0.25	0.43			0.000*
D	MS v. EU/MS	0.51	0.50			

*Indicates levels of statistical significance of the difference between groups at the 1% level; these results are robust for different post hoc tests (i.e. the Sidak method, Scheffé's method, and the Bonferroni procedure)

MS) is significantly different from all other groups. This empirical pattern does not support the constrained court narrative. It does, however, support our argument, which is that these different litigant configurations tend to arise in different situations.

Take group four in Fig. 7.2 (MS v. EU/MS), where member state governments appear on both sides of the conflict. In line with the arguments presented in the previous chapter, these configurations tend to arise more often in cases that are not only perceived as important by member state governments (for whatever reasons). They also include a sufficiently unclear legal situation as to make the Court's ruling quite difficult to predict. This is reflected in a success rate of 51% for the applicant member state government(s). In situations of institutional turbulence, it is more likely that complex constellations comprise actors that are drawn to the conflict by different motivations. Put differently, cases that fall in the MS v. EU/MS category are not simply characterized by a different litigant configuration than cases that fall in the category MS v. EU. Rather, they represent a different underlying situation. The former constellation is more likely to emerge in situations of turbulence and greater legal uncertainty. Accordingly, member state governments do not have a better chance of winning when facing an alliance between an EU institution and (an)other member state government(s). Instead, in these cases, court behaviour is simply harder to predict. Consequently, the success rate for these cases is closer to 50:50.

We believe that this argument also helps to explain the patterns displayed in Fig. 7.3. When court rulings are easier to foresee, cases are unlikely to attract a high number of litigants. Actors in anticipation of losing are reluctant to invest the necessary resources just as actors anticipating sure success will rather free ride on the outcome of the case. Therefore, simple litigant configurations are more likely to emerge when the outcomes of court rulings are easy to foresee. In contrast, conflicts and related legal questions that invite complex applicant and defendant configurations are typically characterized by a high level of political relevance and a high level of legal uncertainty; legal uncertainty and emerging policy junctures ensure that plausible legal arguments can be brought forward on both sides of the conflict, possibly making a difference in the ruling.

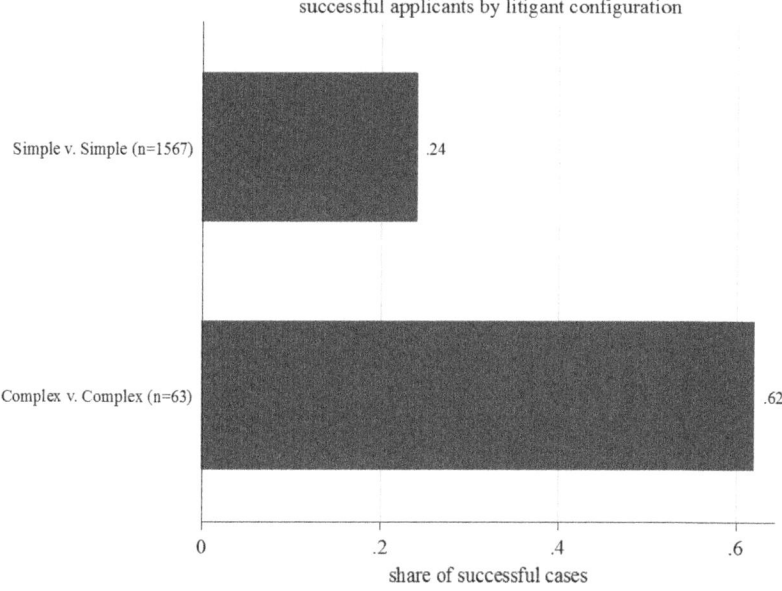

Fig. 7.3 Success rates for simple and complex configurations (*Note* A one-way ANOVA indicates that this difference is statistically significant [$F=48.1$, $p=0.000$])

DISTRIBUTIVE EFFECTS AND FEEDBACK OF WINNING OR LOSING A CASE

Now that we have explored the sequence that links policy conflict with litigation, litigation with litigant configurations, and litigant configurations to judicial outcomes, we come back to the origin. What is the feedback effect of the Court's rulings on the political context out of which the legal action emerged in the first place? Our multilevel policy approach to litigation compels us to reflect on the policy impacts of rulings. How do the Court's rulings feed back into policy arrangements and institutional settings that had led to conflict? What kind of redistributive effects among policy actors can rulings have? We saw that actors generally initiate annulment actions for material gain, to protect or improve decision making competences, to maximize ideological preferences, or to improve political trust. To what extent do court rulings contribute to the achievement of these objectives that motivated policy actors to engage in litigation in the first place?

Typically, when referring to winners and losers, the literature frequently sets success in court equal to winning. Far less attention has been devoted to distributive effects of CJEU rulings (but see Cappelletti et al. 1986). We contend that courts also have distributive impacts that may or may not correspond to success or failure in the judicial conflict. As we have argued in an earlier publication, 'it's not always about winning' (Adam et al. 2015). Losing the legal argument can, at times, be irrelevant for the political utility associated with litigation. Even more, losing can even be positively related to the political utility of rulings. Acknowledging this compels us to explore how court rulings contribute to the objective pursued by policy actors when engaging in litigation.

WINNING CAN BE ALIGNED WITH LEGAL SUCCESS

Success in court and winning of the underlying conflict can be, and most of the time is, inherently connected. This is particularly the case when ideological opposition to specific supranational legal acts drives litigation, when litigation is motivated by direct material concerns, and when litigation is motivated by the wish to obtain or protect decision-making competences.

Material Gains

The connection between judicial success and the maximization of the utility of litigation is particularly evident where litigation is motivated by a concern for material resources. Most of the private claimants seek direct material benefits when going to court. Clearly, where they have success in court, they win. We saw in Chapter 5 that public actors also hold direct economic interests that can be pursued via annulment actions. Virtually all annulment actions in the area of agriculture and regional funds involve financial issues. Here, member states litigate against the Commission's decisions to impose financial correction, consisting in refusing to reimburse to the member states a sum they spent under the Common Agriculture Policy or EU cohesion policies when the Commission's auditors find that national authorities have committed irregularities. EU rules on how EU funds must be spent are complex.

This increases the likelihood of irregularities. When a member state challenges a Commission decision denying the transfer of funds corresponding to the irregularity found, the member state expects that the Court will force the Commission to proceed to the transfer. When the Court rules that the member state is right, the Commission's decision denying the transfer is annulled and the Commission has to reimburse the money spent. Here, the correspondence between judicial success and policy objective is very clear.

Institutional Competences

We have seen that a public actor may litigate in order to protect its decision-making competences from an over-reaching EU institution. There are many cases in state aid, for example, where the member states or regional governments raised an annulment action against a Commission decision that was perceived as a clear instance of competence creep. Often, the member state loses. In Chapter 5, we mentioned the *Leipzig-Halle* and *Dresden Airport* cases (T-396/08, T-215/9), where the Saxon government litigated in order to put a halt on what was perceived as a competence creep of the Commission. In this case, for the first time, the Commission considered the construction of airport infrastructure as an economic activity in the sense of EU state aid law and posited that the Commission thus needed to be notified. This was new; up to this moment, the Commission had never put out this interpretation. Saxony's decision to litigate was mainly driven by the attempt to fend off the Commission's attempt to become more strongly involved in regional infrastructure projects. Yet it remained unsuccessful.

The ruling had a highly significant effect on the redistribution of competences between the member states and the Commission in the field of infrastructure construction. After the ruling, Joaquim Almunia, then the Commissioner for Competition, declared that the Court's judgement was applicable to all kinds of infrastructure, independent of the sector concerned. Such an extrapolation from airports to any kind of infrastructure was unexpected because state aid law is sector specific. This led to a huge increase in the number of state aid case notifications submitted to the Commission, which became overwhelmed by the increase in workload (MIN_SA_1). Nevertheless, the Commission further consolidated its new and enhanced ability to influence regional infrastructure projects by adopting several on sector-specific guidelines for regional infrastructure projects.[3]

Particularly in the area of state aid, annulment litigation was not able to sustainably limit the Commission's competence creep. A series of cases dealing with a Spanish tax scheme that would grant tax deductions to Spanish companies that acquire shares of companies located outside the EU (T-219/10, T-399/11). In these cases, Autogrill SA, Banco Santander, and other companies attacked the Commission for declaring this provision in the Spanish tax code to be incompatible with EU law. According to the EU's state aid law, aid granted selectively to some companies but not to others is generally illegal unless the aid meets a number of exceptional criteria. In a very broad interpretation of this provision, the Commission saw this criterion to be fulfilled since only companies that acquire foreign companies benefit from the tax benefit but not companies that acquire Spanish firms. The applicants perceived this to be an erroneous application of the selectivity concept and went to court. Specifically, the applicants went to the General Court in first instance. The General Court shared the view of the applicants and developed stricter conditions that would have to be met by the Commission when trying to assess the selectivity of tax measures. For the private companies, legal success in court meant a clear victory since it helped them to realize their tax benefits. Also, the Spanish government welcomed this ruling as it effectively constrained the Commission's ability to intrude on its national tax policy.

Yet the Commission appealed the decision of the General Court before the Court of Justice. Given the high redistributive effects at stake for the member states, three of them—Spain, Germany, and Ireland— joined the case in support of the private companies in appeal. The Court overturned the ruling of the General Court based on the argument that the General Court had misapplied the selectivity criterion. 'For state aid specialists and tax lawyers, this decision was bound to be a landmark case, whatever it would turn out to hold'.[4] Legal defeat for the Commission would seriously compromise its impact on state aid provided through national tax measures, while legal success would pave the way for stronger influence in this area. The case was effectively seen as widely stretching the concept of selectivity,[5] which, mechanically, leads to a wide stretch of the Commission's capacity to use EU state aid law to veto national fiscal mechanisms. This redistribution of competences between the Commission and the member states in the field of tax policy was directly connected to legal success and legal defeat in this particular case.

Another policy area where annulment litigation has resulted in clear-cut competence gains for the Commission, here acting as a plaintiff, is external policy. Importantly, the first annulment case ever launched between EU institutions falls into this category. Traditionally, member states would negotiate international agreements in all areas that do not fall within the EU's competence, such as in external trade deals. The *ERTA* case (C-22/70), launched by the Commission against the Council, deals with this right of the Commission to negotiate international agreements (see our discussion of this case in Chapter 5). The Council had authorized member states to negotiate and conclude an international transport agreement that included social rules for the protection of drivers (today, Article 95 TFEU). It did so by claiming that transport was an area of member state competence. The Commission felt that the Council had overstepped its competences and launched an annulment to shift the legal base so negotiation powers would fall on the Commission (Article 207, ex. Article 133 Treaty on European Union). The Court agreed that the existence of *acquis communitaire* harmonizing social provisions in transport (Council Regulation [EEC] No. 543/69[6]) necessarily vested any international agreement that concerned transport in community powers, consequently excluding concurring powers of member states. Winning this case enabled the Commission to expand external policy competences to areas where the Community holds internal competences. This became known as the principle of implied powers and was further developed and fixed in the Nice Treaty (Cremona 2011). Success in court thus meant winning competences beyond the more narrow right to negotiate trade agreements and altered the relationship of the EU institutions.

Ideological and Policy Preferences

Furthermore, winning tends to be closely connected to legal success in court if the motivation to litigate is dominated by the wish to challenge a supranational legal act due to ideological opposition. Where a supranational legal act directly interferes with core beliefs of what is right and wrong as well as with policies that are built on these normative beliefs, then winning a conflict is inherently tied to the ability to win the legal case and thereby abolish the ideological threat.

A good example is the passenger rights case (cf. cases C-317/04 and C-318/04, discussed in Chapter 5). The European Parliament

(EP) challenged agreements that the Council and the Commission had negotiated internationally. The Parliament considered these agreements to violate fundamental individual rights related to data privacy. In an attempt to avoid litigation, the Commission actively approached members of Parliament by trying to convince them that litigation 'was not a good idea' (COM_2). Yet the Commission failed to dissolve ideological concerns over data privacy simply based on strategic concerns. The EP won this case in court. This legal success was also a political success as it helped the Parliament to push forward the legislative agenda on the General Data Protection Regulation.[7]

An example of an unsuccessful attempt to promote ideological preferences is the Spanish coal case (T-57/11), discussed in Chapter 6. This case was triggered by a decree adopted by the Spanish government that altered the rules of the Spanish electricity market in favour of Spanish coal mines. This was seen as one important step in trying to save the Spanish coal sector from further decay. The Commission considered that the Spanish measure was not contrary to EU state aid law and authorized the measure. This decision sparked controversy within Spain. Castelnou, a small company that felt discriminated against by the Spanish decree, raised an annulment action against the Commission's authorization, and several national actors, both private and public, joined the conflict to intervene in favour of either the applicant or the defendant. Greenpeace intervened in support of Castelnou in the hope of further containing attempts to subsidize the exploitation of fossil fuels in the EU. 'Non-governmental organizations like Greenpeace are only very rarely given an opportunity to argue before the EU Courts. This case is therefore a special opportunity to challenge some three-quarters of energy subsidies in the EU that still go towards fossil fuels' (Simons 2014). Greenpeace's legal objective was thus to promote a rebalancing of the interaction between environmental rules and state aid law in favour of the former. Yet the Court's conclusion was unfavourable to this ideologically motivated view promoted by Greenpeace. In the ruling, the Court specified that where the Commission 'assesses an aid measure which does not pursue an environmental objective, the Commission is not required to take account of EU rules on protection of the environment', and 'limits the verification of compliance with the rules, other than those relating to State aid, solely to those rules capable of having a negative impact on the internal market' (General Court 2014, 2). This ruling clearly circumscribed the extent to which environmental objectives can trump other policy objectives in the context of state aid law. While the Commission had not pushed to extend its decision criteria to evaluate state aid in this specific context, the Court's judgement creates a barrier to do so in the future.

WINNING CAN BE DISCONNECTED FROM LEGAL SUCCESS

Policy actors may benefit from a ruling of the Court in which they lose. Cases abound where the redistributive effect of the rulings on policy actors do not coincide strictly with the Court's decision about who the winner of the judicial conflict is. This disconnection between redistributive effect and ruling is particularly clear when the annulment action is raised with a view to maximize political trust domestically or to clarify (in addition to maximize) the distribution of institutional competences. This has specific implications for complex litigant constellations. As argued above, complex constellations are more likely to comprise compound motivations, particularly in cases with different types of actors involved. But where actors seek different objectives, the very same ruling can produce more than one winner or more than one loser on these different grounds. Consequently, annulment conflicts characterized by complex actor constellations are likely to be more nuanced in terms of winners and loser. In a way, rather than producing only winners or only losers, success and defeat are likely to be multidimensional.

Material Gains

When a member state loses a case over state aid against the Commission, legal defeat typically implies that the money flows back into the pockets of the state. In such cases where the state's aid measures are declared illegal retrospectively, the ministry responsible for budget easily feels like a winner (MIN_D_3). While we tend to treat member states as unitary actors before the Court because of their status as litigant, they host important internal tensions and policy conflicts. Here, we see that a court ruling rejecting the action of the state can have a redistributive effect between ministerial departments. A concrete example is the *Apple* case (T-892/16) we discussed in the introduction to this book. While we can assume the Irish Ministry of Finance to be delighted to see huge amounts of tax money being flushed into its coffers, the Ministry of Economic Affairs should certainly be less happy about gloomy investor prospects.

Institutional Competences

Also, cases in which decision-making competences are disputed, success in court might not always generate clear-cut winners. In *Council v. Commission* (C-409/13), the Council and Commission were at loggerheads over the right to withdraw proposals from the legislative process. Along with its quasi monopoly to propose legislation, the Commission has the right to withdraw legal acts from the inter-institutional decision-making process. Installed to allow checks and balances in the EU political system, this right has seldom been used. Therefore, the Council was astonished when the Commission withdrew its proposal for a regulation on general provisions for macro-financial assistance to third countries that face short-term balance-of-payment difficulties after it had altered its content. The Council criticized the Commission by noting that the Commission's right to initiate legislative initiatives did not imply a symmetrical right to withdraw proposals, particularly not for mere political reasons. Consequently, the Council challenged the Commission's decision to withdraw the proposal in court. The Court's judgement had ambivalent effects. One the one hand, the Commission won the legal case and successfully defended its right to withdraw this specific legislative proposal (COM_1). On the other hand, the Court also narrowed the Commission's ability to withdraw proposals in the future by 'clarifying that while this right exists, the Commission cannot invoke this right under any condition and in any kind of way it wants' (EP_1). The Commission's short-term success has thus also had a restricting effect in the long-term as the Court used the ruling to clarify the conditions under which the Commission would effectively be able to withdraw legislative proposals. There was thus a disconnection between imminent success in court and the winning of the general competence conflict.

Furthermore, disconnections between legal outcome and political success emerge in situations in which legal clarification is seen as a second best in cases motivated by the willingness to maximize decision-making competences. In those cases, litigants typically have a clear preference for winning the case. However, they also considered that losing this particular case would not be so bad either, as long as the judgement would clarify unclear rules and ambiguous distributions of competences (MIN_ES_7). This way, even legal defeat is not conceived as a complete loss since the legal certainty produced by the judgements will help to avoid unnecessary conflict and work in the future.

Actually, this situation often emerges after treaty changes (Bauer and Hartlapp 2010). Here, the simple manifestation of a ruling can, in fact, produce winners across the board of litigants. For example, the new comitology system coming into force with the Lisbon Treaty troubled the Commission (Brandsma and Blom-Hansen 2017). Here, the EP claimed that any comitology act had to be considered an implementing act and thus had to be agreed upon according to a procedure endowing it with relatively more influence. The Council, in contrast, had an institutional interest in declaring all comitology acts to be delegated acts. Sitting uneasily between these two options, the Commission feared that it would be exploited by the two as 'a kind of a bargaining chip' (COM_1). A number of annulment actions were launched by the EP and the Commission on the usage of delegated or implementing powers (see, for example, cases C-427/12; C-65/13; and C-88/14). The situation was characterized by general disagreement over the concept of implementation versus delegation as well as uncertainty about what rules would apply. The Commission claimed, for example, that the concept of implementing powers would apply to the online platform *EURES* that allowed for EU-wide job advertisements and job searches to promote job mobility. It claimed that this was the case despite the narrowing of its usage under the Lisbon Treaty. While the Commission was not successful in court, it gained legal certainty for further practices. 'The judgement was useful to that extent, because the Court—actually it was dismissed so we lost the case—but we obtained clarification and the Court said very clearly what an implementing act can do and what it cannot do' (EP_1). The ruling also had consequences at the level of administrative practices. In an attempt to be better able to secure its substantial interests in the altered setting, the Commission secretariat general with the legal service and the secretary general issued an internal guideline advising Commission staff on how to deal with the situation from now on (COM_1). Thus, this case shows how CJEU rulings (indirectly) affect the daily practice of the EU institutions in their interaction.

Political Trust

Finally, where litigation is motivated by gains in political trust, the ruling itself might be of little relevance to determine winners and losers. In these cases, the value of the legal conflict for a plaintiff can be independent of legal success in court. Analytically, these conflicts are best conceptualized as being part of a two-level game (Putnam 1988), where actors can be indifferent towards legal defeat at the supranational level because the mere act of going to court helps them carry home political benefit at the domestic level. The decoupling of the decision to take an active part in judicial proceedings from expectations about the outcome of such proceedings is thus a result of the long duration of the proceedings and the short time horizons of elected officials who are able to reap immediate benefits from the initiation of litigation. When politicians opt for legal conflict based on its value for populist signalling and not on the probability of winning, legal defeat is likely to be more frequent.

A case that illustrates this is the Austrian transit (C-356/01) conflict. In this case, the Austrian government found it worthwhile to initiate annulment litigation against the Commission for refusing to reduce the quota of freight trucks that could legally transit through Austria. This quota had been introduced before Austria joined the EU in order to reduce the country's environmental burden from haulage companies travelling back and forth between Germany and Italy. Generally, this provision held that if the number of trucks in transit through Austria exceeded a certain threshold in any one year, the quota would be lowered for the following year to compensate for the excess. To implement this provision, the Austrian authorities installed a system whereby trucks in transit were counted electronically. In 2001, Austria demanded that the Commission lower the quota based on this data. However, the Commission refused to accommodate Austria's application because it had doubts about the correctness of the data the country had presented. The CJEU subsequently supported the Commission's decision. Following public protest, including several blockades of the Brenner motorway (the most important transit route through the Austrian Alps that connects Germany and Italy) in 1998 and 2000, the formation of social movements such as Transitforum Tirol and the involvement of environmental interest organizations (e.g. Alpenforum), transit traffic became a highly politicized issue in Austria. With the electorate organizing around this issue, Austria's government likely feared that accepting the Commission's position would endanger its perceived integrity, particularly in the affected regions. The annulment actions thus enabled the government to communicate its loyalty and commitment to national constituents and made the legal conflict public via the media. Signalling commitment to affected constituents was a more dominant rationale for the initiation of litigation than the prospect of legal success. Austria's transport minister, Hubert Gorbach, calmly explained in 2003 that the Court's dismissal of Austria's action for annulment had no implications for the country anyway, and thereby openly voiced the government's indifference towards the legal outcome of the dispute.[8,9]

Conclusion

This chapter addressed the last step in our sequential chain argumentation. Having explored different motivations underlying judicial conflict and how they translate into litigant constellations, we turned to the question of how such complex configurations relate to legal success and broader policy and institutional outcomes.

In line with strategic models of judicial behaviour, we also argued that success rates in court vary systematically across different kinds of litigant configurations. Importantly, however, we developed a radically different interpretation of the relationship between litigants' configurations and ruling outcomes. While litigant configurations are typically treated as exogenous factors, we highlighted the need for models of judicial behaviour to endogenize these configurations. Only when we take into account that different litigant configurations tend to emerge in different legal conflict situations, will we be able to understand the empirical association between litigant configuration and court rulings.

More specifically, we argued that complex constellations are more likely to be characterized by higher legal uncertainty and greater variety of legal perspectives presented to and evaluated by the Court when adopting its ruling. This is what explains the substantially greater share of claimant success in complex as opposed to simple conflict configurations. Our statistical analyses, as well as the case study evidence, support this argument.

This argument reflects a similar idea to the one promoted by Davies (2018). Davies claims that the CJEU's recent tendency to side with member states rather than private litigants over questions of rights associated with EU citizenship cannot easily be attributed to a changing judicial perspective or to increasing member state influence. Rather, one has to consider that it is not the Court that has changed, but the cases. With less meritorious cases brought by private litigants, lower success rates are inevitable.

This chapter also brought new insights to the relationship between litigation and broader policy and institutional impacts. It is important to assess the different kinds of impacts that rulings may have, beyond the immediate success or defeat before the courts (Scheingold 1974; Lobel 1994; McCann 1994; NeJaime 2011). We followed up on this approach, extending it to all types of actors raising annulment actions in the EU, while linking it more explicitly with the multilevel policy conflict from which litigation emerges. Starting from the premise that there are a variety of political goods sought by litigants when raising an annulment action (material gains, institutional power, ideology, and political trust), we assessed the relationship between a favourable ruling and the litigant's achievement of the primary goal underpinning its decision to litigate. We found that legal success is often directly related to the litigant's broader objectives; especially when seeking the maximization of material gain, institutional power, and ideological preferences. Legal success can, however, also be entirely disconnected from the litigant's genuine victory in terms of it achieving the objectives underlying its motivation to go to court. Since 'it is not always about winning' (Adam et al. 2015), a litigant may be perfectly satisfied, even in case of legal defeat, as long as the action has allowed it to reach its objectives. We posit that this disconnection between legal success and genuine achievement is particularly likely when, first, litigants use litigation as a way to maximize political trust. Here, litigation is conceived as a symbolic act, more than as a way to change the legal order. Second, this is the case when litigants are seeking, as a secondary objective, legal clarification in situations of unclear distribution of competences. By emphasizing this relationship between legal success and a rulings' broader redistribution impacts, we link back ruling outcomes to the policy conflict from which litigation emerges in the first place, thereby closing the cycle through which litigation and courts intervene in multilevel policy conflicts in the EU. In the following final chapter, we summarize the individual sequences of our argument and our main findings. Moreover, we discuss the implications our study may have for further research in this area.

CASES CITED

See Table 7.2.

Table 7.2 Cases cited in this chapter

C-356/01	Judgment of 20 November 2003, *Austria v. Commission*, C-356/01, EU:C:2003:630
C-317/04; C-318/04	Judgment of 30 May 2006, *Parliament v. Council*, Joined Cases C-317/04 and C-318/04, EU:C:2006:346
C-427/12	Judgment of 18 March 2014, *Commission and Parliament v. Council*, C-427/12, EU:C:2014:170
C-65/13	Judgment of 15 October 2014, *Parliament v. Commission*, C-65/13, EU:C:2014:2289
C-409/13	Judgment of 14 April 2015, *Council v. Commission*, C-409/13, EU:C:2015:217
C-88/14	Judgment of 16 July 2015, *Commission v. Parliament and Council*, C-88/14, EU:C:2015:499
T-396/08	Judgment of 8 July 2010, *Sachsen and Sachsen-Anhalt v. Commission*, T-396/08, EU:T:2010:297
T-215/9	Order of 18 March 2013, *Sachsen v. Commission*, T-215/09, EU:T:2013:132
T-219/10	Judgment of 7 November 2014, *Autogrill España v. Commission*, T-219/10, EU:T:2014:939
T-57/11	Judgment of 3 December 2014, *Castelnou Energia v. Commission*, T-57/11, EU:T:2014:1021
T-399/11	Judgment of 5 December 2014, *Banco Santander v. Commission*, T-399/11, EU:T:2014:938
T-134/14	Order of 8 June 2015, *Germany v. Commission*, T-134/14, EU:T:2015:392
T-671/14	Judgment of 12 September 2017, *BMW v. Commission*, T-671/14, EU:T:2017:599
T-47/15	Judgment of 10 May 2016, *Germany v. Commission*, T-47/15, EU:T:2016:281
T-683/15	Judgment of 12 December 2018, *Freistaat Bayern v. Commission*, EU:T:2018:916
T-892/16	Order of 15 December 2017, *Apple v. Commission*, T-892/16, EU:T:2017:925f

Notes

1. Exchange of information and of legal arguments need not always be strategic. In a case related to a decision of the Commission declaring a clause in German tax law as incompatible with EU state aid law (T-205/11), about twenty German companies raised an annulment action, and the German government intervened as a supporter in these actions. Within the German tax law scene, which organizes meetings gathering German tax law specialists and involving lawyers of the German ministry of economy, the restructuring clause case has been discussed, and legal arguments were

exchanged. However, no information specific to each annulment action was exchanged; the discussions remained general, focusing on the German clause attacked by the Commission (COMP_4).
2. Essentially, this analysis helps us to compare means across different groups. To do so, it compares the variance of means between different groups to the variance within these groups. If the variance across groups is substantially larger than the variance within groups, we dare to assume these groups to be in fact distinct from each other.
3. European Commission, 'Guidance on the notion of State aid'. Accessed 21 February 2017. http://ec.europa.eu/competition/state_aid/modernisation/notice_aid_en.html.
4. Raymond Luja, 'Clarifying the scope of selectivity: How to (Auto) grill a Commission decision on fiscal state aid?', Maastricht University Blog, 23 December 2016, https://www.maastrichtuniversity.nl/blog/2016/12/clarifying-scope-selectivity-how-autogrill-commission-decision-fiscal-state-aid.
5. Phedon Nicolaides, 'Selectivity stretched'. State Aid Blog, 24 January 2017, http://stateaidhub.eu/blogs/stateaiduncovered/post/7842.
6. Regulation (EEC) No 543/69 of the Council of 25 March 1969 on the harmonisation of certain social legislation relating to road transport, Official Journal L 77, 29.3.1969, pp. 49–60
7. Regulation (EU) 2016/679 of the European Parliament and of the Council of 27 April 2016 on the protection of natural persons with regard to the processing of personal data and on the free movement of such data, and repealing Directive 95/46/EC (General Data Protection Regulation), Official Journal L 119, 4.5.2016, pp. 1–88.
8. Ökopunkte-Urteil: EU zählt richtig', Die Presse, 20 November 2003
9. This case description can also be found in Adam et al. (2015).

REFERENCES

Adam, C., Bauer, M. W., & Hartlapp, M. (2015). It's not always about winning: Domestic politics and legal success in EU annulment litigation. *Journal of Common Market Studies, 53*(2), 185–200.

Bauer, M. W., & Hartlapp, M. (2010). Much ado about money and how to spend it! Analysing 40 years of annulment cases against the European Union Commission. *European Journal of Political Research, 49*, 202–222.

Brandsma, G. J., & Blom-Hansen, J. (2017). *Controling the EU executive? The politics of delegation in the European Union*. Oxford, UK: Oxford University Press.

Burley, A.-M., & Mattli, W. (1993). Europe before the court: A political theory of legal integration. *International Organization, 47*(1), 41–76.

Cappelletti, M., Seccombe, M., & Weiler, J. H. H. (Eds.). (1986). *Integration through law: Europe and the American Federal Experience: Vol. 1, Methods, tools and institutions, Book 2, Political organs, integration techniques and judicial process*. Berlin: Walter De Gruyter.

Carrubba, C. J., Gabel, M., & Hankla, C. (2008). Judicial behavior under political constraints: Evidence from the European Court of Justice. *American Political Science Review, 102*(4), 435–452.

Carrubba, C. J., Gabel, M., & Hankla, C. (2012). Understanding the role of the European Court of Justice in European integration. *American Political Science Review, 106*(1), 214–224.

Cremona, M. (2011). External relations and external competences of the European Union: The emergence of an integrated policy. In P. Craig & G. de Burca (Eds.), *The evolution of EU law* (pp. 217–268). Oxford, UK: Oxford University Press.

Davies, G. (2018). Has the Court changed, or have the cases? The deservingness of litigants as an element in Court of Justice citizenship adjudication. *Journal of European Public Policy, 25*, 1442–1460.

Davis, C. L., & Bermeo, S. B. (2009). Who files? Developing country participation in GATT/WTO adjudication. *The Journal of Politics, 71*(3), 1033–1049.

Epp, C. R. (1998). *The rights revolution: Lawyers, activists, and supreme courts in comparative perspective*. Chicago: University of Chicago Press.

Farole, D. J. (1999). Reexamining litigant success in state supreme courts. *Law and Society Review, 33*(4), 1043–1058. https://doi.org/10.2307/3115158.

Galanter, M. (1974). Why the "haves" come out ahead: Speculations on the limits of legal change. *Law and Society Review, 9*(1), 95–160.

Garrett, G., Kelemen, R. D., & Schulz, H. (1998). The European Court of Justice, national governments, and legal integration in the European Union. *International Organization, 52*(1), 149–176.

Garrett, G., & Weingast, B. R. (1993). Ideas, interests, and institutions: Constructing the European Community's internal market. In J. Goldstein & R. O. Keohane (Eds.), *Ideas in foreign policy: Beliefs, institutions, and political change* (pp. 173–206). Ithaca, NY: Cornell University Press.

General Court of the European Union. (2014, December 3). Press Release No. 165/14. Judgement in Case T-57/11 *Castelnou Energia SL v. Commission*. Luxembourg.

Haire, S. B., Lindquist, S. A., & Hartley, R. (1999). Attorney expertise, litigant success, and judicial decision-making in the U.S. Courts of Appeals. *Law and Society Review, 33*(3), 667–685. https://doi.org/10.2307/3115107.

Höpner, M. (2011). Der europäische Gerichtshof als Motor der europäischen Integration: Eine akteursbezogene Erklärung. *Berliner Journal für Soziologie, 21*(2), 203–229.

Kim, M. (2008). Costly procedures: Divergent effects of legalization in the GATT/WTO dispute settlement procedures. *International Studies Quarterly, 52*(3), 657–686.

Larsson, O., & Naurin, D. (2016). Judicial independence and political uncertainty: Assessing the effect of legislative override on the European Court of Justice. *International Organization, 70*(2), 377–408.

Lobel, J. (1994). Losers fools and prophets: Justice as struggle. *Cornell Law Review 80*, 1331–1421.

Malecki, M. (2012). Do ECJ judges all speak with the same voice? Evidence of divergent preferences from the judgments of chambers. *Journal of European Public Policy, 19*(1), 59–75.

McCann, M. W. (1994). *Rights at work: Pay equity reform and the politics of legal mobilization*. Chicago: University of Chicago Press.

McGuire, K. T. (1995). Repeat players in the Supreme Court: The role of experienced lawyers in litigation success. *The Journal of Politics, 57*(1), 187–196. https://doi.org/10.2307/2960277.

NeJaime, D. (2011). Winning through losing. *Iowa Law Review, 96*, 941–1012.

Putnam, R. D. (1988). Diplomacy and domestic politics: The logic of two-level games. *International Organization, 42*(3), 427–460. https://doi.org/10.1017/S0020818300027697.

Scharpf, F. W. (2002). The European social model: Coping with the challenges of diversity. *Journal of Common Market Studies, 40*(4), 645–670.

Scharpf, F. W. (2007). Europe's neo-liberal bias. In A. Hemerijck, B. Knapen, & E. van Doorne (Eds.), *Economic crisis and institutional choice* (pp. 228–234). Amsterdam: Amsterdam University Press.

Scheingold, S. (1974). *The politics of rights: Lawyers, public policy, and social change*. New Haven, CT: Yale University Press.

Segal, J. A., & Spaeth, H. J. (2002). *The Supreme Court and the attitudinal model revisited*. Cambridge, UK: Cambridge University Press.

Shapiro, M. (1980). Comparative law and comparative politics. *Southern California Law Review, 53*, 537–542.

Sheehan, R. S., Mishler, W., & Songer, D. R. (1992). Ideology, status, and the differential success of direct parties before the Supreme Court. *American Political Science Review, 86*(2), 464–471. https://doi.org/10.2307/1964234.

Simons, D. (2014). *Should the European Commission wear green goggles more often? Greenpeace International.* http://www.greenpeace.org/international/en/news/Blogs/makingwaves/Castelnou-Energia-v-Commission/blog/50868/. Accessed 22 August 2017.

Skiple, J. K., Grendstad, G., Shaffer, W. R., & Waltenburg, E. N. (2016). Supreme Court justices economic behaviour: A multilevel model analysis. *Scandinavian Political Studies, 39*(1), 73–94. https://doi.org/10.1111/1467-9477.12060.

Stone Sweet, A., & Brunell, T. L. (2012). The European Court of Justice, state noncompliance, and the politics of override. *American Political Science Review, 106,* 204–213.

Stone Sweet, A., & Brunell, T. L. (2013). Trustee courts and the judicialization of international regimes: The politics of majoritarian activism in the ECHR, the EU, and the WTO. *Journal of Law and Courts, 1*(1), 61–88.

Tridimas, G., & Tridimas, T. (2004). National courts and the European Court of Justice: A public choice analysis of the preliminary reference procedure. *International Review of Law and Economics, 24*(2), 125–145. https://doi.org/10.1016/j.irle.2004.08.003.

Vauchez, A. (2012). Keeping the dream alive: The European Court of Justice and the transnational fabric of integrationist jurisprudence. *European Political Science Review, 4*(1), 51–71.

Open Access This chapter is licensed under the terms of the Creative Commons Attribution 4.0 International License (http://creativecommons.org/licenses/by/4.0/), which permits use, sharing, adaptation, distribution and reproduction in any medium or format, as long as you give appropriate credit to the original author(s) and the source, provide a link to the Creative Commons license and indicate if changes were made.

The images or other third party material in this chapter are included in the chapter's Creative Commons license, unless indicated otherwise in a credit line to the material. If material is not included in the chapter's Creative Commons license and your intended use is not permitted by statutory regulation or exceeds the permitted use, you will need to obtain permission directly from the copyright holder.

CHAPTER 8

The Political Side of EU Annulment Litigation

There is more to annulment actions than political science or legal scholarship have so far brought to our attention. As we showed in this book, annulment actions are part of the struggle about money, policies, competences, and votes in the emerging multilevel political order of the European Union (EU). Annulment actions embody vertical and horizontal tensions among public and private actors that purposefully take their conflicts to the European judicial arena. Annulment litigation works as a defence attempt of last resort; annulments are regularly the last chance to undo actions by supranational institutions. Against this backdrop, we have investigated the genuine political nature of annulment litigation with three analytical focal points: actors' motivations to litigate, actor configurations in court, and the outcome and impacts of annulment judgements. We now turn to the insights gleaned from our empirical analysis regarding these three aspects of annulment litigation dealing with the emergence, structure, and outcome of annulment actions.

While we separated these aspects of annulment litigation analytically by discussing them within individual chapters, our argument and analysis overall is driven by the assumption that it is crucial to understand the interrelatedness of emergence, structure, and outcomes of annulment litigation. Together, these aspects constitute a causal chain. To separate them is, of course, vital for analytical reasons. However, emergence, structure, and outcome of annulment actions are not independent from one another. Rather, they co-determine each other. A major insight of our analysis is that the three-fold elements of the annulment struggle feed into each other, thereby amalgamating the legal with the political struggle of EU multilevel policy making. This is why throughout this study we have developed a sequential approach to analyse annulment litigation.

THE MOTIVATIONS BEHIND ANNULMENT ACTIONS

The first set of questions we raised dealt with the motivations of policy actors to take legal steps and turn to the Court. The EU policy process involves many distinct actors located at different governmental levels and active in different arenas. As a result, a wide array of interests, political preferences, values, cultures, and understandings interact and often clash. Annulment actions constitute one possible legal channel for transferring policy conflicts into the judicial arena, and annulments are raised regularly by a large variety of private and public actors that can be located on the subnational, national, European, or—in the case of multinational companies—even the global level.

While the litigation literature generally investigates the conditions under which specific actors decide to litigate, we focus on their motivations for litigating. In other words, since we already know from existing literature when actors are likely to go to court, we decided to focus on the 'why' question. Why do actors raise annulment cases in front of the Court and what are their objectives? What kind of utility do they associate with annulment litigation? What are they really after?

These questions are usually hidden as implicit assumptions in the litigation literature, which has essentially focussed on companies and non-governmental organizations (NGOs) (Gould 1973; Bouwen and McCown 2007; Vanhala 2011). While companies are generally assumed to litigate to maximize material gains, NGOs are seen to litigate to push for their ideological and policy preferences. These assumptions are plausible; however, they do still need to be substantiated empirically— especially when other actor categories come into play. Indeed, we also have some indications in the litigation literature that financial and ideological payoffs may not always be what litigants seek when turning to the courts. Influencing a court's legal doctrine or gaining bargaining power (Galanter 1974; Schmidt 2000; Granger 2004) can also be important objectives for litigants when turning to courts. Assuming a dominance of financial concerns and ideology in litigation decisions seems, especially for public actors, overly simplistic. Public actors are, after all, committed to a variety of objectives, not least keeping or expanding political power and institutional competences in addition to securing financial resources.

This study showed that in annulment actions, it is the multilevel political context that prompts litigants' decisions to turn to court. Locating actors' action in the context of the struggles they go through in the multilevel policy process allows identifying their needs and subsequently the utility they associate with litigation. We found four types of motivations driving the use of annulment actions; litigants turn to the EU Court to maximize material gains, institutional competences, ideological and policy preferences, and political trust. While these four motivations constitute real types, they are not mutually exclusive at the level of empirical cases; in other words, one annulment action can be driven by more than one motivation. Yet our case studies allowed for the identification of the single most dominant motivation underlying a particular case.

First, material gains constitute the quantitatively most important motivation. In these cases, litigation is pursued when success in court would significantly improve the litigant's budget situation, by either avoiding substantial expenses or maximising revenue. This motivation is crucial for governments and for regional, subnational authorities confronted with Commission decisions imposing financial corrections in agriculture or cohesion policies. This motivation is also important for companies having benefitted from domestic state aid that is later declared illegal by the Commission. In these cases, litigating is often the only option that can help to avoid having to pay back subsidies.

Second, litigation is pursued when the Court's interpretation of unclear legal concepts may significantly improve the litigant's institutional and decision-making competences. This motivation is often found among public actors, both national and European, in the face of a measure adopted that appears to the litigant as a competence-stretch threatening to reduce its own institutional powers.

Third, ideology drives litigation when this provides an opportunity to defend or promote an important ideological or policy position by establishing or keeping a normative order. In the cases we have explored here, ideology is most likely to show when strongly politicized actors such as NGOs (private litigants) become involved or public actors engage in party politics.

Fourth and finally, annulment litigation can also be used as a political symbol to signal responsiveness and trustworthiness to the litigant's electorate or to important political partners. This motivation is current among actors that are directly elected at the subnational, national, or supranational level, such as governments or the European Parliament. Analysing annulment actions with the frame developed in this book thus allows capturing the conflictive dimension of EU multilevel governance. Annulment politics highlights that multilevel interaction in the EU has more to it than the processes of cooperation and coordination often dominating scholarly focus.

We have emphasized the political character of annulment actions. This is not to say that legal factors are irrelevant. On the contrary, legal aspects do play a crucial role in actor's decisions to engage in litigation. Legal factors, however, usually relate to the 'when' question; they are located on a different analytical plane as the identification of actors' motivations to engage in litigation. Even when actors are motivated to litigate, very bleak chances of legal success can nevertheless lead them to dismiss this option. As we showed, once we understand what actors are seeking, we can clarify the conditions for their decision to opt for litigation in order to achieve their objective. This is where legal factors come in.

The literature on litigation economics emphasizes the probability of winning as an essential element in litigants' risk-benefit analysis underpinning their decision to litigate (Gould 1973). While this is hard to refute, our findings give more nuanced insights into its role in the litigation decision. More often than not, the benefit considered is political rather than financial. This considerably limits litigants' capacity to quantify the benefits they expect to gain. Consequently, risk-benefit assessments of the utility of litigation often need to be far less scientific and objective as assumed within economic models of litigation.

Second, we found that chances of legal success in front of the Court—though important—are not systematically considered as such by potential litigants. Often—and this is particularly true for public actors—litigants are satisfied with the presence of a certain legal uncertainty, while the exact scope of legal uncertainty hardly plays a role in their decision to litigate. Since the economics of litigation literature refers implicitly to chances of success, it considers that legal uncertainty is measurable in one way or another and that the scope of legal uncertainty—the litigant's chances of success—is a determinant factor in the decision to litigate (Gould 1973; Landes 1974). By contrast, as soon as the financial, institutional, ideological, or political stakes of the case become important, most of the public actors we talked to were satisfied with a small degree of legal uncertainty that would allow them to present decent legal arguments in court without risking their reputation in Luxembourg. When limited resources force them to select cases for litigation among several conflicts, it is more the political, institutional, or material relevance of the case than its legal merits that dominates the filtering process.

The importance of the legal factor, in the form of chances of success, also varies depending on the litigant. The risk-benefit analysis found in the economics of litigation literature is certainly important to private actors, particularly to companies. For them, the costs of preparing annulment litigation are non-trivial, and the expected benefits strongly depend on judicial success. In contrast, as we show in the case studies, public actors' individual decisions of litigation do not impose significant additional costs, and the utility of annulment litigation does not systematically require judicial success. Hence, as public actors are facing different incentives and constraints, their decisions to litigate are much less dependent on the scope of legal uncertainty surrounding the case than for private companies. While the legal uncertainty surrounding the conflicts does play an important role, this role is not as dominant as economic models of litigation suggest.

Last but not least, our findings emphasize the multilevel and multi-actor nature of annulment actions. Far from being restricted to conflicts between the Commission and the member states (in the case of infringement proceedings) or formally channelled through an interaction between national and European judges (like preliminary rulings), annulment actions are a direct strategy to 'judicialise' (as we refer to the process) conflicts between a wide variety of actors located on different governmental levels in the European Union. The material gains motivation for litigation coins conflicts between member states governments and EU institutions and between national companies and the Commission. The institutional competences motivation generally drives conflicts between member states governments and the EU and between EU institutions among themselves; the ideological motivation is found in vertical conflicts between member states or NGOs and EU institutions and among EU institutions. The political trust motivation generally underpins annulment actions in which national or regional governments judicialise conflict with an EU institution to send a positive signal to their constituency at home. In sum, annulment actions truly are a judicial manifestation of the multilevel and multidimensional nature of the EU policy process.

Actor Configurations in Annulment Conflicts

The multilevel governance approach conceives EU governance as composed of a variety of interactions between a wide range of actors in the EU public policy process (Benz and Eberlein 1999; Benz 2007; Schakel et al. 2015). Judicial proceedings can involve several actors and may feature private companies, NGOs, subnational governments, and other EU institutions, such as the European Central Bank or the European Parliament. In a large number of cases, the number of actors engaged in the legal conflict rises beyond the typical face-to-face duel between one applicant and one defendant as other actors join the conflict to support either applicant or defendant.

Often, it is not only the number of actors engaged in the conflict that increases, but also the variety of types of actors involved and governmental levels they are associated with. We often see highly complex multilevel actors' configurations, where different conflict lines and litigation motivations overlap and interact. As discussed in Chapter 6, litigant configurations in the context of annulment litigation are highly diverse. We employed a rather basic distinction between simple (1 v. 1) configurations and complex configurations (all other constellations). Complex constellations amount to around 26% of all vertical annulment conflicts. They come in many different forms and while they are more frequent in horizontal conflicts—a vast majority of all horizontal annulment cases are by our definition complex (81%)—they generally emerge in various different contexts. How can we explain their emergence? How can we account for the rise of multilevel complexity in annulment actions?

We are far from claiming the ability to predict the emergence of a complex actor constellation in a specific case. What we do see is that complex litigant configurations often emerge in situations of institutional turbulence. In situations in which existing institutional arrangements are in flux or are going through a phase of substantial revision, annulment litigation dealing with these unsettled institutional arrangements often involves more than just two actors. Why is this the case? First, the status quo represents a negotiated temporary equilibrium situation that tends to involve a substantial number of stakeholders. This temporary equilibrium comprises a financial dimension, an ideological dimension, an institutional or competence-related dimension, and a political or electoral dimension. Therefore, threats of disrupting the status quo hold the potential to trigger litigation by actors based on all four motivations we described in Chapter 5. Institutional turbulence unsettles the established order in many different ways. Hence, a wide range of actors, each for its own reasons, are likely to be discontented with the change and to engage in a struggle to maintain the status quo through litigation. Likewise, the multidimensional character of institutional turbulence is likely to appeal to a wide range of stakeholders interested in moving away from the status quo and ready to engage in the conflict to protect the disrupting measure. In short, as institutional turbulence disrupts different dimensions of the existing status quo, turbulence increases the stakes in different regards and affects a wide variety of policy stakeholders. Annulment litigation gives them a chance to shape their prerogatives within the emerging order.

Secondly, situations of institutional turbulence are more likely to produce legal uncertainty. Unstable situations are critical junctures where it is not yet clear which (legal) path will be chosen by a ruling. As contested measures represent a move away from the preexisting legal and policy path, whether and how the preexisting case law applies is largely unclear. The existing legal stock does not allow drawing clear conclusions and making safe predictions regarding the Court's reaction. For applicants, which have to consider an overall success rate of 24.7%, and in view of the legal uncertainty of those cases, which pushes the chances of success towards 50%, turbulence thus creates higher incentives to litigate. After all, as seen in Chapter 5, the chance of legal success is an important factor encouraging the use of litigation—although relatively more determinant for private actors and regional authorities than for member states and EU institutions. Likewise, in a situation of high legal uncertainty, actors whose interests align with those of the defendant cannot rely so much on the Court's tendency to protect EU measures challenged via annulment actions. The unpredictability of the Court's ruling serves as an incentive for these actors to actively engage in the litigation in support of the defendant, hoping their intervention can make a difference in the ruling. Put differently, whenever the status quo is disrupted, the unclear legal situation holds a substantial potential for triggering judicial law making (Adam 2016). Situations of institutional turbulence increase not only the stakes for many different policy stakeholders, they also increase the uncertainty about how the Court will rule. That, in turn, increases policy stakeholders' incentives for getting actively involved in the legal conflict. While we have highlighted above the danger of overstressing the role of expected chances of legal success promoted by economic models of litigation, it is similarly problematic to assume that legal uncertainty and the legal merits of a case systematically affect neither litigants nor the Court. In this sense, we believe legal uncertainty has to be taken into account much more than is currently the case in political models of litigation and judicial behaviour.

In sum, conflicts that take place at critical institutional junctures or at critical policy junctures are most-likely cases to attract not only one but several actors. There is a greater probability that different motivations are coming into the play. At the same time, there are higher incentives to take the conflict emerging from these motivations to court. Taking treaty changes as manifestations of potential turbulence, we found strong empirical evidence for this theorized nexus between institutional turbulences and complex actor constellations. For years with treaty modifications entering into force, we observe an average of 15% of annulment conflicts featuring a complex litigant configuration where we observe only an average of around 7% for years without such events. Our case studies further support this argument and interpretation.

The finding that institutional turbulence plays an important role in triggering such complex multilevel litigant configurations highlights one important difference between the cooperative and the conflictive dimension of multilevel governance in the EU. Multilevel governance refers to a process dominated by the superposition of coordination and interaction practices among different types of policy stakeholders located on different levels. While the cooperative side of this multilevel process seems to be a pervasive feature of the day-to-day functioning of the EU, conflicts within this process—particularly judicialised conflict—are more limited and reserved to specific situations, such as situations of institutional turbulence.

Success, Failure, and Feedback Effects

The third analytical focal point of the book is the analysis of effects of annulment actions analysed in Chapter 7. We differentiated between legal outcomes, based on who was successful in the legal case, and the more far-reaching implications of rulings on the multilevel political context from which litigation emerged.

Legal outcomes, in terms of applicants' success rates, differ substantially depending on the actor configuration involved. We have seen that in cases with certain complex litigant constellations, success rates are slightly elevated (for example, to about 32% when at least one member state and at least one private litigant jointly accuse an individual EU institution). Strategic approaches to judicial decision making assume a causal impact of litigant configurations on judicial behaviour since many powerful litigants might be able to effectively constrain the Court. We propose a fundamentally different explanation for observed correlations between litigant configurations and legal outcomes: the relationship between complex actor constellations and higher success rates in annulment actions is not primarily a causal relationship. Instead, the empirical association is merely a result of the fact that specific conflict situations not only affect the emergence of specific litigant configurations but also the emergence of certain rulings. More specifically, situations of institutional turbulence not only foster legal uncertainty. Such situations also facilitate the emergence of complex actor configurations. In this sense, we promote a similar argument as Davies (2018), who claims that the recent tendency of the Court of Justice of the European Union (CJEU) to side with member states rather than with private litigants over questions of rights associated with EU citizenship cannot easily be attributed to a changing judicial perspective or increasing member state influence. Rather, one has to consider that it has not been the Court that has changed but rather the cases that have been brought before it. With less meritorious cases brought by private litigants, lower success rates are inevitable.

We do not refute the possibility of a causal effect of litigant configurations on legal outcomes completely. Yet we do focus on the ability of litigant configurations to influence judicial behaviour by increasing the variety of legal arguments presented to the Court rather than by putting political pressure on the Court. While political models of judicial behaviour typically treat actor constellations as exogenous factors, we see it as important to integrate the theorization of the emergence of these configurations into these models. Different policy conflicts not only come with various degrees of legal certainty and predictability of court behaviour; they also attract different litigant configurations. Assuming that litigant constellations are completely independent from the legal merits of cases is therefore misleading.

Our findings suggest heading for a new approach of judicial politics. Up to now, research on judicial decision making has downplayed the impact of the political context and the nature of the conflict at stake, in particular the legal uncertainty underpinning the case, on judges' decisions. Yet if one acknowledges that case law creates legal path dependence (Schmidt 2012), one has to recognize the highly constraining power of the existing legal stock on judges' decisions. We agree in this context with Susanne K. Schmidt, who has pointed out the crucial role played by litigants in activating case law to their advantage and, thereby, pushing judges into forging and consolidating a given legal path (Schmidt 2012, 2018).

We are not, however, simply trying to reiterate the conditioning effect of case law or Schmidt's argument about the role of litigants' legal strategies in creating legal paths. Rather, we emphasize the crucial role of the nature of the conflict situation and of the specific political context in influencing the eventual impact of case law. The activation of existing case law is dependent not only on litigant's legal strategies. Litigants' capacity to mobilize existing case law highly depends on whether the case at hand lends itself to it. When annulment actions are directed against a supranational act that is very similar to previous acts and was adopted on the same legal basis, applicants enjoy a relatively high level of legal certainty. The Court's past decisions on these similar acts form well-informed expectations about their ability to win the respective case. As soon as previously established case law becomes less instructive—because of a changing legal basis or as a result of a changing content of the legal act—the less predictable judicial behaviour becomes. Consequently, a political context characterized by institutional turbulence produces legal uncertainty, which reduces the predictability of rulings and ultimately brings success rates closer to 50%.

In this sense, research that analyses the relationship between litigant configurations and legal outcomes without taking legal uncertainty into account risks suffering from a substantial omitted variable problem. In the context of annulment litigation, institutional turbulence and the legal uncertainty that comes with it act as a confounding variable that influences litigant configurations as well as legal outcomes. This only comes to light when the political context—most importantly in terms of actor motivations and institutional turbulence—is given appropriate analytical space. As a result, our approach can contribute to better understand court agency (Saurugger and Terpan 2017) and to the debate about court constraint and legislative override (Carrubba et al. 2008, 2012).

Moreover, our cases also provide insights into the wider redistributive political effects of annulment actions—beyond judicial success or defeat. In this respect, two observations stand out. First, we showed that successful litigation does not necessarily rely on winning legal proceedings. We argue that the success of litigation should always be conceptualized broadly and assessed based on litigants' general objectives and motives for entering into conflict. Chapter 5 showed that actors seek different objectives when going to court. Hence, there are many cases where the redistributive effect of the rulings on policy actors does not coincide strictly with the Court's decision about who the winner of the judicial conflict is. This disconnection between redistributive effect and ruling is particularly clear when the annulment action is raised with a view to maximize political trust domestically or to clarify (rather than maximize) the distribution of competences. This finding echoes the literature on the legal mobilization of social movements, which highlights the beneficial (secondary) effects of litigation for social movements even in case of judicial defeat (Scheingold 1974; McCann 1998; Lobel 2003; NeJaime 2011; Vanhala 2011). We go one step further by explicitly underlining that litigants' major objective, and therefore major benefit from litigation, does not need to be connected with judicial success. This argument further highlights the potential disconnection between judicial success and the functional utility of litigation. We argue that understanding this particular functional utility of litigation requires delving into the multilevel political context from which the conflict emerges. Policy stakeholders use litigation, as one tool among others, to navigate the complex EU's multilevel system. This further underlines the relevance of our multilevel policy approach to litigation.

Second, complex constellations, as they involve a higher number of litigating actors, tend to involve different types of motivations for litigation, which is particularly visible in cases featuring the involvement of different types of actors. In other words, different actors, because of their diverse positioning in the multilevel political context responsible for the rise of the conflict, seek different objectives in the judicial proceeding. When several actors intervene, several litigation motivations overlap and several conflict lines are intertwined in a single judicial proceeding, the redistributive impact of the ruling is multidimensional. The very same ruling can produce more than one winner—and more than one loser—on these different dimensions. Wider policy impacts of annulment conflicts with complex configurations are thus particularly nuanced and likely to reflect the complexity of their actor configuration.

In Chapter 1 of this book, we underlined the relevance of annulments for seizing substantial impacts on policy and actor relationships. We traced these feedback effects on the bases of cases studies. Our case studies range from constitutionalisation to adjustment to policy change. Examples for constitutionalisation are the insertion of trade negotiations related to implied powers into the treaty (Cremona 2011)—EU level— and the modification of the German constitution following the suckler-cow premiums case (Adam et al. 2015). Adjustments of procedural rules governing the interaction of institutions are constituted by Articles 290 and 291 of the Treaty on the Functioning of the European Union on delegation in comitology. Policy changes are found in the Autogrill and Banco Santander cases, which significantly expanded the scope of EU competition law to the detriment of national autonomy in fiscal policies. Discussing such broader feedback effects, we conclude that annulments are politically as well as economically highly relevant and that the increasing frequency with which annulments are used reflects their rising importance as a genuine feature of the emerging multilevel conflict over supranational decision making and implementation in the European integration process.

BEYOND THE STATE OF THE ART: HOW EXPLAINING ANNULMENT CASES CHALLENGE COMMON RESEARCH PERSPECTIVES

Annulment actions have received substantially less attention than other forms of legal conflicts in the EU—wrongly so, as our study hopefully showed. The patterns of when and how annulments matter have important implications beyond specific empirical analysis. Annulment actions are more than technical review mechanisms. They are constitutive elements of the multilevel struggle for policy making in the EU. As soon as one opens annulment analysis beyond the examination of the ruling in a narrow sense and engages with the earlier steps feeding into litigation and with the feedback effects, the importance of underlying policy conflicts as a constitutive force in the EU multilevel system comes to the fore. Rather than a constraint (Scharpf 2006; Falkner 2011), the multilevel interaction, coordination, and cooperation of governments and non-state actors in the judicial arena can be understood as a continuation

8 THE POLITICAL SIDE OF EU ANNULMENT LITIGATION   201

of actors' attempts to influence specific outcomes in the policy-making arena. Analysing the sequence connecting conflict to resulting new dynamics, feedback effects, and structuring elements for policy and polity allows us to integrate judicial processes into the functioning of the EU multilevel system of governance. At a time when the rise of tensions and crises on the global scene have intensified the potential for conflict within the EU, developing this line of reasoning will further gain relevance in the European multilevel system.

Other scholars have studied the chain from societal conflict to legal disputes. Referring to a filtering process (Van Waarden and Hildebrand 2009), a delta (Glenn 1999), or a funnel (Klages 1983), these works all look at the chain as a narrowing passageway and seek to understand what shapes the amount of litigation at its end. In contrast, the contribution of this book consists in promoting a comprehensive approach to judicial proceedings as an element of the multilevel policy process. In essence, what distinguishes our argument from existing accounts is that we try to analytically connect the motivations underlying litigation, the conditions that promote the legal actions to unfold, the litigant configurations in court, the imminent legal outcomes of litigation, and the larger judicial impact of rulings on the multilevel political context.

Our findings reveal the important mediating role of institutional turbulence in the way judicial proceedings integrate into the multilevel policy process. The deeper the disruption of the status quo initiated by policy measures adopted by EU institutional actors, the wider the range of actors concerned by the impacts of the disrupting measure and the higher the legal uncertainty of the situation. This has two consequences. First, legal uncertainty goes with low legal predictability. Such cases are characterized by higher success rates; about half of these EU measures end up being annulled by the Court. In other words, the institutional turbulence created by the disrupting act creates legal uncertainty, which is then further amplified by the difficulty to anticipate the Court's annulment ruling—whether it will defend or annul the destabilizing measure. The chain that links policy conflict to judicial conflict to feedback into political contexts shows that status quo disruption is not the end of the story; destabilization inevitably comes with a certain level of uncertainty as to what the future will bring. Second, situations of institutional turbulence create multidimensional stakes for a wide variety of stakeholders. Consequently, annulment rulings also have multidimensional feedback effects on the various actors that are part of the multilevel policy conflict.

The use of judicial proceedings in situations of institutional turbulence thus mediate—and therefore amplify—highly instable, unpredictable, and multidimensional equilibria between a wide range of actors located on different governmental levels.

Analysing annulment litigation from a perspective of multilevel governance, as has been done in this book, complements extant research on the nexus between courts and compliance in the EU based on infringements and preliminary rulings (Carrubba and Murrah 2005; Thomson et al. 2007; Hartlapp 2008; Hartlapp and Falkner 2009; Broberg and Fenger 2013; Kelemen and Pavone 2016). Our focus on annulments needs to transcend the top-down perspective typically applied to infringement rulings and the typical bottom-up perspective on preliminary references. Annulment actions are manifestations of conflict that are neither captured by preliminary rulings, which have to be handed up by national courts, nor lead to infringements procedures that EU institutions launch against noncompliant member states. After all, annulment actions represent a direct channel to the CJEU that can be used by a most diverse set of actors willing to challenge supranational actions. The conceptual contributions offered by this book reflect the resulting need for a truly multilevel perspective. We introduce the distinctions between horizontal and vertical conflicts, as well as the distinction between simple and complex conflict configurations, to capture essential features of this multilevel process while minimizing the risk of getting lost in the vast heterogeneity of these conflicts.

Future research might want to compare the use, functioning, and impact of these different legal roads to Luxembourg. Comparing the frequency with which annulment actions, infringement procedures, and preliminary references are used within different political contexts can be an interesting first analytical step in this direction. After all, there is interesting variation. In 2016, most infringement procedures were opened in the political contexts of the internal market, environment, financial services, mobility, and transport.[1] Preliminary rulings most frequently dealt with questions of the freedom of movement and establishment in the internal market as well as with intellectual property (Court of Justice of the European Union 2017, 28). Vertical annulment conflicts continue to be dominated by agricultural and state aid cases (Bauer and Hartlapp 2010), while horizontal annulment conflicts emerge most often in the area of external affairs (Hartlapp 2018). By analysing quantitative and qualitative differences between these different channels, future research should develop a more nuanced understanding of the political role of litigation and the Court within different political contexts in the European Union. This should be of interest not only to scholars of judicial politics in the EU but also to scholars interested in policy implementation and compliance. We hope our book can contribute to these debates.

Note

1. Out of the 1657 infringement cases open in 2016, 270 emerge on questions of the internal market, industry, entrepreneurship, and SME; 269 on environmental policies; 230 from financial stability, financial services, and capital markets union; and 191 from mobility and transport. See COM (2017) 370 final report from the European Commission monitoring the application of European Union law 2016 Annual Report, p. 26.

References

Adam, C. (2016). *The politics of judicial review: Supranational administrative acts and judicialized compliance conflict in the EU*. Basingstoke, UK: Palgrave Macmillan.

Adam, C., Bauer, M. W., & Hartlapp, M. (2015). It's not always about winning: Domestic politics and legal success in EU annulment litigation. *Journal of Common Market Studies, 53*(2), 185–200.

Bauer, M. W., & Hartlapp, M. (2010). Much ado about money and how to spend it! Analysing 40 years of annulment cases against the European Union Commission. *European Journal of Political Research, 49*, 202–222.

Benz, A. (2007). Accountable multilevel governance by the open method of coordination? *European Law Journal, 13*(4), 505–522.

Benz, A., & Eberlein, B. (1999). The Europeanization of regional policies: Patterns of multi-level governance. *Journal of European Public Policy, 6*(2), 329–348.

Bouwen, P., & Mccown, M. (2007). Lobbying versus litigation: Political and legal strategies of interest representation in the European Union. *Journal of European Public Policy, 14*(3), 422–443.

Broberg, M., & Fenger, N. (2013). Variations in member states' preliminary references to the court of justice—Are structural factors (part of) the explanation? *European Law Journal, 19*(4), 488–501. https://doi.org/10.1111/eulj.12045.

Carrubba, C. J., Gabel, M., & Hankla, C. (2008). Judicial behavior under political constraints: Evidence from the European Court of Justice. *American Political Science Review, 102*(4), 435–452.

Carrubba, C. J., Gabel, M., & Hankla, C. (2012). Understanding the role of the European Court of Justice in European integration. *American Political Science Review, 106*(1), 214–224.
Carrubba, C. J., & Murrah, L. (2005). Legal integration and use of the preliminary ruling process in the European Union. *International Organization, 59*(2), 399–418.
Court of Justice of the European Union. (2017). Communications Directorate—Electronic Publications and Media Unit. *Annual report 2016: The year in review.*
Cremona, M. (2011). External relations and external competences of the European Union: The emergence of an integrated policy. In P. Craig & G. de Burca (Eds.), *The Evolution of EU Law* (pp. 217–268). Oxford, UK: Oxford University Press.
Davies, G. (2018). Has the Court changed, or have the cases? The deservingness of litigants as an element in Court of Justice citizenship adjudication. *Journal of European Public Policy, 25,* 1442–1460.
Falkner, G. (Ed.). (2011). *The EU's decision traps: Comparing policies.* Oxford, UK: Oxford University Press.
Galanter, M. (1974). Why the "haves" come out ahead: Speculations on the limits of legal change. *Law and Society Review, 9*(1), 95–160.
Glenn, H. (1999). *Paths to justice: What people do and think about going to law.* Oxford, UK: Hart Publishing.
Gould, J. P. (1973). The economics of legal conflicts. *Journal of Legal Studies, 2*(2), 279–300.
Granger, M. (2004). When governments go to Luxembourg…: The influence of governments on the European Court of Justice. *European Law Review, 29,* 1–31.
Hartlapp, M. (2008). Extended governance: Implementation of EU social policy in the member states. In I. Tömmel & A. Verdun (Eds.), *Innovative governance in the European Union: The politics of multilevel policymaking* (pp. 221–236). Boulder, CO: Lynne Rienner.
Hartlapp, M. (2018). Power shifts via the judicial arena: How annulments cases between EU institutions shape competence allocation. *Journal of Common Market Studies, 56*(6), 1429–1445.
Hartlapp, M., & Falkner, G. (2009). Problems of operationalisation and data in EU compliance research. *European Union Politics, 10*(2), 291–315.
Kelemen, R. D., & Pavone, T. (2016). Mapping European law. *Journal of European Public Policy, 23*(8), 1–21. https://doi.org/10.1080/13501763.2016.1186211.
Klages, H. (1983). Ursachenfaktoren der Inspruchnahme der Ziviljustiz. *Deutsche Richterzeitung, 10,* 395–436.
Landes, William M. (1974). An economic analysis of the courts. In Gary S. Becker & William M. Landes (Eds.), *Essays in the economics of crime and punishment* (pp. 164–214). New York: Columbia University Press.

Lobel, J. (2003). *Success without victory: Lost legal battles and the long road to justice in America*. New York: New York University Press.

McCann, M. W. (1998). How does law matter for social movements? In B. G. Garth & A. Sarat (Eds.), *How does law matter?* Evanston, IL: Northwestern University Press.

NeJaime, D. (2011). Winning through losing. *Iowa Law Review, 96,* 941–1012.

Saurugger, S., & Terpan, F. (2017). *The Court of Justice of the European Union and the politics of law*. London: Palgrave.

Schakel, A. H., Hooghe, L., & Marks, G. (2015). Multilevel governance and the state. In S. Leibfried, E. Huber, M. Lange, J. D. Levy, & F. Nullmeier (Eds.), *The Oxford handbook of transformation of the state* (pp. 269–285). Oxford, UK: Oxford University Press.

Scharpf, F. W. (2006). The joint-decision trap revisited. *Journal of Common Market Studies, 44*(4), 845–864.

Scheingold, S. (1974). *The politics of rights: Lawyers, public policy, and social change*. New Haven, CT: Yale University Press.

Schmidt, S. K. (2000). Only an agenda setter? The European Commissions power over the council of ministers. *European Union Politics, 1*(1), 37–61.

Schmidt, S. K. (2012). Who cares about nationality? The path-dependent case law of the ECJ from goods to citizens. *Journal of European Public Policy, 19*(1), 8–24. https://doi.org/10.1080/13501763.2012.632122.

Schmidt, S. K. (2018). *The European Court of Justice and the policy process*. Oxford, UK: Oxford University Press.

Thomson, R., Torenvlied, R., & Arregui, J. (2007). The paradox of compliance: Infringements and delays in transposing European Union directives. *British Journal of Political Science, 37*(4), 685–709.

Van Waarden, F., & Hildebrand, Y. (2009). From corporatism to lawyocracy? On liberalization and juridification. *Regulation and Governance, 3*(3), 259–286. https://doi.org/10.1111/j.1748-5991.2009.01059.x.

Vanhala, L. (2011). *Making rights a reality? Disability rights activists and legal mobilization*. Cambridge, UK: Cambridge University Press.

Open Access This chapter is licensed under the terms of the Creative Commons Attribution 4.0 International License (http://creativecommons.org/licenses/by/4.0/), which permits use, sharing, adaptation, distribution and reproduction in any medium or format, as long as you give appropriate credit to the original author(s) and the source, provide a link to the Creative Commons license and indicate if changes were made.

The images or other third party material in this chapter are included in the chapter's Creative Commons license, unless indicated otherwise in a credit line to the material. If material is not included in the chapter's Creative Commons license and your intended use is not permitted by statutory regulation or exceeds the permitted use, you will need to obtain permission directly from the copyright holder.

Correction to: Taking the EU to Court

Correction to:
C. Adam et al., *Taking the EU to Court*,
Palgrave Studies in European Union Politics,
https://doi.org/10.1007/978-3-030-21629-0

The original version of the book was inadvertently published without incorporating the corrections in "Funding details and List of figures" which have been now incorporated. This correction to the book has been updated with the changes.

The updated version of the book can be found at
https://doi.org/10.1007/978-3-030-21629-0

© The Author(s) 2020
C. Adam et al., *Taking the EU to Court*,
Palgrave Studies in European Union Politics,
https://doi.org/10.1007/978-3-030-21629-0_9

Annexes

See Table A.1.
Guidelines for Interviews

Case-specific questions:

- What is the background of the case (Technical/economic/juridical/political background, actors involved, etc.)?
- What did the controverted Commission decision consist of?
- What kind of economic or political impact did it have on Spanish/German/regional public or private actors?
- Who made the request for initiating an action and why?
- Was there support (or opposition) by other actors affected by the decisions regarding the possibility to raise an action?
- Was there some consultation/cooperation/coordination done with these other actors? (for example, exchanging information/legal arguments or raising parallel actions or arranging intervention into the case).
- Who were the actors involved in the decision to bring an annulment action and what was their position?
- In case of divergence of positions, how has the final decision been made?

Table A.1 List of interviews

Organization	Date	Abbreviation
European Commission, Legal Service	16.06.16	COM_1
European Commission, Legal Service	16.06.16	COM_2
European Commission, DG TRADE	17.06.16	COM_3
European Parliament, Legal Service	17.06.16	EP_1
Council, Legal Service	17.06.16	CONS_1
Ministry of Agriculture, Germany	15.04.09	MIN_DE_1
Ministry of Agriculture, Germany	15.04.09	MIN_DE_2
Ministry of Economic Affairs, Germany	04.05.09	MIN_DE_3
Ministry of Economic Affairs, Germany	21.02.16	MIN_DE_4
Ministry of Food and Agriculture, Germany	10.05.16	MIN_DE_5
Ministry for Economic Affairs, Germany	17.05.16	MIN_DE_6
Ministry for Economic Affairs, Germany	17.05.16	MIN_DE_7
Ministry for Economic Affairs, Germany	17.05.16	MIN_DE_8
Ministry of Food and Agriculture, Germany	17.05.16	MIN_DE_9
Ministry of Foreign Affairs, Spain	29.06.15	MIN_ES_1
Ministry of Justice, Spain	30.06.15	MIN_ES_2
(Former) Ministry of Foreign Affairs, Spain	01.07.15	MIN_ES_3
Ministry of Agriculture, Spain	02.07.15	MIN_ES_4
Ministry of Foreign Affairs, Spain	02.07.15	MIN_ES_5
(Former) Ministry of Foreign Affairs, Spain	21.09.15	MIN_ES_6
Ministry of Finances, Spain	21.09.15	MIN_ES_7
Ministry of Energy, Tourism and Digital Agenda, Spain	21.09.15	MIN_ES_8
Ministry of Energy, Tourism and Digital Agenda, Spain	22.09.15	MIN_ES_9
Ministry for the Economy, Germany	20.05.16	MIN_SA_1
Ministry for Rural Development, Bayern, Germany	23.05.16	MIN_BA_1
Ministry for Rural Development, Galicia, Spain	10.09.15	MIN_GA_1
Ministry of the Presidency, Galicia, Spain	10.09.15	MIN_GA_2
Ministry of the Economy, Galicia, Spain	11.09.15	MIN_GA_3
Ministry of the Presidency, Galicia, Spain	11.09.15	MIN_GA_4
Ministry for the Sea, Galicia, Spain	21.09.15	MIN_GA_5
Ministry of the Presidency, Galicia, Spain	22.09.15	MIN_GA_6
Private Law Firm, Spain	01.07.15	LAW_1
Private Law Firm, Spain	03.07.15	LAW_2
Private Law Firm, Spain	07.09.15	LAW_3
Private Law Firm, Brussels	24.09.15	LAW_4
Private Law Firm, Germany	18.05.16	LAW_5
Private company, Spain	30.06.15	COMP_1
Public Company, Spain	07.09.15	COMP_2
Private Company, Spain	22.09.15	COMP_3
Private Company, Germany	04.07.16	COMP_4

- What were the criteria considered when making the decision to litigate (e.g. probability of success, financial considerations, securing citizen support, defend interests of national companies, etc.)?
- If several criteria were involved in the decision, which was the most important one?

General questions (for interviews with state attorneys):

- Brief description of the decision-making process for initiation of annulment actions against commission (procedure, actors, criteria).
- Are annulment actions against the Commission sometimes initiated for the following criteria, and if so, can you give examples and indicate an approximate frequency/share of such cases?
  - Governmental finances/budget?
  - Finances/budget of an autonomous community?
  - Achieving policy change at EU level (if difficult through legislative route)?
  - Influencing long-term development of the ECJ's legal doctrine?
  - Ensuring popular/citizen support?
  - Defend the interests of national companies?
  - Increase bargaining power/influence vis-à-vis the Commission?
  - Increase bargaining power/influence vis-à-vis another actor (e.g. autonomous communities, companies, etc.)?
  - Increase bargaining power/influence in a context of internal divisions (e.g. intra-party or intra-government divisions)?
- Are there sometimes cases where an actor's request for initiating an annulment action is NOT followed up with an annulment action? If so, examples & approximate frequency/rate of such cases?
- Are there sometimes contact/cooperation/coordination with other private or public actors affected by the controverted Commission's decision? If so, examples and approximate frequency/rate?
- To what extent are their interests taken over by the state in the decision to raise an action, i.e. to what extent are they counterbalanced by other considerations?
- Are there sometimes divergent positions among actors taking part in the decision to raise an action? If so, example and approximate frequency/rate?
- In case of divergent positions, how is the final decision made? Who are the decisive actors and/or which are the decisive criteria?

REFERENCES

Abend, L. (2010). Spain's coal miners fight for the right to keep digging. *Time*.http://content.time.com/time/world/article/0,8599,2020555,00.html. Accessed 22 August 2017.
Aberbach, J. D., & Rockman, B. A. (2002). Conducting and coding elite interviews. *Political Science and Politics, 35*, 673–676.
Adam, C. (2015). Gambling: Erosion and persistence of domestic sports betting monopolies. In C. Knill, C. Adam, & S. Hurka (Eds.), *On the road to permissiveness? Change and convergence of moral regulation in Europe* (pp. 206–233). Oxford, UK: Oxford University Press.
Adam, C. (2016). *The politics of judicial review: Supranational administrative acts and judicialized compliance conflict in the EU*. Basingstoke, UK: Palgrave Macmillan.
Adam, C. (2018). Multilevel conflict over policy application—Detecting changing cleavage patterns. *Journal of European Integration, 40*(6), 683–700.
Adam, C., Bauer, M. W., & Hartlapp, M. (2015). It's not always about winning: Domestic politics and legal success in EU annulment litigation. *Journal of Common Market Studies, 53*(2), 185–200.
Aiken, K. D., Liu, B. S., Mackoy, R. D., & Osland, G. E. (2004). Building internet trust: Signalling through trustmarks. *International Journal of Internet Marketing and Advertising, 1*(3), 251–267.
Alter, K. J. (1998). Who are the "masters of the treaty"? European governments and the European Court of Justice. *International Organization, 52*(1), 121–147.

© The Editor(s) (if applicable) and The Author(s) 2020
C. Adam et al., *Taking the EU to Court*,
Palgrave Studies in European Union Politics,
https://doi.org/10.1007/978-3-030-21629-0

Alter, K. J. (2003). Do international courts enhance compliance with international law? *Review of Asian and Pacific Studies 25*, 51–78.
Alter, K. J., & Meunier-Aitsahalia, S. (1994). Judicial politics in the European Community: European integration and the pathbreaking Cassis de Dijon decision. *Comparative Political Studies, 26*(4), 535–561.
Alter, K. J., & Vargas, J. (2000). Explaining variation in the use of European litigation strategies: European Community law and British gender equality policy. *Comparative Political Studies, 33*(4), 452–482.
Amaral, D. A., & Neave, D. G. (2009). On Bologna, weasels and creeping competence. In A. Amaral, G. Neave, C. Musselin, & P. Maassen (Eds.), *European integration and the governance of higher education and research* (pp. 281–299). Dordrecht, The Netherlands: Springer.
Andersen, E. A. (2005). *Out of the closets and into the courts legal opportunity structure and gay rights litigation*. Ann Arbor: The University of Michigan Press.
Andersen, E. A. (2006). *Out of the closets and into the courts: Legal opportunity structure and gay rights litigation*. Ann Arbor: University of Michigan Press.
Ansell, C. K., Trondal, J., & Øgård, M. (Eds.). (2017). *Governance in turbulent times*. Oxford, UK: Oxford University Press.
Arnull, A. (1995). Private applicants and the action for annulment under Article 173 of the EC treaty. *Common Market Law Review, 32*, 7–49.
Arnull, A. (2000). The action for annulment: A case of double standards? In D. O'Keefe (Ed.), *Judicial review in European Union law* (pp. 177–190). The Hague: Kluwer Law International.
Arnull, A. (2001). Private applicants and the action for annulment since CODORNIU. *Common Market Law Review, 38*, 7–52.
Arnull, A. (2006). *The European Union and its Court of Justice*. Oxford, UK: Oxford University Press.
Arnull, A. (2011). The principle of effective judicial protection in EU law: An unruly horse. *European Law Review, 1*, 51–70.
Bacharach, M., & Gambetta, D. (2001). Trust in signs. In K. Cook (Ed.), *Trust in society* (pp. 148–184). New York: Sage.
Baier, G. (2006). *Courts and federalism: Judicial doctrine in the United States, Australia, and Canada*. Vancouver, BC: University of British Columbia Press.
Baker, L. A., & Young, E. A. (2001). Federalism and the double standard of judicial review. *Duke Law Journal, 51*(1), 75–164.
Barav, A. (1974). Direct and individual concern: An almost insurmountable barrier to the admissibility of individual appeal to the EEC court. *Common Market Law Review, 11*(2), 191–198.
Barav, A. (1979). The judicial power of the European Economic Community Symposium: Conference on comparative constitutional law. *Southern California Law Review 53*, 461–526.

Barrett, S., & Fudge, C. (Eds.). (1981). *Policy and action*. London: Methuen.
Bauer, M. W. (1996). Die Verbindungsbüros der Deutschen Länder bei der Europäischen Union in Brüssel. *Verwaltungsrundschau, 42*(12), 417–420.
Bauer, M. W. (2001). *A creeping transformation? The European Commission and the management of EU structural funds in Germany*. Dordrecht, The Netherlands: Kluwer Academic (Library of Public Policy and Public Administration).
Bauer, M. W. (2002). The EU 'partnership principle': Still a sustainable governance device across multiple administrative arenas? *Public Administration, 80*(4), 769–789.
Bauer, M. W., & Becker, S. (2014). The unexpected winner of the crisis: The European Commissions strengthened role in economic governance. *Journal of European Integration, 36*(3), 213–229.
Bauer, M. W., & Becker, S. (2015). Subnational administrations in the EU multilevel system: Perspectives from the bureaucratic elite. In M. W. Bauer & J. Trondal (Eds.), *The Palgrave handbook on the European administrative system* (pp. 432–448). Basingstoke: Palgrave Macmillan.
Bauer, M. W., & Börzel, T. A. (2010). Regions and the European Union. In H. Enderlein, S. Wälti, & M. Zürn (Eds.), *Handbook on multi-level governance* (pp. 253–263). Cheltenham, UK: Edward Elgar.
Bauer, M. W., & Ege, J. (2012). Politicization within the European Commissions bureaucracy. *International Review of Administrative Sciences, 78*(3), 403–424.
Bauer, M. W., & Ege, J. (2016). Bureaucratic autonomy of international organizations secretariats. *Journal of European Public Policy, 23*(7), 1019–1037.
Bauer, M. W., & Hartlapp, M. (2010). Much ado about money and how to spend it! Analysing 40 years of annulment cases against the European Union Commission. *European Journal of Political Research, 49,* 202–222.
Bauer, M. W., & Knill, C. (2007). Politikabbau im europäischen Mehrebenensystem: Nationale Beendigungseffekte europäischer Politik. In I. Tömmel (Ed.), *Die Europäische Union: Governance und Policy-Making: PVS-Sonderheft* (Special Issue No. 40 of the official quarterly of the German Political Science Association) (pp. 185–206). Wiesbaden, Germany: VS Verlag.
Bauer, M. W., & Knill, C. (2014). A conceptual framework for the comparative analysis of policy change: Measurement, explanation, and strategies of policy dismantling. *Journal of Comparative Policy Analysis: Research and Practice, 16*(3), 28–44.
Bauer, M. W., & Tatham, M. (2015). The state, the economy, and the regions: Theories of preference formation in times of crisis. *Journal of Public Administration Research and Theory, 26*(4), 631–646.
Bauer, M. W., & Trondal, J. (Eds.). (2015a). *The Palgrave handbook of the European administrative system*. Basingstoke: Palgrave Macmillan.

Bauer, M. W., & Trondal, J. (2015b). The administrative system of the European Union. In M. W. Bauer & J. Trondal (Eds.), *The Palgrave handbook of the European administrative system* (pp. 1–28). Basingstoke: Palgrave Macmillan.

Bebchuk, L. A. (1984). Litigation and settlement under imperfect information. *The RAND Journal of Economics, 15*(3), 404–415.

Becker, S., & Bauer, M. W. (2016). Horizontale Gewaltenteilung in der EU-Haushaltspolitik– Determinanten des Einflusses des Europäischen Parlaments. *Zeitschrift für Politikwissenschaft, 26*(1) (Sonderheft Gewaltenteilung und Demokratie im Mehrebenensystem der EU), 99–114.

Becker, S., Bauer, M. W., Connolly, S., & Kassim, H. (2016). The Commission: Boxed in and constrained, but still an engine of integration. *West European Politics, 39*(5), 1011–1031.

Becker, S., Bauer, M. W., & De Feo, A. (Eds.). (2017). *The new politics of the European Union budget*. Nomos Publisher: Baden-Baden, Germany: Nomos (Series Studies on the European Union).

Bellamy, C. (2010). An EU competition court: The continuing debate. In I. Kokkoris & I. Lianos (Eds.), *The reform of EC competition law: New challenges* (pp. 33–52). Alphen aan den Rijn, The Netherlands: Kluwer Law International.

Benz, A. (2007). Accountable multilevel governance by the open method of coordination? *European Law Journal, 13*(4), 505–522.

Benz, A., & Eberlein, B. (1999). The Europeanization of regional policies: Patterns of multi-level governance. *Journal of European Public Policy, 6*(2), 329–348.

Bergström, C.-F., Farrell, H., & Héritier, A. (2007). Legislate or delegate? Bargaining over implementation and legislative authority in the EU. *West European Politics, 30*(2), 338–366.

Berry, J. M. (2002). Validity and reliability issues in elite interviewing. *Political Science and Politics, 35*, 679–682.

Beyers, J., de Bruycker, I., & Baller, I. (2015). The alignment of parties and interest groups in EU legislative politics: A tale of two different worlds? *Journal of European Public Policy, 22*(4), 534–551.

Biesenbender, J. (2011). The dynamics of treaty change: Measuring the distribution of power in the European Union. *European Integration Online Papers (EIoP), 15*(5), 1–24.

Blau, P. M. (1977). *Inequality and heterogeneity: A primitive theory of social structure*. London: Macmillan.

Blauberger, M. (2012). With Luxembourg in mind … the remaking of national policies in the face of ECJ jurisprudence. *Journal of European Public Policy, 19*(1), 109–126.

Blauberger, M. (2014). National responses to European court jurisprudence: West European politics. *West European Politics, 37*(3), 457–474. https://doi.org/10.1080/01402382.2013.830464.

Blauberger, M., & Weiss, M. (2013). If you can't beat me, join me! How the Commission pushed and pulled member states into legislating defence procurement. *Journal of European Public Policy, 20*(8), 1120–1138.

Börzel, T. A. (2000). Why there is no southern problem: On environmental leaders and laggards in the European Union. *Journal of European Public Policy, 7,* 141–162.

Börzel, T. A. (2003). Guarding the treaty: The compliance strategies of the European Commission. In T. A. Börzel & R. A. Cichowski (Eds.), *The state of the European Union* (6th ed., pp. 197–220). Oxford, UK: Oxford University Press.

Börzel, T. A. (2005). Mind the gap! European integration between level and scope. *Journal of European Public Policy, 12*(2), 217–236.

Börzel, T. A., Hofmann, T., & Panke, D. (2012). Caving in or sitting it out? Longitudinal patterns of non-compliance in the European Union. *Journal of European Public Policy, 19*(4), 454–471.

Börzel, T. A., Hofmann, T., Panke, D., & Sprungk, C. (2010). Obstinate and inefficient: Why member states do not comply with European law. *Comparative Political Studies, 43*(11), 1363–1390. https://doi.org/10.1177/0010414010376910.

Bourdieu, P. (1991). La représentation politique. Elements pour une théorie du champ politique. *Actes de Recherche En Sciences Sociales, 36–37,* 3–24.

Boutcher, S. A. (2013). Law and social movements: It's more than just litigation and courts. *Blog Post.* https://mobilizingideas.wordpress.com/2013/02/18/law-and-social-movements-its-more-than-just-litigation-and-courts/. Accessed 9 March 2017.

Bouwen, P., & Mccown, M. (2007). Lobbying versus litigation: Political and legal strategies of interest representation in the European Union. *Journal of European Public Policy, 14*(3), 422–443.

Boyle, E. H. (1998). Political frames and legal activity: The case of nuclear power in four countries. *Law and Society Review, 32*(1), 141–174.

Brandsma, G. J., & Blom-Hansen, J. (2017). *Controlling the EU executive? The politics of delegation in the European Union.* Oxford, UK: Oxford University Press.

Brennan, G., & Buchanan, J. M. (1980). *The power to tax: Analytic foundations of a fiscal constitution.* Cambridge, UK: Cambridge University Press.

Brigham, J. (2000). *The constitution of interests: Beyond the politics of rights.* New York: New York University Press.

British American Tobacco. (2014). *Science-tobacco blend.* http://www.bat-science.com/groupms/sites/BAT_9GVJXS.nsf/vwPagesWebLive/DO7AXG65. Accessed 22 August 2017.

Broberg, M., & Fenger, N. (2013). Variations in member states' preliminary references to the court of justice—Are structural factors (part of) the explanation? *European Law Journal, 19*(4), 488–501. https://doi.org/10.1111/eulj.12045.

Burley, A.-M., & Mattli, W. (1993). Europe before the court: A political theory of legal integration. *International Organization, 47*(1), 41–76.
Burns, T., & Stalker, G. M. (1961). *The management of innovation.* London: Tavistock.
Cameron, K. S., Kim, M. U., & Whetten, D. A. (1987). Organizational effects of decline and turbulence. *Administrative Science Quarterly, 32*(2), 222–240.
Camia, V., & Caramani, D. (2012). Family meetings: Ideological convergence within party families across Europe, 1945–2009. *Comparative European Politics, 10*(1), 48–85.
Canadian Coalition for Action on Tobacco. (2004). *A win-win: Enhancing public health and public revenue—Recommendations to increase tobacco taxes submitted to the minister of finance.* http://www.smoke-free.ca/pdf_1/2004taxreport.pdf. Accessed 7 December 2017.
Cappelletti, M., Seccombe, M., & Weiler, J. H. H. (Eds.). (1986). *Integration through law: Europe and the American Federal Experience: Vol. 1, Methods, tools and institutions, Book 2, Political organs, integration techniques and judicial process.* Berlin: Walter De Gruyter.
Carrubba, C. J., Gabel, M., & Hankla, C. (2008). Judicial behavior under political constraints: Evidence from the European Court of Justice. *American Political Science Review, 102*(4), 435–452.
Carrubba, C. J., Gabel, M., & Hankla, C. (2012). Understanding the role of the European Court of Justice in European integration. *American Political Science Review, 106*(1), 214–224.
Carrubba, C. J., & Murrah, L. (2005). Legal integration and use of the preliminary ruling process in the European Union. *International Organization, 59*(2), 399–418.
Chanley, V. A. (2002). Trust in government in the aftermath of 9/11: Determinants and consequences. *Political Psychology, 23*(3), 469–483.
Chanley, V. A., Rudolph, T. J., & Rahn, W. M. (2000). The origins and consequences of public trust in government: A time series analysis. *Public Opinion Quarterly, 64*(3), 239–256.
Christiansen, T., & Kirchner, E. J. (2000). *Committee governance in the European Union.* Manchester, UK: Manchester University Press.
Christensen, T., & Laegreid, P. (2005). Trust in government: The relative importance of service satisfaction, political factors, and demography. *Public Performance and Management Review, 28*(4), 487–511.
Christiansen, T., & Neuhold, C. (2013). Informal politics in the EU. *Journal of Common Market Studies, 51*(6), 1196–1206.
Cichowski, R. A. (2007). *The European court and civil society.* Cambridge, UK: Cambridge University Press.
Cini, M., & McGowan, L. (2008). *The competition policy in the European Union* (2nd ed.). Basingstoke, UK: Palgrave Macmillan.

Cisnal De Ugarte, S., & Di Masi, L. (2016). The European antitrust review 2016. *Crowell*.https://www.crowell.com/files/European-Union-Energy.pdf. *Accessed 22 August 2017.*

Citrin, J. (1974). Comment: The political relevance of trust in government. *American Political Science Review, 68*(3), 973–988.

Citrin, J., & Green, D. P. (1986). Presidential leadership and the resurgence of trust in government. *British Journal of Political Science, 16*(4), 431–453.

Coleman, J. S. (1994). *Foundations of social theory.* Cambridge, MA: Harvard University Press.

Conant, L. J. (2002). *Justice contained: Law and politics in the European Union.* Ithaca, NY: Cornell University Press.

Conant, L. J. (2006). Individuals, courts, and the development of European social rights. *Comparative Political Studies, 39*(1), 76–100.

Conant, L. J., Hofmann, A., Soennecken, D., & Vanhala, L. (2017). Mobilizing European law. *Journal of European Public Policy, 25*(9), 1–14. https://doi.org/10.1080/13501763.2017.1329846.

Corbett, R., Jacobs, F., & Shackleton, M. (2011). *The European Parliament.* London: John Harper.

Court of Justice of the European Union. (2001). Judgment of the Court of First Instance of 10 October 2001 on *British American Tobacco International Investments Ltd. v. Commission* in Case T-111/00. *European Court Reports 2001*(II), 02997.

Court of Justice of the European Union. (2014). Judgment of the Court of 4 September 2014 in *European Commission v. Council of the European Union* Case C-114/12. *Official Journal of the European Union 57*, C 395.

Court of Justice of the European Union. (2017). Communications Directorate—Electronic Publications and Media Unit. *Annual report 2016: The year in review.*

Craig, P. (2010). *The Lisbon Treaty: Law, politics, and treaty reform.* Oxford, UK: Oxford University Press.

Craig, P., & de Búrca, G. (2011). *EU law: Text, cases, and materials.* Oxford, UK: Oxford University Press.

Cremona, M. (2011). External relations and external competences of the European Union: The emergence of an integrated policy. In P. Craig & G. de Burca (Eds.), *The Evolution of EU Law* (pp. 217–268). Oxford, UK: Oxford University Press.

Crespy, A., & Saurugger, S. (2014). Resistance to policy change in the European Union: An actor-centered perspective. *Cahiers Du Cevipol, 2014*(1), 1–20.

Davis, C. L., & Bermeo, S. B. (2009). Who files? Developing country participation in GATT/WTO adjudication. *The Journal of Politics, 71*(3), 1033–1049.

Davis, D. W., & Silver, B. D. (2004). Civil liberties vs. security: Public opinion in the context of the terrorist attacks on America. *American Journal of Political Science, 48*(1), 28–46.

Davies, G. (2018). Has the Court changed, or have the cases? The deservingness of litigants as an element in Court of Justice citizenship adjudication. *Journal of European Public Policy, 25*, 1442–1460.

Dederke, J., & Naurin, D. (2018). Friends of the Court? Why EU governments file observations before the Court of Justice. *European Journal of Political Research, 57*(4), 867–882. https://doi.org/10.1111/1475-6765.12255.

De Fazio, G. (2012). Legal opportunity structure and social movement strategy in Northern Ireland and Southern United States. *International Journal of Comparative Sociology, 53*(1), 3–22. https://doi.org/10.1177/0020715212439311.

Dehousse, R. (1997). Regulation by networks in the European Community: The role of European agencies. *Journal of European Public Policy, 4*(2), 246–261.

De Swaan, A. (1973). *Coalition theories of democracy*. New York: Harper and Row.

Deutsch, K. G. (1998). Aktuelle Themen: Perspektiven einer EU-Richtlinie zu Pensionsfonds. *Deutsche Bank Research Bulletin, 103*, 1–10.

Doherty, B., & Hayes, G. (2014). Having your day in court: Judicial opportunity and tactical choice in anti-GMO campaigns in France and the United Kingdom. *Comparative Political Studies, 47*(1), 3–29. https://doi.org/10.1177/0010414012439184.

Downs, A. (1957). *An economic theory of democracy*. New York: Harper and Row.

Downs, A. (1967). *Inside bureaucracy*. Santa Monica, CA: RAND.

Dunsire, A. (1978). *The execution process: Implementation in a bureaucracy*. Los Gatos, CA: Martin Robertson.

Easton, D. (1965). *A framework for political analysis*. Englewood Cliffs, NJ: Prentice Hall/Harvester Wheatsheaf.

Ege, J., Bauer, M. W., & Becker, S. (2018). *The European Commission in turbulent times: Assessing organizational change and policy impact*. Baden-Baden, Germany: Nomos.

Egeberg, M. (2006). *Multilevel Union administration: The transformation of executive politics in Europe*. New York: Palgrave Macmillan.

Eisenberg, T. (1990). Testing the selection effect: A new theoretical framework with empirical tests. *The Journal of Legal Studies, 19*, 337–358.

Eliantonio, M., & Kas, B. (2010). Private parties and the annulment procedure: Can the gap in the European system of judicial protection be closed? *Journal of Politics and Law, 3*(2), 2–121.

Elmore, R. F. (1979). Backward mapping: Implementation research and policy decisions. *Political Science Quarterly, 94*(4), 601–616.

Ennis, B. J. (1984). Effective amicus briefs. *Catholic University Law Review, 33*, 603–609.

Epp, C. R. (1998). *The rights revolution: Lawyers, activists, and supreme courts in comparative perspective*. Chicago: University of Chicago Press.

European Commission. (1991). Proposal for a Council directive relating to the freedom of management and investment of funds held by institutions for retirement provision. COM (91) 301 final—SYN 363, *Official Journal of the European Communities 1991 C 312 34*, 3.

European Commission. (2005, June 7). State aid action plan—Less and better targeted state aid: A roadmap for state aid reform 2005–2009. COM (2005) 107 final. http://eur-lex.europa.eu/LexUriServ/LexUriServ.do?uri=CELEX:52005DC0107:EN:NOT. Accessed 9 April 2013.

Evans, J. S. B. T. (2003). In two minds: Dual-process accounts of reasoning. *Trends in Cognitive Sciences, 7*(10), 454–459. https://doi.org/10.1016/j.tics.2003.08.012.

Fairhurst, J. (2010). *Law of the European Union*. London: Pearson Education.

Falkner, G. (Ed.). (2011). *The EU's decision traps: Comparing policies*. Oxford, UK: Oxford University Press.

Falkner, G. (2018). A causal loop? The Commissions new enforcement approach in the context of non-compliance with EU law even after CJEU judgments. *Journal of European Integration, 40*, 769–784.

Falkner, G., Treib, O., Hartlapp, M., & Leiber, S. (2005). *Complying with Europe: EU harmonisation and soft law in the member states*. Cambridge, UK: Cambridge University Press.

Farole, D. J. (1999). Reexamining litigant success in state supreme courts. *Law and Society Review, 33*(4), 1043–1058. https://doi.org/10.2307/3115158.

Farrell, H., & Héritier, A. (2007). Contested competences in the European Union. *West European Politics, 30*(2), 227–243.

Federal Republic of Germany (2005). *Stellungnahme der Bundesregierung der Bundesrepublik Deutschland zum Aktionsplan staatliche Beihilfen vom*. http://ec.europa.eu/competition/state_aid/reform/comments_saap/37982.pdf. Accessed 7 December 2017.

Franchino, F. (2007). *The powers of the Union: Delegation in the EU*. Cambridge, UK: Cambridge University Press.

Galanter, M. (1974). Why the "haves" come out ahead: Speculations on the limits of legal change. *Law and Society Review, 9*(1), 95–160.

Gambetta, D. (1998). *Trust: Making and breaking cooperative relations*. Hoboken, NJ: Blackwell.

Gambetta, D. (2000). Can we trust trust? In D. Gambetta (Ed.), *Trust: Making and breaking cooperative relations* (pp. 213–237). Hoboken, NJ: Blackwell.

Garrett, G., Kelemen, R. D., & Schulz, H. (1998). The European Court of Justice, national governments, and legal integration in the European Union. *International Organization, 52*(1), 149–176.

Garrett, G., & Weingast, B. R. (1993). Ideas, interests, and institutions: Constructing the European Community's internal market. In J. Goldstein & R. O. Keohane (Eds.), *Ideas in foreign policy: Beliefs, institutions, and political change* (pp. 173–206). Ithaca, NY: Cornell University Press.

Geerts, T. (2012). Partnering with Belgian news publishers. *Google Europe Blog*. https://europe.googleblog.com/2012/12/partnering-with-belgian-news-publishers.html. Accessed 22 August 2017.
General Court of the European Union. (2014, December 3). Press Release No. 165/14. Judgement in Case T-57/11 *Castelnou Energia SL v. Commission*. Luxembourg.
Gil Ibañez, A. (1998). *Commission tools for the supervision and enforcement of EC Law other than Article 169 EC Treaty: An attempt at systematization* (Jean Monnet Working Papers No. 12/98).
Glenn, H. (1999). *Paths to justice: What people do and think about going to law*. Oxford, UK: Hart Publishing.
Glöckler, G., Lindner, J., & Salines, M. (2016). Explaining the sudden creation of a banking supervisor for the euro area. *Journal of European Public Policy*, 24(8), 1135–1153. https://doi.org/10.1080/13501763.2016.1184296.
Gould, J. P. (1973). The economics of legal conflicts. *Journal of Legal Studies*, 2(2), 279–300.
Granger, M. (2004). When governments go to Luxembourg...: The influence of governments on the European Court of Justice. *European Law Review*, 29, 1–31.
Grønbech-Jensen, C. (1998). The Scandinavian tradition of open government and the European Union: Problems of compatibility? *Journal of European Public Policy*, 5(1), 185–199.
Guiliani, M. (2003). Europeanization in comparative perspective: Institutional fit and national adaptation. In K. Featherstone & C. M. Radaelli (Eds.), *The politics of Europeanization* (pp. 134–155). Oxford, UK: Oxford University Press.
Haas, P. M. (1998). Compliance with EU directives: Insights from international relations and comparative politics. *Journal of European Public Policy*, 5(1), 17–37.
Hadfield, G. K. (1994). Judicial competence and the interpretation of incomplete contracts. *The Journal of Legal Studies*, 23(1), 159–184.
Haire, S. B., Lindquist, S. A., & Hartley, R. (1999). Attorney expertise, litigant success, and judicial decision-making in the U.S. Courts of Appeals. *Law and Society Review*, 33(3), 667–685. https://doi.org/10.2307/3115107.
Hall, P. A., & Taylor, R. C. R. (1996). Political science and the three new institutionalisms. *Political Studies*, 44, 936–957.
Handler, J. F. (1978). *Social movements and the legal system: A theory of law reform and social change*. Cambridge, MA: Academic Press.
Harlow, C., & Rawlings, R. (2013). *Pressure through law*. London: Routledge.
Hartlapp, M. (2005). *Die Kontrolle der nationalen Rechtsdurchsetzung durch die Europäische Kommission*. Frankfurt: Campus Verlag.
Hartlapp, M. (2008a). Extended governance: Implementation of EU social policy in the member states. In I. Tömmel & A. Verdun (Eds.), *Innovative governance in the European Union: The politics of multilevel policymaking* (pp. 221–236). Boulder, CO: Lynne Rienner.

Hartlapp, M. (2008b). Intra-Kommissionsdynamik im policy-making. EU-Politiken angesichts des demographischen Wandels. *Politische Vierteljahresschrift, 40* (PVS-Sonderheft 2007/2), 139–160.
Hartlapp, M. (2015). Politicization of the European Commission. When, how and with what impact? In M. W. Bauer & J. Trondal (Eds.), *The Palgrave handbook of the European administrative system* (pp. 145–160). Basingstoke, UK: Palgrave.
Hartlapp, M. (2018). Power shifts via the judicial arena: How annulments cases between EU institutions shape competence allocation. *Journal of Common Market Studies, 56*(6), 1429–1445.
Hartlapp, M., & Falkner, G. (2009). Problems of operationalisation and data in EU compliance research. *European Union Politics, 10*(2), 291–315.
Hartley, T. C. (2007). *The foundations of European Community law: An introduction to the constitutional and administrative law of the European Community*. Oxford, UK: Oxford University Press.
Haverland, M. (2000). National adaptation to European integration: The importance of institutional veto points. *Journal of Public Policy, 20*(1), 83–103.
Haverland, M. (2007). When the welfare state meets the regulatory state: EU occupational pension policy. *Journal of European Public Policy, 14*(6), 886–904.
Haydon, P. (2012, October 29). In Sweden, smokers have another option—Snus. *The Guardian*.https://www.theguardian.com/commentisfree/2012/oct/29/sweden-smokers-option-snus.
Hetherington, M. J. (1998). The political relevance of political trust. *American Political Science Review, 92*(4), 791–808.
Hetherington, M. J. (2005). *Why trust matters: Declining political trust and the demise of American liberalism*. Princeton, NJ: Princeton University Press.
Hetherington, M. J., & Rudolph, T. J. (2008). Priming, performance, and the dynamics of political trust. *The Journal of Politics, 70*(2), 498–512.
Hillion, C., & Wessel, R. A. (2009). Competence distribution in EU external relations after ECOWAS: Clarification or continued fuzziness? *Common Market Law Review, 46*(2), 551–586.
Hilson, C. (2002). New social movements: The role of legal opportunity. *Journal of European Public Policy, 9*(2), 238–255.
Hilson, C. (2017). *Protest and litigation against nuclear power in the 1970s: Exploring political and legal opportunity structure*. Paper presented at CES Glasgow 2017.
Hirschl, R. (2008). The judicialization of politics. In K. E. Whittington, D. R. Kelemen, & G. A. Caldeira (Eds.), *The Oxford handbook of law and politics* (pp. 1–23). Oxford, UK: Oxford University Press. https://dx.doi.org/10.1093/oxfordhb/9780199604456.013.0013.

Hix, S. (2008). Towards a partisan theory of EU politics. *Journal of European Public Policy, 15*(8), 1254–1265.

Hix, S. (2011). *The political system of the European Union* (3rd ed.). Basingstoke, UK: Palgrave Macmillan.

Hofmann, A. (2016). Legal rights and practical effect: Why the European Commission supports access to justice for interest groups. Conference Paper: Workshop implementation and judicial politics: Conflict and compliance in the EU multi-level system.

Hofmann, H. C. H., Rowe, G. C., & Türk, A. H. (2011). *Administrative law and policy of the European Union*. Oxford, UK: Oxford University Press.

Holzinger, K., & Schimmelfennig, F. (2012). Differentiated integration in the European Union: Many concepts, sparse theory, few data. *Journal of European Public Policy, 19*(2), 292–305.

Hooghe, L. (1996). *Cohesion policy and European integration: Building multi-level governance*. Oxford, UK: Oxford University Press.

Hooghe, L., & Marks, G. (2001). *Multi-level governance and European integration*. Lanham, MD: Rowman & Littlefield.

Hooghe, L., & Marks, G. (2009). A postfunctionalist theory of European integration: From permissive consensus to constraining. *British Journal of Political Science, 39*(1), 1–23.

Höpner, M. (2011). Der europäische Gerichtshof als Motor der europäischen Integration: Eine akteursbezogene Erklärung. *Berliner Journal für Soziologie, 21*(2), 203–229.

Horowitz, D. L. (1985). *Ethnic groups in conflict*. Berkeley, CA: University of California Press.

Horspool, M., & Humphreys, M. (2012). *European Union law*. Oxford, UK: Oxford University Press.

Houlder, V., Barker, A., & Beesley, A. (2016, August 30). Apple's EU tax dispute explained: The consequences of the commissions complaint and the wider implications of its ruling. *Financial Times*.https://www.ft.com/content/3e0172a0-6e1b-11e6-9ac1-1055824ca907.

Hughes, C. E. (1928). *The Supreme Court of the United States: Its foundation, methods and achievements*. Washington, DC: Beard Books.

Hutter, S., & Grande, E. (2014). Politicizing Europe in the national electoral arena: A comparative analysis of five West European countries, 1970–2010. *Journal of Common Market Studies, 52*(5), 1002–1018.

Jupille, J. (2004). *Procedural politics: Issues, influence, and institutional choice in the European Union*. Cambridge, UK: Cambridge University Press.

Jupille, J. (2007). Contested procedures: Ambiguities, interstices and EU institutional change. *West European Politics, 30*(2), 301–320.

Kahneman, D. (2012). *Thinking, fast and slow* (1st ed.). New York: Farrar, Straus and Giroux.

Keele, L. (2007). Social capital and the dynamics of trust in government. *American Journal of Political Science, 51*(2), 241–254.
Kelemen, R. D. (2011). *Eurolegalism*. Cambridge, MA: Harvard University Press.
Kelemen, R. D., & Pavone, T. (2016). Mapping European law. *Journal of European Public Policy, 23*(8), 1–21. https://doi.org/10.1080/13501763.2016.1186211.
Klages, H. (1983). Ursachenfaktoren der Inanspruchnahme der Ziviljustiz. *Deutsche Richterzeitung, 10*, 395–436.
Kim, M. (2008). Costly procedures: Divergent effects of legalization in the GATT/WTO dispute settlement procedures. *International Studies Quarterly, 52*(3), 657–686.
Kitschelt, H. P. (1986). Political opportunity structures and political protest: Anti-nuclear movements in four democracies. *British Journal of Political Science, 16*(1), 57–85.
Kornezov, A. (2014). Locus standi of private parties in actions for annulment: Has the gap been closed? *The Cambridge Law Journal, 73*, 25–28.
Kreppel, A. (2000). Rules, ideology, and coalition formation in the European Parliament past, present and future. *European Union Politics, 1*(3), 340–362.
Kvist, J. (2004). Does EU enlargement start a race to the bottom? Strategic interaction among EU member states in social policy. *Journal of European Social Policy, 14*(3), 301–318.
Lampinen, R., & Uusikylä, P. (1998). Implementation deficit—why member states do not comply with EU directives? *Scandinavian Political Studies, 21*(3), 231–251.
Landes, William M. (1974). An economic analysis of the courts. In Gary S. Becker & William M. Landes (Eds.), *Essays in the economics of crime and punishment* (pp. 164–214). New York: Columbia University Press.
Larsson, O., & Naurin, D. (2016). Judicial independence and political uncertainty: Assessing the effect of legislative override on the European Court of Justice. *International Organization, 70*(2), 377–408.
Laufer, H., & Münch, U. (1998). *Das föderative System der Bundesrepublik Deutschland*. Stuttgart, Germany: UTB.
Levi, M., & Stoker, L. (2000). Political trust and trustworthiness. *Annual Review of Political Science, 3*(1), 475–507.
Lijphart, A. (1999). *Patterns of democracy: Government forms and performance in thirty-six countries*. New Haven, CT: Yale University Press.
Lipsky, M. (1971). Street-level bureaucracy and the analysis of urban reform. *Urban Affairs Quarterly, 6*, 391–409.
Lipsky, M. (1980). *Street-level bureaucracy*. New York: Sage.
Lobel, J. (1994). Losers fools and prophets: Justice as struggle. *Cornell Law Review, 80*, 1331–1421.

Lobel, J. (1995). Losers fools and prophets: Justice as struggle. *Cornell Law Review, 80,* 1331–1421.

Lobel, J. (2003). *Success without victory: Lost legal battles and the long road to justice in America.* New York: New York University Press.

Long, W. J., & Quek, M. P. (2002). Personal data privacy protection in an age of globalization: The US-EU safe harbor compromise. *Journal of European Public Policy, 9,* 325–344.

Lowi, T. J. (1972). Four systems of policy, politics, and choice. *Public Administration Review, 32,* 298–310.

Lynggaard, K., & Nedergaard, P. (2009). The logic of policy development: Lessons learned from reform and routine within the CAP 1980–2003. *Journal of European Integration, 31*(3), 291–309.

Macoubrie, J. (2006). Nanotechnology: Public concerns, reasoning, and trust in government. *Public Understanding of Science, 15*(2), 221–241.

Majone, G. (1993). The European Community between social policy and social regulation. *Journal of Common Market Studies, 31*(2), 153–170.

Malecki, M. (2012). Do ECJ judges all speak with the same voice? Evidence of divergent preferences from the judgments of chambers. *Journal of European Public Policy, 19*(1), 59–75.

Maor, M., Gilad, S., & Bloom, P. B.-N. (2013). Organizational reputation, regulatory talk, and strategic silence. *Journal of Public Administration Research and Theory, 23*(3), 581–608.

Marks, G. (1993). Structural policy and multilevel governance in the EC. In A. Cafruny & G. Rosenthal (Eds.), *The state of the European Community: The Maastricht debates and beyond* (Vol. 2, pp. 391–410). Harlow, UK: Longman.

Marks, G., Scharpf, F. W., Schmitter, P. C., & Streek, W. (Eds.). (1996). *Governance in the European Union.* Thousand Oaks, CA: Sage.

Martinsen, D. S. (2015). *An ever more powerful court? The political constraints of legal integration in the European Union.* Oxford, UK: Oxford University Press.

Martinsen, D. S., & Falkner, G. (2011). Social policy: Problem solving gaps, partial exits and court-decision traps. In G. Falkner (Ed.), *The EUs decision traps: Comparing policies* (pp. 128–145). Oxford, UK: Oxford University Press.

Mathieu, E., Adam, C., & Hartlapp, M. (2018). From high judges to policy stakeholders: A public policy approach to the CJEUs power. *Journal of European Integration, 40*(6), 653–666.

Mathieu, E., & Bauer, W. M. (2018). Domestic resistance against EU policy implementation: Member states motives to take the Commission to court. *Journal of European Integration, 40*(6), 667–682.

Mattli, W., & Slaughter, A.-M. (1998). Revisiting the European Court of Justice. *International Organization, 52*(1), 177–209. https://doi.org/10.1162/002081898550590.

Mazey, S., & Richardson, J. J. (1993). *Lobbying in the European Community*. Oxford, UK: Oxford University Press.

Mbaye, H. A. D. (2001). Why national states comply with supranational law: Explaining implementation infringements in the European Union 1972–1993. *European Union Politics, 2*(3), 259–281.

McCann, M. W. (1994). *Rights at work: Pay equity reform and the politics of legal mobilization*. Chicago: University of Chicago Press.

McCann, M. W. (1998). How does law matter for social movements? In B. G. Garth & A. Sarat (Eds.), *How does law matter?* Evanston, IL: Northwestern University Press.

McCann, M. W. (2008). Litigation and legal mobilization. In K. E. Whittington, D. R. Kelemen, & G. A. Caldeira (Eds.), *The Oxford handbook of law and politics* (pp. 1–25). Oxford, UK: Oxford University Press. https://dx.doi.org/10.1093/oxfordhb/9780199208425.003.0030.

McCown, M. (2003). The European Parliament before the bench: ECJ precedent and EP litigation strategies. *Journal of European Public Policy, 10*(6), 974–995.

McGuire, K. T. (1995). Repeat players in the Supreme Court: The role of experienced lawyers in litigation success. *The Journal of Politics, 57*(1), 187–196. https://doi.org/10.2307/2960277.

McLaughlin, A., & Greenwood, J. (1995). The management of interest representation in the European Union. *Journal of Common Market Studies, 33*, 143–156.

Meardi, G. (2000). Trojan horse for the Americanization of Europe? Polish industrial relations towards the EU. *European Journal of Industrial Relations, 8*(1), 77–99.

Meyer, D., & Boutcher, S. (2007). Signals and spillover: Brown vs. Board of Education and other social movements. *Perspectives on Politics, 1*, 81–93.

Miller, A. H. (1974). Political issues and trust in government: 1964–1970. *The American Political Science Review, 68*(3), 951–972.

Miller, D. (2013). TRP starts DIET plant. *Tobacco Reporter*.http://www.tobaccoreporter.com/2013/08/trp-starts-diet-plant/. *Accessed 7 December 2017.*

Mishler, W., & Rose, R. (2001). What are the origins of political trust? Testing institutional and cultural theories in post-communist societies. *Comparative Political Studies, 34*(1), 30–62.

Moravcsik, A. (1991). Negotiating the single European act: National interests and conventional statecraft in the European Community. *International Organization, 45*(1), 9–56.

Moser, P., & Sawyer, K. (Eds.). (2008). *Making community law: The legacy of Advocate General Jacobs at the European Court of Justice*. Cheltenham, UK: Edward Elgar.

Mühlböck, M. (2013). Linking Council and European Parliament? Voting unity of national parties in bicameral EU decision-making. *Journal of European Public Policy, 20*(4), 571–588.
Müller, W. C., & Strøm, K. (1999). *Policy, office, or votes? How political parties in Western Europe make hard decisions.* Cambridge, UK: Cambridge University Press.
Naurin, D., & Wallace, H. (Eds.). (2008). *Unveiling the Council of the European Union: Games governments play in Brussels.* Basingstoke: Palgrave Macmillan.
NeJaime, D. (2011). Winning through losing. *Iowa Law Review, 96,* 941–1012.
Newman, A. L. (2008). Building transnational civil liberties: Transgovernmental entrepreneurs and the European data privacy directive. *International Organization, 62*(1), 103–130. https://doi.org/10.1017/S0020818308080041.
Newton, K., & Norris, P. (1999). *Confidence in public institutions: Faith, culture or performance?* Presented at the American Political Science Association, Atlanta, GA.
Niskanen, W. A. (1971). *Bureaucracy and representative government.* Chicago: Transaction Publishers.
Pedersen, H. S., Floristean, A., Iseppi, L., Dawkins, R., Smith, C., Morup, C., et al. (2012). *Study on the measuring and reducing of administrative costs for economic operators and tax authorities and obtaining in parallel a higher level of compliance and security in imposing excise duties on tobacco products.* http://ec.europa.eu/smart-regulation/evaluation/search/download.do?documentId=11702485. Accessed 7 December 2017.
Peers, S., & Costa, M. (2012). Court of Justice of the European Union (General Chamber), Judicial review of EU Acts after the Treaty of Lisbon; Order of 6 September 2011, Case T-18/10 Inuit Tapiriit Kanatami and Others vs. Commission & Judgment of 25 October 2011, Case T-262/10 Microban vs. Commission. *European Constitutional Law Review, 8*(1), 82–104.
Pierson, P. (2004). *Politics in time: History, institutions, and social analysis.* Princeton, NJ: Princeton University Press.
Pluemper, T., & Schneider, C. J. (2007). Discriminatory European Union membership and the redistribution of enlargement gains. *Journal of Conflict Resolution, 51*(4), 568–587.
Pollack, M. A. (1994). Creeping competence: The expanding agenda of the European Community. *Journal of Public Policy, 14*(2), 95–145.
Posner, R. A. (1973). An economic approach to legal procedure and judicial administration. *Journal of Legal Studies, 2*(2), 399–458.
Prechal, S. (2010). Competence creep and general principles of law. *Review of European Administrative Law, 3*(1), 5–22.

Pressman, J. L., & Wildavsky, A. B. (1973). *Implementation: How great expectations in Washington are dashed in Oakland—Or, why it's amazing that federal programs work at all, this being a saga of the Economic Development Administration as told by two sympathetic observers who seek to build morals on a foundation of ruined hopes*. Berkeley: University of California Press.

Priest, G. L., & Klein, B. (1984). The selection of disputes for litigation. *The Journal of Legal Studies, 13*(1), 1–55.

Putnam, R. D. (1988). Diplomacy and domestic politics: The logic of two-level games. *International Organization, 42*(3), 427–460. https://doi.org/10.1017/S0020818300027697.

Rauh, C. (2019). EU politicization and policy initiatives of the European Commission: The case of consumer policy. *Journal of European Public Policy, 26*(3), 1–22.

Redelmeier, D. A. (2005). The cognitive psychology of missed diagnoses. *Annals of Internal Medicine, 142*(2), 115–120. https://doi.org/10.7326/0003-4819-142-2-200501180-00010.

Redelmeier, D. A., & Shafir, E. (1995). Medical decision-making in situations that offer multiple alternatives. *JAMA, 273*(4), 302–305. https://doi.org/10.1001/jama.1995.03520280048038.

Riddervold, M., & Rosén, G. (2016). Trick and treat: How the Commission and the European Parliament exert influence in EU foreign and security policies. *Journal of European Integration, 38*(6), 1–16. https://doi.org/10.1080/07036337.2016.1178737.

Rieger, E. (2005). Agricultural policy. In E. Wallace, W. Wallace, & M. A. Pollack (Eds.), *Policy-making in the European Union* (5th ed., pp. 161–190). Oxford, UK: Oxford University Press.

Risse, T., Engelmann-Martin, D., Knope, H.-J., & Roscher, K. (1999). To euro or not to euro? The EMU and identity politics in the European Union. *European Journal of International Relations, 5*(2), 147–187.

Rosati, E. (2016). Neighbouring rights for publishers: Are national (possible) EU initiatives lawful? *International Review of Intellectual Property and Competition Law, 47*(5), 569–594.

Rosenberg, G. N. (1991). *The hollow hope: Can courts bring about social change?* (1st ed.). Chicago: University of Chicago Press.

Rudolph, T. J., & Evans, J. (2005). Political trust, ideology, and public support for government spending. *American Journal of Political Science, 49*(3), 660–671.

Ryan, E. (2011). Negotiating federalism. *Boston College Law Review, 52*(1), 1–136.

Sabatier, P., & Mazmanian, D. (1979). The conditions of effective implementation: A guide to accomplishing policy objectives. *Policy Analysis, 5*(4), 481–504.

Sandholtz, W., & Stone Sweet, A. (1998). *European integration and supranational governance*. Oxford, UK: Oxford University Press.
Saurugger, S., & Terpan, F. (2013). Analyser les résistances nationales à la mise en œuvre des normes européennes: une étude des instruments daction publique. *Quaderni, 80*, 5–24.
Saurugger, S., & Terpan, F. (2017). *The Court of Justice of the European Union and the politics of law*. London: Palgrave.
Schakel, A. H., Hooghe, L., & Marks, G. (2015). Multilevel governance and the state. In S. Leibfried, E. Huber, M. Lange, J. D. Levy, & F. Nullmeier (Eds.), *The Oxford handbook of transformation of the state* (pp. 269–285). Oxford, UK: Oxford University Press.
Scharpf, F. W. (1985). Die Politikverflechtungs-Falle. Europäische Integration und deutscher Föderalismus im Vergleich. *Politische Vierteljahresschrift, 26*(4), 323–356.
Scharpf, F. W. (2002). The European social model: Coping with the challenges of diversity. *Journal of Common Market Studies, 40*(4), 645–670.
Scharpf, F. W. (2006). The joint-decision trap revisited. *Journal of Common Market Studies, 44*(4), 845–864.
Scharpf, F. W. (2007). Europe's neo-liberal bias. In A. Hemerijck, B. Knapen, & E. van Doorne (Eds.), *Economic crisis and institutional choice* (pp. 228–234). Amsterdam: Amsterdam University Press.
Scharpf, F. W. (2010). The asymmetry of European integration, or why the EU cannot be a social market economy. *Socio-Economic Review, 8*(2), 211–250.
Scharpf, F. W. (2017). *Vom asymmetrischen Euro-Regime in die Transferunion – und was die deutsche Politik dagegen tun könnte* (MPIfG Discussion Paper 17/15). Cologne, Germany: Max Planck Institute for the Study of Societies.
Scheingold, S. (1974). *The politics of rights: Lawyers, public policy, and social change*. New Haven, CT: Yale University Press.
Schmidt, S. K. (1998). Commission activism: Subsuming telecommunications and electricity under European competition law. *Journal of European Public Policy, 5*(1), 169–184.
Schmidt, S. K. (2000). Only an agenda setter? The European Commissions power over the council of ministers. *European Union Politics, 1*(1), 37–61.
Schmidt, S. K. (2012). Who cares about nationality? The path-dependent case law of the ECJ from goods to citizens. *Journal of European Public Policy, 19*(1), 8–24. https://doi.org/10.1080/13501763.2012.632122.
Schmidt, S. K. (2014). Judicial Europeanisation: The case of Zambrano in Ireland. *West European Politics, 37*(4), 769–785. https://doi.org/10.1080/01402382.2014.919775.
Schmidt, S. K. (2018). *The European Court of Justice and the policy process*. Oxford, UK: Oxford University Press.

Segal, J. A., & Spaeth, H. J. (2002). *The Supreme Court and the attitudinal model revisited*. Cambridge, UK: Cambridge University Press.
Segovia Arancibia, C. (2008). *Political trust in Latin America* (PhD thesis), University of Michigan.
Shapiro, M. (1964). Political jurisprudence. *Kentucky Law Journal, 52*, 294–345.
Shapiro, M. (1980). Comparative law and comparative politics. *Southern California Law Review, 53*, 537–542.
Sheehan, R. S., Mishler, W., & Songer, D. R. (1992). Ideology, status, and the differential success of direct parties before the Supreme Court. *American Political Science Review, 86*(2), 464–471. https://doi.org/10.2307/1964234.
Silverstein, G. (2009). *Laws allure: How law shapes, constrains, saves, and kills politics*. Cambridge, UK: Cambridge University Press.
Simons, D. (2014). Should the European Commission wear green goggles more often? *Greenpeace International*. http://www.greenpeace.org/international/en/news/Blogs/makingwaves/Castelnou-Energia-v-Commission/blog/50868/. Accessed 22 August 2017.
Skiadas, D. V. (2002). *Judicial review of the budgetary authority during the enactment of the European Unions Budget* (SSRN Scholarly Paper No. ID 302757). Rochester, NY: Social Science Research Network.
Skiple, J. K., Grendstad, G., Shaffer, W. R., & Waltenburg, E. N. (2016). Supreme Court justices economic behaviour: A multilevel model analysis. *Scandinavian Political Studies, 39*(1), 73–94. https://doi.org/10.1111/1467-9477.12060.
Steunenberg, B., & Rhinard, M. (2010). The transposition of European law in EU member states: Between process and politics. *European Political Science Review, 2*(3), 495–520.
Stone Sweet, A. (1999). Judicialization and the construction of governance. *Comparative Political Studies, 32*(2), 147–184.
Stone Sweet, A., & Brunell, T. L. (1998). Constructing a supranational constitution: Dispute resolution and governance in the European Community. *American Political Science Review, 92*(1), 63–81.
Stone Sweet, A., & Brunell, T. L. (1999). *Data set on preliminary references in EC law*. San Domenico di Fiesole, Italy: Robert Schuman Centre, European University Institute.
Stone Sweet, A., & Brunell, T. L. (2007). *Data set on actions under Article 230: 1954–2006. NEWGOV Project*. San Domenico di Fiesole, Italy: Robert Schuman Centre, European University Institute.
Stone Sweet, A., & Brunell, T. L. (2012). The European Court of Justice, state noncompliance, and the politics of override. *American Political Science Review, 106*, 204–213.

Stone Sweet, A., & Brunell, T. L. (2013). Trustee courts and the judicialization of international regimes: The politics of majoritarian activism in the ECHR, the EU, and the WTO. *Journal of Law and Courts, 1*(1), 61–88.
Swenden, W. (2006). *Federalism and regionalism in Western Europe: A comparative and thematic analysis.* Basingstoke: Palgrave.
Tallberg, J. (2002). Paths to compliance: Enforcement, management, and the European Union. *International Organization, 56,* 609–643.
Tatham, M., & Bauer, M. W. (2014). Competence ring-fencing from below? The drivers of regional demands for control over upwards dispersion. *Journal of European Public Policy, 21*(9), 1367–1385.
Tatham, M., & Bauer, M. W. (2014). Support from below? Supranational institutions, regional élites, and governance preferences. *Journal of Public Policy, 34*(2), 237–267.
Terpan, F. (2015). Soft law in the European Union—The changing nature of EU Law. *European Law Journal, 21*(1), 68–96. https://doi.org/10.1111/eulj.12090.
Thomson, R., Torenvlied, R., & Arregui, J. (2007). The paradox of compliance: Infringements and delays in transposing European Union directives. *British Journal of Political Science, 37*(4), 685–709.
Tobacco Tactics. (2017). *Snus: EU ban on snus sales.* University of Bath. http://www.tobaccotactics.org/index.php/Snus:_EU_Ban_on_Snus_Sales. Accessed 22 August 2017.
Tömmel, I., & Verdun, A. (Eds.). (2008). *Innovative governance in the European Union: The politics of multilevel policymaking.* Boulder, CO: Lynne Rienner.
Treib, O. (2003). Die Umsetzung von EU-Richtlinien im Zeichen der Parteipolitik: Eine akteurszentrierte Antwort auf die Misfit-These. *Politische Vierteljahresschrift, 44*(4), 506–528.
Treib, O. (2010). Party politics, national interests, and government—Opposition dynamics cleavage structures in the convention negotiations on EU social policy. *European Union Politics, 11*(1), 119–142.
Tridimas, G., & Tridimas, T. (2002). The European Court of Justice and the annulment of the Tobacco Advertisement Directive: Friend of national sovereignty or foe of public health? *European Journal of Law and Economics, 14*(2), 171–183.
Tridimas, G., & Tridimas, T. (2004). National courts and the European Court of Justice: A public choice analysis of the preliminary reference procedure. *International Review of Law and Economics, 24*(2), 125–145. https://doi.org/10.1016/j.irle.2004.08.003.
Trondal, J., & Bauer, M. W. (2017). Conceptualizing the European multilevel administrative order: Capturing variation in the European administrative system. *European Political Science Review, 9*(1), 73–94.
Türk, A. (2009). *Judicial review in EU law.* Cheltenham, UK: Edward Elgar.

Van Der Vleuten, A. (2005). Pincers and prestige: Explaining the implementation of EU gender equality legislation. *Comparative European Politics, 3,* 464–488.
Van De Walle, S., & Bouckaert, G. (2003). Public service performance and trust in government: The problem of causality. *International Journal of Public Administration, 26*(8–9), 891–913.
Vanhala, L. (2009). Anti-discrimination policy actors and their use of litigation strategies: The influence of identity politics. *Journal of European Public Policy, 16*(5), 738–754.
Vanhala, L. (2011). *Making rights a reality? Disability rights activists and legal mobilization.* Cambridge, UK: Cambridge University Press.
Vanhala, L. (2012). Legal opportunity structures and the paradox of legal mobilization by the environmental movement in the UK. *Law and Society Review, 46*(3), 523–556.
Vanhala, L. (2017). Is legal mobilization for the birds? Legal opportunity structures and environmental nongovernmental organizations in the United Kingdom, France, Finland, and Italy. *Comparative Political Studies.* https://doi.org/10.1177/0010414017710257.
Van Waarden, F., & Hildebrand, Y. (2009). From corporatism to lawyocracy? On liberalization and juridification. *Regulation and Governance, 3*(3), 259–286. https://doi.org/10.1111/j.1748-5991.2009.01059.x.
van Zimmeren, E., Mathieu, E., & Verhoest, K. (2015). The interaction between agencies, networks and the European Commission in emerging regulatory constellations: A comparative analysis of the European telecom sector and the European patent system. In E. Ongaro (Ed.), *Multi-level governance: The missing linkages* (pp. 125–162). Bingley, UK: Emerald.
Vauchez, A. (2012). Keeping the dream alive: The European Court of Justice and the transnational fabric of integrationist jurisprudence. *European Political Science Review, 4*(1), 51–71.
Vauchez, A. (2015). Methodological Europeanism at the cradle: Eur-lex, the Acquis and the making of Europe's cognitive equipment. *Journal of European Integration, 37*(2), 193–210.
Vauchez, A., & de Witte, B. (Eds.). (2013). *Lawyering Europe: European law as a transnational social field.* Oxford, UK: Oxford University Press.
Weatherill, S. (2004). Competence creep and competence control. *Yearbook of European Law, 23*(1), 1–55.
Wilson, B., & Rodriguez Cordero, J. C. (2006). Legal opportunity structures and social movements: The effects of institutional change on Costa Rican politics. *Comparative Political Studies, 39*(3), 325–351.
Woods, L., & Peers, S. (2014). Copyright: Anything left of member states external competence? *EU Law Analysis.* http://eulawanalysis.blogspot.de/2014/09/copyright-anything-left-of-member.html. Accessed 22 August 2017.

Index

A
access to court, 29, 53
Adjustment of Salaries and Pensions of Eurocrats (C-196/12, C-66/12, C-63/12), 98
Admissibility, 61–63, 66. *See also* access to court
adversarial style of policy-making, 27
Agricultural policy, 84, 95, 136. *See also* Common Agriculture Policy (CAP)
Alpenforum, 181
Amici curiae. See intervener
annulment litigation, 3–5, 7, 8, 13–16, 21, 22, 32–34, 36, 39, 51–53, 59, 60, 66, 73, 75, 76, 80, 81, 83, 84, 91, 99, 102, 104, 110, 113, 116, 117, 128, 129, 138, 142, 149, 162–164, 167, 175, 176, 181, 189–191, 193–195, 198, 202
Apple Case (T-892/16), 178
applicant, 4, 13–15, 27, 28, 36, 37, 52, 54, 56–58, 61–63, 66, 96, 107, 127, 129, 144, 148, 161, 162, 165, 167, 169–171, 175, 177, 194–196, 198
attitudinal model, 33, 156
attitudinal approach, 159
Austrian transit (C-356/01), 181
Autogrill Case (T-219/10), 106

B
Banco Santander Case (T-399/11), 106
Basque country, 105
Bavaria, 80, 115
BMW Case (T-671/14), 115, 166
Brandenburg, 98
British American Tobacco, 143–146, 150
Broadcasting, 7, 10, 136, 141, 150, 151. *See also* Broadcasting organizations
Broadcasting organizations, 140, 141
business, companies, 1, 143

C

Case selection, 74, 76–78
case studies, 74, 79, 95, 99, 163, 191, 193, 196, 200
Castelnou, 177
Castile and León, 147, 148
causal chain, 75, 76, 161, 189
Chernobyl Case (C-70/88), 15, 62, 69
Citizens support, 209
Clarification, 102, 140, 179, 180, 183. *See also* clarify
clarify, 8, 102, 178, 179, 192, 199
Coal, 147. *See also* energy
Cohesion policy, 77, 84, 112, 173, 191
Comitology, 10, 111, 113, 143, 144, 146, 180, 200
Commission, 1, 2, 5–10, 12, 14, 15, 17, 25, 27, 30–32, 34, 37, 51, 54, 56–62, 64, 68, 79, 84, 87–89, 95–106, 108–115, 127, 128, 130–132, 136, 138, 140–148, 150, 166, 173–181, 184, 185, 191, 193, 203
Committee of the Regions, 61, 62, 68
Common Agriculture Policy (CAP), 95, 173
Common Foreign and Security Policy (CFSP), 105
Company, 1, 2, 4, 102, 105, 106, 109, 115, 144, 177. *See also* business, companies
Competence creep, 88, 99, 101, 102, 105, 174, 175
Competition law, 60, 101, 200. *See also* competition policy
competition policy, 12, 54, 148
complex conflict, 37, 129, 134, 202
Complex constellation, 5, 37, 133, 140, 155, 165, 171, 178, 182, 194, 199. *See also* complex conflict

conflict constellation, 23
Constellation, 5, 15, 16, 34, 40, 52, 67, 76, 85, 106, 110, 129–132, 134, 149, 155, 163, 169–171, 178, 182, 194, 196, 197. *See also* conflict constellation
Constitutionalization, 52
Constrained court, 157, 168, 170, 171. *See also* strategic model
consumer policy, 100
Consumer protection, 111, 112. *See also* consumer policy
Council, 4, 9, 10, 12, 14, 25, 27, 30–32, 35, 38, 54, 55, 57–59, 61, 62, 64, 68, 79, 80, 87, 90, 98, 99, 104, 105, 108, 109, 119, 130, 132, 140–143, 150, 151, 159, 164, 176, 177, 179, 180, 184, 185
Court agency, 28, 198
Court of Auditors, 61, 62, 66, 68
Court of First Instance, 54

D

Data privacy, 38, 108, 110, 177
Data Protection Supervisor, 38, 145, 146
data set, 74, 78
Decision making competences, 4, 172. *See also* institutional competences
Defendant, 4, 13, 27, 28, 36–38, 59, 60, 67, 79, 80, 99, 127–131, 136, 142, 148, 162–164, 167, 171, 177, 194, 195
Deutsche Bank, 109
Distributive effect, 155, 172, 173, 199. *See also* redistributive effect
distributive policies, 95
Dresden Airport (T-215/9), 174

E

electoral concern, 93
Electorate, 93, 116, 146, 181, 192. *See also* electoral concern
emission allowances, 104
Endogeneity, 76, 169. *See also* endogenous factors
endogenous factors, 76
Energy, 78, 100–102, 127, 147, 148, 165, 177. *See also* coal; emission allowances; renewables
Environment, 78, 148, 163, 177, 181, 202. *See also* environmental policy, environmental law
environmental law, 148
environmental policy, 147
EPSO and Patent Package Cases (T-148/13, T-149/13, T-191/13, C-274/11, T-146/13, 147/13), 107
ERTA Case (C-22/70), 9, 104, 176
EU institutions, 2–4, 6, 9, 11–15, 17, 30, 34–38, 52, 54–56, 59–63, 65, 67, 75, 77, 79, 80, 83, 87, 89–91, 93–95, 98, 99, 107, 110, 128, 131, 138, 145, 162, 168–171, 174, 176, 180, 193–195, 197, 202
EU policy-making, 32
Eurolegalism, 24
European Central Bank (ECB), 12, 15, 25, 54, 57–59, 61, 62, 66, 150, 194
European Commission. *See* Commission
European integration, 6, 33, 52, 67, 75, 90, 157, 160, 161, 200
European Parliament (EP), 10–12, 15, 25, 27, 30, 35, 37, 38, 54, 55, 57, 59–63, 66, 79, 80, 85, 87, 90, 93, 98, 104, 105, 108, 132, 142, 176, 177, 180, 192, 194

Europe Economics, 144
Expanded Tobacco Case, 143
expert interviews, 74, 79
external affairs, 10, 12, 77, 78, 104, 140, 202
external policy, 9, 10, 176. *See also* external trade policy; external affairs
external trade policy, 104

F

federal states, 10, 88, 96
feedback effect, 24, 81, 83, 104, 172, 200, 201
financial concerns, 145, 190
financial corrections, 9, 84, 95–98, 112, 173, 191
financial dimension, 128, 147, 194
financial resources. *See* material gains, 86, 87, 95, 128, 191
France, 64, 68, 97, 108–110, 119, 141
free-rider, 162

G

Galicia, 80, 113, 114, 147, 148
Germany, 7–10, 76, 77, 84, 95–98, 100, 101, 103, 105, 106, 111, 112, 118, 127, 141, 150, 175, 181, 184
governments, 1–3, 5, 8, 9, 12–14, 17, 23, 25–27, 34–38, 58, 85, 86, 89, 90, 92, 93, 97, 100, 102, 103, 106, 107, 110–115, 117, 128, 131, 142, 145–148, 157–161, 163, 166, 169–171, 175, 177, 181, 182, 184, 191–194, 200
Greenpeace, 147, 148, 177

H

horizontal conflict, 35–37, 76, 77, 130–132, 194

I

IBM Case (C-60/81), 58, 67
ideological dimension, 128, 194
ideology, 4, 83, 85, 89–91, 93, 95, 107, 117, 138, 183, 190, 191. *See also* ideological dimension; policy preference
implied powers, 9, 10, 55, 69, 104, 176, 200
infringement procedure, 31, 51, 52, 56, 87, 202
institutional competences, 4–6, 83, 87–89, 93–95, 99, 100, 102, 106, 117, 133, 178, 191, 193
institutional junctures, 196
institutional turbulence, 5, 128, 129, 135–138, 140, 142, 143, 145–147, 149, 161, 171, 194–198, 201, 202
interest group, 2, 3, 6, 13, 25, 26, 34, 52, 61, 65, 147, 148, 158. *See also* organized interests
intergovernmentalism, 157
intervene, 26, 28, 40, 73, 74, 76, 99, 106, 129, 136, 162, 177, 183, 199
intervener, 26, 36, 103, 115, 164, 165. *See also* intervene
interviews, 17, 74, 80, 81, 94, 99, 113, 134, 164, 165. *See also* expert interviews; semi structured interviews

J

joint case, 79, 130
judicial behaviour, 33, 34, 73, 75, 134, 156, 158, 159, 162, 182, 196–198

judicialization, 87
judicial politics, 15, 22, 33, 84, 86, 197, 203
judicial protection, 51, 66
judicial review, 6, 7, 11, 15, 27, 29, 52, 63, 87, 88, 91, 116, 150, 200. *See also* technical review mechanism
junctures, 135–138, 142, 148, 149, 195, 196. *See also* institutional junctures; policy junctures

L

law and politics, 6, 16
legal arguments, 2, 97, 134, 137, 155, 160, 164–167, 171, 173, 184, 193, 197
legal conflict, 22, 24, 38, 73, 112, 127, 129, 131–133, 180–182, 194, 195, 200
legal experts, 165
legal factor, 29, 94, 97, 116, 192, 193. *See also* legal stock; merits of a case
legal flux, 5, 138. *See also* Treaty change
legalisation, 156
legalistic perspective, 156. *See also* legal model
legal model, 156
legal narratives, 167
legal opportunity structure, 4, 29, 52, 127
legal path dependency, 198
Legal reasoning, 163, 167. *See also* legal arguments; legal narratives
legal stock. *See* legal factor, 29, 134, 137, 164, 167, 195, 198
legal success, 4, 23, 84, 155, 156, 160, 161, 164, 167, 175–177, 180, 182, 183, 192, 195, 196
legal (un)certainty, 4, 5, 136–138, 144, 148, 149, 155, 161–163,

INDEX 237

167, 171, 182, 192, 193, 195–198, 201
legislative override, 34, 159, 160, 168, 170, 198
Leipzig Halle airport (T-396/08), 102, 103
Les Verts v European Parliament (C-294/83), 59, 67
litigant configuration. *See* conflict constellation
litigants budget. *See* material gains
litigation, 3–5, 15, 21, 23–25, 27–32, 34, 39, 51–53, 56, 73, 75–77, 79–81, 84–88, 90–96, 98, 99, 102, 107, 112, 114, 116, 117, 128, 129, 134, 136, 138, 145, 146, 150, 155, 156, 158, 161, 163, 172, 173, 177, 180, 181, 183, 190–196, 199–201, 203

M
Majoritarian activism, 159
material benefits, 98, 173
Material gains, 4–6, 83, 86, 87, 89, 93–95, 117, 128, 134, 172, 183, 190, 191, 193. *See also* financial concerns; financial dimension; financial resources; material benefits
merits of a case, 4, 33, 99, 134, 164, 196
milk quality Case (T-683/15), 166
Molluscs Case (T-204/11), 112, 113
Motivations, 3–5, 15, 16, 21, 22, 28, 29, 40, 67, 73, 75, 76, 79, 80, 84–91, 93–95, 99–101, 106–108, 110, 112, 113, 117, 119, 128, 129, 133, 134, 136, 138, 145–148, 161–163, 171, 176, 178, 182, 183, 189–194, 196, 198, 199, 201

Multilevel governance, 2, 15, 21–24, 27, 28, 31, 32, 38, 73, 75, 99, 192, 194, 196, 202. *See also* multilevel system
multilevel system, 2, 3, 10, 35, 36, 39, 66, 73–76, 81, 85, 87, 89, 117, 127, 199–201

N
Non-governmental organization (NGO), 4, 90, 128, 177, 190
non-privileged applicant, 54, 61–63, 69, 96, 148

O
organized interests, 158
original data set, 74

P
partisan politics, 93
party political orientation, 89. *See also* partisan politics, party politics
party politics, 117, 191
Passenger rights (C-317/04 and C-318/04), 108, 110, 176
Plaumann Case (C-25/62), 63, 67
policy junctures, 129, 138, 142, 146, 171, 196
policy preference, 4, 10, 84, 93, 117, 190, 191
Political system of the EU, 77, 88. *See also* systemic features of the EU
Political trust, 4, 6, 83, 84, 91–95, 110, 112, 113, 116, 128, 133, 134, 138, 146, 149, 172, 178, 180, 183, 191, 193, 199. *See also* political trustworthiness
political trustworthiness, 91
Potato Starch Case (T-557/13), 97, 98

Preliminary reference, 6, 34, 51, 52, 63, 91, 202
Preliminary ruling, 52, 63, 77, 158, 193, 202
private actors, 13, 15, 27, 31, 35, 57, 64, 84, 86, 94, 130, 131, 134, 145, 161, 165, 169, 170, 189, 193, 195
Private litigants, 4, 64, 117, 160, 169, 182, 191, 197. See also private actors
Private Pension Market Case (C-57/95), 108–110
Privileged applicant, 54, 61, 69
probability to win, 86
Procedural Competences in Trade Negotiations (C-22/70 and C-425/13), 104, 105
public actors, 3, 4, 6, 22, 27, 83, 84, 86, 89, 94, 95, 99, 110, 116, 117, 129, 158, 161, 164, 173, 190–193
Public litigants, 4, 5. See also public actors
Public opinion, 26, 93, 110, 111, 157

R
Ramboll Management, 144
redistributive effect, 172, 175, 178, 199
Redistributive policies, 77, 95. See also distributive policies
regional actors, 14
regional authorities, 15, 61, 115, 195
regional governments, 2, 6, 17, 34, 52, 61, 62, 67, 77, 88, 163, 174, 193
Regione Siciliana (C 15/06), 96
Regions, 62, 96, 110, 112–114, 116, 181. See also regional actors; regional governments;

regional authorities; subnational authorities
Renewable energies. See Energy, 101
Renewable Energies Law (T-134/14 and T-47/15), 100, 101
renewables, 100, 101, 147, 165
repeat player, 91, 161
reputation, 93, 94, 161, 193
Research design, 73, 75, 76, 78, 81. See also research strategy
research strategy, 74–76
reviewable acts, 57, 59, 60, 66
Risk-benefit analysis, 4, 86, 116, 161, 192, 193
Roquette (C-138/79), 55

S
Saxony, 102, 103, 115, 166, 174
Semi-privileged applicant, 54, 61, 62
semi structured interviews, 80
Sequential chain, 40, 182
simple conflict, 182
simple constellation, 130. See also simple conflict
snus, 145, 146. See also *snus* ban
snus ban, 145
social movement, 6, 29, 30, 52, 90, 91, 117, 134, 181, 199
standing rights, 14, 15, 29, 61, 63, 128, 149
State aid, 12, 15, 54, 78, 84, 101–103, 105, 106, 115, 136, 148, 166, 174, 175, 177, 178, 191, 202
State attorneys, 79, 94, 96–98, 101, 102, 113, 114
statistical analysis, 182
strategic approach, 33, 157, 158, 168, 170, 197
Strategic model, 157, 159, 160, 182. See also strategic approach

Subnational authorities, 17, 84, 96, 116, 191. *See also* Regions
Success in court, 9, 16, 23, 94, 116, 158, 168, 173, 175, 176, 179, 180, 191. *See also* legal success
suckler cow premiums (C-344/01), 8, 16
systemic features of the EU, 88

T
Tax, 1, 2, 78, 105
technical review mechanism, 200
Temporary equilibrium, 128, 194
Time limit, 54, 56
Tobacco Case (T-170/03), 143–146. *See also* Expanded Tobacco Case
Tobacco Control Research Group, 146
Tobacco Tactics, 146
Toys Safety Case (T-198-12), 111, 112
Transitforum Tirol, 181
Treaty change, 5, 9, 24, 57, 89, 99, 100, 135–140, 142, 180, 196. *See also* legal flux, treaty modification

treaty modification, 138, 139, 142, 143, 146, 196
Trustee, 92, 159
Two-level game, 128, 163, 181

V
Vertical conflict, 35, 36, 39, 76, 94, 128, 131, 132, 193, 202

W
winners, 32, 38, 173, 178–180
Winning, 94, 104, 116, 133, 155, 159, 163, 171, 173, 176, 179, 181, 183, 192, 199. *See also* winners
Withdraw, 109, 115, 179. *See also* withdrawal
withdrawal, 101, 104, 110
Working language, 107

The manufacturer's authorised representative in the EU is Springer Nature Customer Service Centre GmbH, Europaplatz 3, 69115 Heidelberg, Germany. If you have any concerns regarding our products, please contact ProductSafety@springernature.com

Printed and bound by CPI Group (UK) Ltd, Croydon, CR0 4YY
23/03/2026
02076670-0003